INTREPID

INTREPID

Bill White and Robert Gandt

Foreword by Senator John McCain

Broadway Books • New York

THE EPIC STORY OF AMERICA'S MOST LEGENDARY WARSHIP

Published in the United States by Broadway Books, an imprint of
The Doubleday Publishing Group, a division of Random House, Inc.,
New York.
www.broadwaybooks.com

BROADWAY BOOKS and its logo, a letter B bisected on the diagonal, are
trademarks of Random House, Inc.

Pages 347–48 constitute an extension of this copyright page.

Book design by Michael Collica

Library of Congress Cataloging-in-Publication Data
White, Bill, 1967–
Intrepid : the epic story of America's most legendary warship / Bill White and
Robert Gandt.
p.   cm.
1. Intrepid (Aircraft carrier). 2. World War, 1939–1945—Naval operations,
American. 3. Vietnam War, 1961–1975—Naval operations, American.
I. Gandt, Robert L. II. Title.

VA65.I57W45 2008
359.9'4350973—dc22
2008011353

ISBN 978-0-7679-2989-9

PRINTED IN THE UNITED STATES OF AMERICA

1 3 5 7 9 10 8 6 4 2

First Edition

To all the brave men and women in uniform who have served in the defense of freedom, and to their families. May our nation never forget your sacrifice.

★ CONTENTS ★

Contents

★ FOREWORD ★

by Senator John McCain

This book by Bill White and Robert Gandt is more than just a tribute to a famous ship. The story of USS *Intrepid* is, above all else, a story about people. In the thirty years of *Intrepid*'s military career, some 55,000 Americans served aboard her. She is an amalgam of all their stories, some incredibly heroic, some poignant, some heartbreakingly sad. It is the spirit of those men that gives life to this great warship. Her history is our history; her story tells us not just about a ship but also about a country.

For me, the story of USS *Intrepid* is a personal journey. My relationship with this remarkable vessel spans three generations. My grandfather, Adm. John S. "Slew" McCain, commanded Carrier Task Force 38 during the final, decisive sea battles of World War II. *Intrepid* was one of the fast carriers of his task force. She fought under his command in the Philippines in 1944, and he stood aboard her after she endured a near-fatal kamikaze attack in November 1944.

More than two decades later, during *Intrepid*'s third deployment to Vietnam, she served under my father, Adm. John S. McCain Jr., who was commander in chief of U.S. forces in the Pacific. Under his command, *Intrepid*'s aircraft flew hundreds of combat sorties and bombing runs over North Vietnam, while I, coincidentally, resided in a Hanoi prison. On Christmas Day, 1968, my father went aboard *Intrepid* to celebrate the holiday with the crew in the Tonkin Gulf.

My own first contact with *Intrepid* came early in my career. As a newly winged naval aviator—a "nugget," in Navy parlance—*Intrepid* was my first carrier. I was assigned to Attack Squadron 65 and flew the venerable Douglas AD-6 Skyraider. I can still hear the loud throbbing noise of the Skyraider's Wright engine starting up, and I remember clearly that first catapult launch from *Intrepid*— a wild, exhilarating ride, like being shot from a cannon. Like every fledgling carrier pilot, I remember staring in awe at *Intrepid's* postage-stamp-sized deck as I closed in to make my first arrested landing.

I made several deployments aboard *Intrepid*, including two to the Mediterranean Sea. As an older, *Essex*-class carrier, she was overshadowed by the big-deck supercarriers such as *Forrestal* and *Saratoga*. She had only two catapults versus their four, and yet she consistently beat them at their own game, launching and recovering aircraft as fast as and often faster than her bigger and newer rivals. *Intrepid's* crew and her air group comprised an efficient, tightly knit team, and we were all proud to serve aboard her.

This legendary ship ended her active-duty life in 1974. After languishing for several years in a shipyard, this old ship—the survivor of kamikaze and torpedo attacks—looked to meet her final fate at the scrap yard. But then came a hero—and a city—to rescue and transform *Intrepid*. She now stands as a proud sea, air, and space museum, moored near the heart of one of our greatest cities.

Famous warships, like consecrated battlefields and military museums, have the power to capture our imaginations. When you walk the decks of *Intrepid*, study the exhibits, touch the gray steel of her bulkheads, it is impossible not to sense the closeness of history. You feel yourself being transported in time. You may hear the thunder of gunfire. You can feel the deck once again resonate with the throb of engines. Your nerves may sense the approach of kamikazes or the silent danger of an incoming torpedo.

A great ship such as *Intrepid* also has the power to educate. From her dramatic story, our citizens learn the vital lessons of their own history. They understand the sacrifices made by their fathers and grandfathers in the most cataclysmic of all wars. They grasp how ordinary Americans like themselves were sent into the smoke and chaos of battle and rose to greatness, achieving a victory that changed the course of humankind. *Intrepid* serves as a visible tribute to that greatest generation of heroes.

Intrepid is also a stage from which we honor today's heroes. There is no better place than on the decks of this veteran warship to salute our present generation of soldiers, sailors, airmen, marines, and coast guardsmen, those brave Americans who risk everything on our behalf. *Intrepid* stands as a living connection between our heroes of the past and those of the present.

It is also the namesake for the world's most technologically advanced rehabilitation center for amputees and burn victims. The Center for the Intrepid, made possible by the generosity of so many to the Intrepid Fallen Heroes Fund, and particularly the Fisher family, helps Americans who have sacrificed so much for our sake to have the care they deserve and the comfort of their families as they recover from wounds and rebuild their lives.

Of all *Intrepid*'s missions, perhaps her most important is to inspire our heroes of tomorrow. Our nation's future is bright and boundless, but not guaranteed. Only through the heroic efforts of a new generation of Americans will our liberty and ideals be preserved. The USS *Intrepid* and her educational programs present a powerful and tangible representation of that age-old virtue—love of country, pride in America.

I urge you to read this story of the magnificent *Intrepid*, and then, armed with the knowledge of her glorious past, take the opportunity to visit her in person. Let yourself be immersed in the sights and sounds and feel of history. The story of the *Intrepid* is a classic American saga. Long may she serve as a symbol of our country's greatness.

John McCain

★ *INTREPID* TIME LINE ★

December 1, 1941: Keel laid at Newport News, Virginia.

December 7, 1941: Japanese attack on Pearl Harbor. United States enters World War II.

April 26, 1943: Launched.

August 16, 1943: Commissioned CV-11.

December 3, 1943: Sailed for Pearl Harbor via Panama Canal and San Francisco.

January–February 1944: Participated in the Marshall Islands invasion, raids on Kwajalein.

February 16, 1944: Participated in attack on Truk Pacific fortress.

February 17, 1944: Struck by Japanese aerial torpedo.

August–October 1944: Supported invasion of the Palaus and landings on Peleliu. Strikes against the Philippines, Formosa, Okinawa.

October 24–26, 1944: Fought in Battle of Leyte Gulf. Helped sink super-battleship Musashi.

October 29, 1944: Struck by kamikaze in Gun Tub 10.

November 25, 1944: Struck by two successive kamikazes—heavily damaged, returned to San Francisco for repair.

March 18, 1945: Strikes against Kyushu and Okinawa. Near miss by a G4M "Betty" kamikaze showers hangar deck in flame.

April 6, 1945: Helped sink the Japanese super-battleship Yamato.

April 16, 1945: Struck by kamikaze off Okinawa. Returned to San Francisco for repair.

August 6, 1945: Reported back to the fast carrier force. Strikes on Wake Island. War ended.

August–December 1945: Policed the coasts of China and Korea, aided in repatriation of Allied POWs.

December 15, 1945: Returned to the United States.

August 15, 1946: Placed in reserve status in San Francisco shipyard.

March 22, 1947: Decommissioned.

February 9, 1952: Recommissioned for voyage to Norfolk, decommissioned again for modernization.

June 18, 1954: Recommissioned, returned to service with modern equipment including steam catapults.

1956: Refitted at the Brooklyn Navy Yard. Angled deck added.

May 24, 1962: Recovery ship for Mercury VII *(astronaut Scott Carpenter).*

March 23, 1965: Recovery ship for Gemini III *(astronauts Gus Grissom and John Young).*

April 1966: Begins first tour with Seventh Fleet off Vietnam.

June 1967: Start of second Vietnam tour. Air group wins a Navy Unit Commendation, Navy's highest group honor.

July 1968: Commences third combat tour in Vietnam. Remains on Yankee Station until cessation of Rolling Thunder, September 1968.

November 1972: Deploys to Mediterranean with multi-mission capability: ASW, air defense, conventional and nuclear strike.

March 15, 1974: Decommissioned at Quonset Point, Rhode Island. Towed to Philadelphia.

October 13, 1975: Declared official vessel of the 1976 U.S. Navy and Marine Corps Bicentennial Exposition.

February 1982: Transferred by act of Congress from Navy rolls to Intrepid Museum Foundation.

August 4, 1982: Opens as the Intrepid Sea, Air, & Space Museum in New York City.

January 1986: Designated National Historic Landmark.

September 11, 2001: Assigned as temporary emergency headquarters for the FBI following attack on World Trade Center.

August 2005: Intrepid Museum welcomes its ten-millionth visitor.

November–December 2006: After failed first attempt, departed New York City for renovations.

October 2008: Returned to New York City.

November 11, 2008: Museum reopened.

INTREPID

Leviathans

October 24, 1944

They were huge, beautiful, and utterly terrifying.

Lt. (jg) Max Adams stared at the apparitions beneath him. He had heard of such warships, but nothing in his imagination prepared him for this. Adams was gazing down at the two mightiest battleships ever to sail the oceans. Their names were *Yamato* and *Musashi*. They were sister ships, and each was carving a long white wake across the Sibuyan Sea.

Adams was a Helldiver pilot in Bombing Squadron 18, based aboard USS *Intrepid*. He and his radioman, Cornelius Clark, escorted by a pair of Hellcat fighters, had been searching the inland sea at the southern end of Mindoro, an island in the eastern Philippines. Clark had picked up a surface radar contact bearing 090 degrees, 25 miles. Adams flew over to check it out.

The night before, a pair of U.S. submarines had encountered a column of Japanese warships passing through the narrow Palawan Strait, headed for the Philippines. The submarines' report was flashed to the bridge of USS *New Jersey*, flagship of Adm. William F. "Bull" Halsey. Halsey commanded the Third Fleet, an armada of more than 200 warships, including the aircraft carrier *Intrepid*. Halsey was responsible for protecting Gen. Douglas MacArthur's 125,000 troops, who had just landed on the southern shore of Leyte Island.

Halsey needed more information. How many Japanese ships? What size? Where were they going? Why?

At 0600, twenty-four search planes took off from *Intrepid*. They were divided into teams, each assigned a different sector in the general area where the submarines had spotted the task force. At a few minutes past 0800, Max Adams and his flight spotted the Japanese task force. His report was relayed by another *Intrepid* Helldiver pilot stationed halfway between Adams and the *New Jersey*, 250 miles away.

The Japanese force amounted to twenty-eight warships, including five battleships. Aboard *New Jersey*, the news had a galvanizing effect. Halsey no longer had any doubt about Japanese intentions. A powerful enemy fleet was heading for Leyte, where MacArthur's landing forces were still digging in.

Of Halsey's four carrier task groups, only one, Task Group 38.2, was within range of the Japanese force. And of the task group, only one fleet carrier was available for immediate action: USS *Intrepid*.

Halsey wasted no time. At 0837 he grabbed the TBS (Talk Between Ships) radiophone and issued a command that would become part of U.S. Navy legend: "Strike! Repeat: Strike! Good luck!"

It was a perfect day for bombing. The morning clouds were dissipating. The ocean was bathed in a pale, almost ethereal light.

The first wave of warplanes from *Intrepid* found the enemy fleet at 1027. Cdr. Bill Ellis, *Intrepid*'s air group commander—CAG, in Navy parlance—was a tough, no-nonsense Virginian who believed a commander's place was in the front of his force. CAG Ellis was leading a group of eleven F6F Hellcat fighters, a dozen SB2C Helldiver bombers, and eight torpedo-carrying TBM Avengers.

Gazing at the armada below them, the pilots were filled with awe. Most had never seen a Japanese battleship. Beneath them were five, including the behemoths *Yamato* and *Musashi*, plus a fleet of heavily armored cruisers and destroyers. Already the Japanese warships were going into a defensive circling formation, the destroyers forming an outer ring, with the cruisers surrounding the battleships at the center. The sky was filling with multi-hued bursts of anti-aircraft fire—some pink, some purple, some exploding in clouds of silvery pellets. It was a Japanese tactic the pilots had heard about but never seen—each ship firing different-colored bursts so the gun directors could track their own fire. The bursts were coming close enough that the *Intrepid* pilots could hear and feel the concussion.

In the number four slot of his division of TBM Avengers, Ens. Ben St. John reflected on his luck. He was there by pure chance. During the briefing in the squadron ready room, five pilots were available to fly the four assigned airplanes. St. John and the other junior pilot flipped a coin to see who would fly the mission. St. John won the toss.

Or lost, he thought, staring at the Japanese warships. It would depend on whether he lived through the next half hour.

Helldiver pilot Lt. (jg) John "Jack" Forsyth, looking at the mammoth battleships, had a thought: the only sane way to attack a battleship was with *two* battleships, or a whole damned *fleet* of battleships, not with a gaggle of aluminum-framed, single-engine airplanes carrying bombs and torpedoes from an aircraft carrier 250 miles away.

Each of the Japanese super-battleships mounted 150 anti-aircraft guns, and each cruiser and destroyer had nearly as many. Every one of those guns was now firing at the warplanes from *Intrepid*. The flak, a Helldiver pilot wrote in his action report, "was so thick you could get out and walk on it."

CAG Ellis had laid out the plan during the briefing that morning. The first to engage would be the Helldivers, diving almost vertically from 12,500 feet. Right behind them would go the Hellcats, strafing with their six .50-caliber guns per airplane. Then the Avengers would swoop down, roaring straight into the muzzles of the Japanese guns to drop their torpedoes.

From Ellis's lead fighter came the order: attack.

At the dawn of the greatest sea battle in history, the 36,000-ton *Essex*-class carrier *Intrepid* was 90 miles off Samar, in the eastern Philippines. The ship's inner spaces still smelled of fresh paint and newly oiled machinery. Measured by a warship's normal longevity, *Intrepid* was still in her infancy. She was in her fourteenth month of commissioned service.

From her flight deck pilots had already delivered thousands of bombs, rockets, and torpedoes on Japanese bases and ships. She had carried the war to the enemy from Kwajalein to Truk to Pelelieu to the islands of the Philippines. Her fighter pilots had lit up the sky with the blazing hulks of Japanese aircraft. *Intrepid* herself had been bloodied, but not badly. Despite taking a torpedo off Truk the previous February, *Intrepid*'s crew still thought of her as a lucky ship.

Most of her 3,300 crew members had been with her since August 16, 1943, the day she entered service. They were "plank owners"—members of the ship's original crew—and they were a cross section of 1944 America.

Many, like eighteen-year-old Seaman Ed Coyne, had dropped out of high school to enlist in the Navy. Fresh from two months at the Navy's Great Lakes boot camp, Coyne and 175 other sailors were bused straight to the Newport News, Virginia, receiving station to join the crew of the newly constructed USS *Intrepid*. Now Coyne was at his battle station at the starboard edge of *Intrepid*'s flight deck, manning a sound-powered phone.

Down in *Intrepid*'s nerve center, the Combat Information Center (CIC), nineteen-year-old Ray Stone sat at a radar scope. Stone, who was a high school graduate, had been sent from boot camp for advanced training at the Fleet Radar School at Virginia Beach, Virginia. His first assignment as a radarman was to the USS *Intrepid*.

At his station in a gun tub on *Intrepid*'s port rail, Alonzo Swann Jr., who had just turned nineteen, was manning an anti-aircraft gun. Officially, Swann wasn't supposed to be there. Nor were the other twenty African American sailors of the gun crew. They were steward's mates, which meant their official duties were to clean spaces and serve meals. This was 1944, and the Navy hadn't yet opened its specialized enlisted ratings to black sailors. They weren't normally assigned to combat stations.

Capt. Joe Bolger, *Intrepid*'s skipper, had rendered his own judgment on the matter. *Intrepid* would use every able-bodied sailor who was willing to fight. Alonzo Swann Jr. and his black shipmates had been trained on the Oerlikon 20-mm anti-aircraft gun and assigned to gunner duty in Gun Tub 10.

From *Intrepid*'s signal bridge, Signalman Lou Valenti, age eighteen, was peering into the sky. As one of *Intrepid*'s plank owners, Valenti hadn't liked his first job, hauling hundred-pound mailbags to the flight deck. Seeing an opportunity, he volunteered for assignment as a signalman. Now Valenti's station was in the island—the carrier's superstructure—where he had a view of the action around him.

After nearly a year and a half of war, the young crewmen of *Intrepid* were ready for whatever the enemy could throw at them. The hazy August day fourteen months before now seemed only a distant memory.

PART ONE

Years of Thunder

in·trep·id *adj*
 fearless and resolute; persistent in the pursuit of
 victory <an *intrepid* warrior>

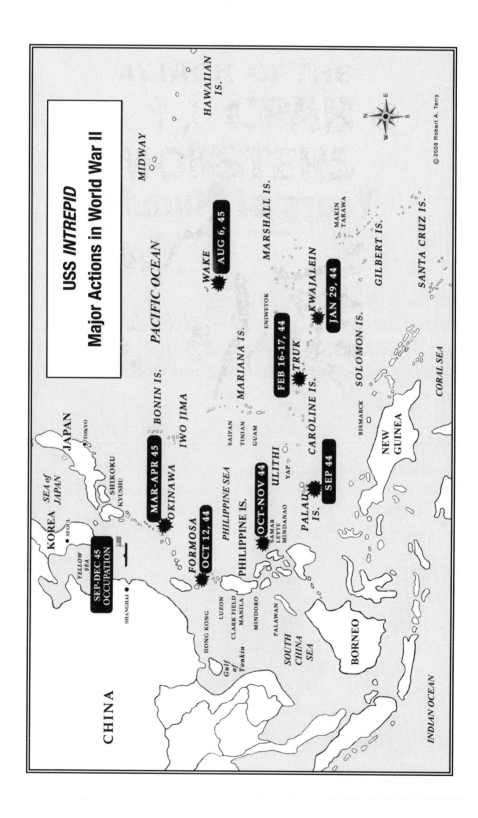

Call to Arms

In mare in coelo (On the sea and in the air)
—Motto given to USS *Intrepid* on her commissioning day

August 16, 1943

Capt. Thomas L. Sprague, USN, squinted in the harsh sunlight. It was a typical Chesapeake summer early afternoon, the humidity clinging to the atmosphere like a damp blanket. Sprague could feel the perspiration trickling beneath the starched white cotton of his service dress uniform.

For nearly three decades Tom Sprague had waited for this day. He had served for what seemed a lifetime in a budget-slashed, promotionless, peacetime Navy. Finally Sprague was getting his first major command.

And what a command. Sprague's new vessel was one of the most formidable warships ever built, the third example of the fast new *Essex*-class aircraft carriers. With a full complement of a hundred warplanes and nearly 4,000 crew, the new carrier displaced 36,000 tons and could slice through the ocean at a speed of 33 knots.

Her name was *Intrepid*, and she was the fourth U.S. Navy ship of the line to bear the distinguished title. This new *Intrepid* was named in honor of an armed ketch that had fought with distinction at Tripoli in 1803. She was constructed at the Newport News Shipbuilding and Dry Dock Co. in Virginia. Her ceremonial keel-laying in December 1941 had nearly coincided with the Japanese attack on the U.S. fleet at Pearl Harbor. Getting *Intrepid* into service became a matter of national urgency. Instead of the normal three years, *Intrepid* had to be ready for duty in a year and a half.

When Tom Sprague entered the Naval Academy in 1913, he couldn't have guessed the historical twists and reversals that would shape his career. He received his commission in 1917, just in time to see duty as a surface officer escorting convoys across the Atlantic in World War I. Correctly sensing the future importance of naval aviation, he applied for flight training and was designated a naval aviator in 1921. During the doldrums of the twenties and thirties, Sprague rotated through a succession of staff jobs, commanded a scouting squadron, became air officer aboard the carrier USS *Saratoga,* and eventually rose to the post of superintendent of naval air training at Pensacola. In 1940 he was assigned as executive officer of the carrier USS *Ranger,* then briefly commanded the newly constructed escort carrier USS *Charger.* Even in the plodding, peacetime Navy, it was clear that Tom Sprague was an officer on his way up.

On this hazy August day, Sprague knew he ought to feel a glow of contentment. This was the crowning moment of a successful military career, the prize he had dreamed about for his entire adult life. But the sweetness of the moment was tinged with a sense of foreboding. Hanging like a dark cloud over the celebration was the news from the Pacific. Four large American aircraft carriers had been lost in battle with the Imperial Japanese Navy. In May of the previous year, USS *Lexington* was torpedoed and sunk during the Battle of the Coral Sea. USS *Yorktown* was lost to Japanese bombers and torpedo planes in the Battle of Midway. USS *Wasp,* torpedoed off Guadalcanal, went down in September 1942. A month later USS *Hornet,* the carrier from whose deck Lt. Col. James H. Doolittle's raiders launched the first attack on Japan, was sunk by dive-bombers and aerial torpedoes in the Battle of Santa Cruz Island. The Navy was desperately short of aircraft carriers.

No other U.S. military service was as steeped in centuries-old tradition as the Navy. The ritual of commissioning a new ship, like many U.S. Navy traditions, was adopted from the British Navy. It was a symbolic birthing, a way of giving "life" to an inanimate, newly constructed vessel. Tom Sprague, as traditional as any sailor of his generation, was sticking with the script.

More than a hundred guests—women in long skirts and sun hats, men in summer suits and in the uniforms of all the services—stood on *Intrepid*'s gleaming flight deck at the Norfolk Navy Yard. Each division of the ship's new crew, resplendent in their dress whites, stood in neat rows facing the elevated podium. The band was playing a medley of Sousa marches and traditional military tunes.

Standing with Sprague on the podium was an assortment of Navy brass, including Rear Adm. Calvin Durgin; Cdr. Dick Gaines, who was *Intrepid*'s new executive officer; and the guest of honor, Assistant Secretary of the Navy Artemus Gates.

The crowd stood for the playing of the national anthem. Then came the invocation, followed by the ceremonial turning over of the ship by the commandant to the new captain. Captain Sprague read the orders appointing him to command the new warship. His first act as *Intrepid*'s new captain was to order the ship's ensign and her commissioning pennant—a long red, white, and blue streamer—hoisted. The ship's bell rang, and the watch was set. Assistant Secretary Gates delivered an address, followed by the pipe-down order and the retreat.

The new ship had just taken on a life of her own. The band struck up, and the crowd broke into applause.

There was a reception on the hangar deck, with more music by the ship's band, congratulatory talk, handshakes, and farewells. Then Tom Sprague and his crew changed uniforms and went to work. They didn't have the luxury of a long shakedown cruise, publicity tours, or visits to exotic ports of call. There was a war on. Time was short.

They had, in fact, less than four months.

First.

First skipper, first day at sea, first round of ammunition fired. In the early life of a new warship, there came a succession of such events. When the warship was an aircraft carrier, there were some unique firsts: first landing, first launch, first combat sortie flown by the carrier's aircraft, first crash.

It was October 16, 1943, and *Intrepid* was about to notch her first arrested landing. Behind the ship trailed a long white wake, glistening in the autumn sun. A steady 20-knot wind blew straight down the flight deck. This was a carrier's raison d'être and her primary function. Her armament, crew, massive displacement, and gleaming flight deck were irrelevant without the ability to launch and recover warplanes.

Turning into the groove—the final approach behind the ship—was a Grumman F6F Hellcat. To no one's surprise, the honor of making *Intrepid*'s first arrested landing was going to Cdr. A. M. Jackson, commander of Air Group 8, *Intrepid*'s newly assigned air group. Under the watchful eye of the LSO—the landing signal officer—on his platform at the aft port deck edge, Jackson landed the Hellcat squarely in the middle of the arresting cables, snatching a wire with his tailhook, logging the first of more than 100,000 arrested landings aboard this ship.

In early October, with Air Group 8's full complement of F6F-3 Hellcats, SB2C-1 dive-bombers, and TBF torpedo bombers aboard, *Intrepid* headed for the benign waters of the Caribbean. In the Gulf of Paria, near Trinidad, *Intrepid*'s crew and airmen began rehearsing the tenuous, intricate choreography of carrier flight operations.

There were mishaps. Bombing Squadron 8 had just received the new and troublesome Curtiss SB2C-1 Helldiver and was still working out the dive-bomber's many handling problems. Many of the air group's aviators were fresh out of flight training. Most of the "traps"—arrested landings—were routine, with the plane's tailhook snagging one of the sixteen arresting cables strung across the deck. But not all. A few missed the wires and careened into the barricade, the cabled fence at the end of the landing area that protected the parked airplanes, equipment, and crewmen on the forward deck. Except for some damage to airplanes, none of the incidents was serious. There was no loss of life.

By October 27 Captain Sprague was satisfied. He turned *Intrepid* to the north and headed back to Norfolk. In the next few weeks there were more sea trials off the Atlantic coast, including a winter trip north to Maine without the air group. On November 30 *Intrepid* went back into port for final storing and provisioning.

Finally, on December 3, 1943, with a full complement of crew and aircraft, *Intrepid* sailed out of Norfolk, bound for the far end of the world. For most of the crew—and for the base where *Intrepid* had come to life—it was a sentimental departure. No one knew what lay ahead, but they all had the clear sense that *Intrepid* would not soon return.

As all seagoing Navy men knew, a new ship headed to war needed luck. Before *Intrepid* had even reached the Pacific, her luck turned bad. Looking back on that day, some would say it was an omen.

The Panama Canal was a tight squeeze for any capital ship. The passage had been completed at the turn of the century, and even then it could barely accommodate the Navy's biggest warships. For *Intrepid*, it turned out to be more than tight.

On December 9, 1943, she left her mooring at Colón, on the Atlantic side of the isthmus, and entered the first lock of the Panama Canal. Most of the crew gathered on deck to watch the arduous process of guiding the ship through the narrow passage. At times the ship appeared to have only a few feet of clearance on either side. Scaffolding was constructed on the flight deck, perpendicular to the bridge, to give the canal pilot better visibility.

The pilot took the carrier into the Gaillard Cut, the twisting waterway leading to the locks at Balboa. What happened next would later be the subject of finger-pointing and speculation. Midway through the narrow passage, while the ship was negotiating a left turn, the bow veered to starboard, toward a steep cliff at the waterway's edge. Though the crew put the engines into full reverse and dropped a bow anchor, the ship's momentum shoved her bow into the rocky cliff. The impact ripped a 4-by-4-foot hole in her bow and buckled several plates in her hull.

Blame for what happened—whether it was the pilot or the captain or, as some suggested, the opening of a lock that caused a surge of water—was never assigned. A later board of inquiry exonerated both the canal pilot and *Intrepid*'s officers. The carrier had to pull into port at Balboa, Panama, where she spent five days receiving a patch job on her hull. *Intrepid* finally reached her destination at Alameda Naval Station in San Francisco Bay three days before Christmas, 1943.

Because of the hull damage from the canal collision, *Intrepid* shed her planes, then steamed 5 miles across the bay to the Hunters Point dry dock to receive a more permanent repair to her bow. It would be the first of many Hunters Point dry dock sessions for *Intrepid*, earning for her the uncomplimentary nickname "Dry I."

Thus did the crew of *Intrepid* celebrate the first of several consecutive holiday seasons in San Francisco. On January 6, repairs complete and the air group's aircraft back aboard, *Intrepid* pulled away from her mooring and slid beneath the Golden Gate Bridge, her bow pointed westward. She was on her way to join Adm. Marc Mitscher's Fifth Fleet in the Pacific, the largest armada of warships ever assembled.

The Pearl Harbor of January 1944 was a beehive of activity. Not only had the naval complex recovered from the devastation of two years earlier, but the harbor was crammed with warships (many newly constructed, like *Intrepid*), ramps covered with seaplanes, and thousands of servicemen, most of them enlisted in the last two years. *Intrepid* glided into Pearl Harbor like a new member of a fast-growing club.

Her stay in Hawaii would be brief, but long enough to make a change in her air group. Air Group 8 had been *Intrepid*'s first, but it wasn't the one she'd take into combat. The air group and its squadrons had new orders: they would be off-loaded in Pearl Harbor and detached to the Naval Air Station in Maui.

Taking their place was Air Group 6, a battle-tested unit whose CAG, Cdr. John Phillips, had taken over from Medal of Honor winner Butch O'Hare, lost on a night fighter mission two months before. The squadrons had fought in almost every major engagement in the Pacific, including the Midway, Guadalcanal, and the Gilbert and Marshall Islands actions.

After conducting qualification landings with her new air group, *Intrepid* put to sea on January 16, bound for the Marshall Islands. Accompanied by the carriers *Cabot* and *Essex* and a screen of escort vessels, she was part of a newly formed task group that would join Task Force 58, the largest U.S. Navy task force yet assembled in World War II.

The first two targets of the operation—the islands of Makin and Tarawa in the Gilbert Islands—had been captured by U.S. Marines in November 1943 after a quick but costly amphibious assault. The next phase of the island-hopping campaign would concentrate on the Kwajalein atoll, Japan's major defense center in the Marshall Islands.

The triangular atoll, 66 miles long and 20 miles across at its widest, was the world's largest enclosed atoll. Within the reefs that rimmed Kwajalein was a landlocked lagoon used by the Japanese as a fueling and repair facility. Nearly a hundred Japanese warplanes were based on the atoll, and the entire complex bristled with fortifications and heavy guns.

The Kwajalein campaign was to be a two-pronged attack with the assault forces divided into Northern and Southern Attack Groups. The Northern Group, units of the 4th Marine Division, would seize the islands that guarded the northern approach to Kwajalein, and the Southern Group with units of the U.S. Army 7th Division would invade Kwajalein itself. Task Group 58.2, with *Intrepid* at its center, was assigned to the Northern Group.

The next day, January 29, 1944, *Intrepid* would log another first in her history: first day of combat.

★ 2 ★

First Blooding

The collective thunder of fifty radial engines split the morning still-ness. One after the other, Air Group 6's warplanes roared down the flight deck and lumbered into the sky. First went the Hellcat fight-ers, followed by the slower, bomb-laden Avengers and Dauntlesses.

Captain Sprague, watching from the nav bridge, couldn't help feeling a sense of satisfaction. After five months of urgent prepara-tion, *Intrepid* and its crew were about to prove their worth. This cool Pacific morning would mark their first engagement with the Japanese.

The targets were the low, brush-covered islands of Roi and Namur, 42 miles north of Kwajalein. On the larger island of Roi, the Japanese had constructed an airfield with three runways and a complex of hangars and support buildings. The islands were ringed with anti-aircraft emplacements, pillboxes, and coast defense guns. On either side of Roi and Namur were islets on which the Japanese had installed heavy guns.

The invasion of Roi and Namur was preceded by a two-day bom-bardment by the battleships *Tennessee*, *Maryland*, and *Colorado*, plus the combined guns of five cruisers and nineteen destroyers. Then came *Intrepid*'s Air Group 6, which would strafe, bomb, and set ablaze every aircraft and building on the islands. Leading the first wave would be the F6F-3 Hellcats of Fighting Squadron 6.

In the opinions of the men who flew it, the Hellcat was the best American fighter of the war. Produced by Grumman as the replacement for the plodding, short-ranged F4F Wildcat, the Hellcat arrived at precisely the right time. The rugged fighter had a top speed of 380 mph, and though less maneuverable than its adversary, the Japanese Zero (code-named "Zeke"), the Hellcat had superior armor and higher altitude capability. Like other products of Grumman, the Hellcat was a fighter that could take terrific punishment from Japanese guns and still keep flying.

The Japanese ace Saburo Sakai described an encounter with a Grumman fighter: "I had full confidence in my ability to destroy the Grumman and decided to finish off the enemy fighter with only my 7.7-mm machine guns. I turned the 20-mm cannon switch to the off position, and closed in. For some strange reason, even after I had poured about five or six hundred rounds of ammunition directly into the Grumman, the airplane did not fall, but kept on flying. I thought this very odd—it had never happened before—and closed the distance between the two airplanes until I could almost reach out and touch the Grumman. To my surprise, the Grumman's rudder and tail were torn to shreds, looking like an old torn piece of rag. With his plane in such condition, no wonder the pilot was unable to continue fighting! A Zero which had taken that many bullets would have been a ball of fire by now."

"These Grummans are beautiful planes," declared a Hellcat pilot after coming back from a mission. "If they could cook, I'd marry one."

One Hellcat pilot in the ready room of Fighting 6 was frustrated. Lt. (jg) Alex Vraciu and his wingman, Ens. Tom Hall, had not been assigned to the first fighter sweep. "The meat is in the morning," fighter pilots liked to say, which meant that the first fighter sweep got the most kills. Vraciu was worried that the air action over Roi and Namur would be finished before he had the chance to get into the air.

Vraciu was twenty-four, a darkly handsome Chicago kid, the son of Romanian immigrants. He'd learned to fly in 1939 while he was still at DePauw University. After graduating in 1941, he entered Navy flight training just before Pearl Harbor. Early in his Navy career he'd come under the tutelage of Butch O'Hare, the legendary VF-6 skipper and later Air Group 6 CAG. As O'Hare's number three in his flight, Vraciu had gotten his first kill over Wake Island in October 1943. He added a Mitsubishi G4M "Betty" bomber to the score at Tarawa.

A month later Vraciu's friend and mentor O'Hare was dead, killed during a night radar-intercept mission off USS *Enterprise*. He and his wingman were flying at low altitude behind a radar-equipped TBM when the Avenger's radar picked up a Japanese Betty moving up behind the Hellcats. In the ensuing, confused cross fire, O'Hare's Hellcat went down. Whether he was killed by the Betty's 7.7-mm nose gun or by accidental fire from the Avenger was never determined.

It didn't matter to Alex Vraciu. Since then, killing Japanese Betty bombers had become his private obsession. "I'm going to get ten of those bastards," he vowed. "For Butch."

That afternoon Vraciu and Hall got their chance. With the rest of the ten-plane VF-6 CAP—combat air patrol—they hurtled down *Intrepid*'s deck and pointed their noses toward Roi and Namur. Vraciu's earlier worry—that the sky would already be swept of Zeroes—turned out to be valid. There were no fighters to be seen. More than a hundred Japanese aircraft had been destroyed on the airfields.

Vraciu and Hall were rolling in to strafe an already shot-up bomber on the ground when Vraciu spotted something: Bettys. They looked like fat geese coming to a pond. The twin-engine bombers were slipping into the area, seemingly oblivious to the Hellcats above them. Diving from 7,000 feet, Vraciu fired one long burst in a high deflection shot from starboard. A Betty burst into flames and crashed into the lagoon from 400 feet.

Then another Betty blundered onto the scene. Seeing the danger, the Betty pilot dived for the water and tried to escape. Vraciu's first burst blew up a wing, and the Betty went down in flames. As the Hellcats were pulling up, they spotted yet another pair of the twin-engine bombers. The Bettys split, with Tom Hall chasing the leader and Vraciu in hot pursuit of the second.

It turned into a long cat-and-mouse chase. Like most Hellcat pilots, Vraciu had a healthy respect for the Betty's deadly rearward-firing 20-mm cannon. Tracers were arcing backward from the tail gunner toward Vraciu's Hellcat. His armament system had already taken damage, and he was down to one gun.

The chase led them out over the water. Vraciu made one firing pass after another, pulling out between passes to recharge his gun. The pursuit went on, with Vraciu determined to shoot down the Betty. After 25 miles over open water, his single .50-caliber gun finally hit a vital spot. He saw the Betty nose over and plunge into the ocean.

Vraciu returned to the ship drained and exhilarated. He'd just gotten three more of the hated Bettys. With five downed enemy airplanes to his credit, Alex Vraciu had become *Intrepid*'s first ace.

In the back of his TBF-1 Avenger, Aviation Radioman First Class Joe Liotta knew they were in trouble. Liotta and the other three men of his crew were on a photo mission at 1,500 feet above the beach at Porcelain Island when he felt the burst from a Japanese 5-inch gun slam into the Avenger. The pilot, Lt. (jg) Tom Vaughn, wrestled to keep the torpedo bomber from going into the water.

With the shot-up airplane leaking fuel and hydraulic fluid, Vaughn headed back to the *Intrepid*. He reassured his crew that they would get aboard okay. "Just let me know when we get back to the ship if the wheels come down," the pilot told them.

The Avenger's landing gear came down, and so did the tailhook. Vaughn landed the Avenger back on *Intrepid*'s deck. As they were exiting the arresting wires, Joe Liotta, in the back compartment, began to relax. He was taking off his seat belt when he felt the airplane lurch to the left. "We spun around on our left wheel," he recalled, "because the hydraulics were shot out on the right wheel."

Realizing they were going over the side, Liotta stood up and braced himself. In the next moment the Avenger somersaulted over the port deck edge and plunged upside down into the ocean 60 feet below. Liotta escaped. So did his two fellow crewmen in the back. In half a minute, the Avenger sank out of sight. "I didn't get a scratch," Liotta remembered. But when they counted heads in the water, one was missing. The pilot, twenty-two-year-old Tom Vaughn, had gone down with the Avenger.

Other *Intrepid* warplanes were also having a bad day. Fighting 6 pilot Lt. (jg) R. A. Hobbs had just finished making his second firing pass on a Betty bomber that he and his section leader had been chasing over the enemy airfield at Nancy Point. Their collective gunfire caused the Betty to burst into flame and crash into the ground, precisely at the intersection of the runways.

And then Hobbs realized that he was low on gasoline. With less than 20 gallons remaining, he headed back to the ship. As he approached, he saw that the decks of both *Intrepid* and *Essex* were covered with airplanes. He flew over the ships, giving the emergency forced-landing signal. Neither carrier seemed inclined to clear its decks for the Hellcat. Out of ideas and gasoline, Hobbs landed his fighter in the water alongside a destroyer escorting the carriers. He scrambled to safety and the destroyer hauled him aboard.

Hellcat pilot Bob Neel was having a worse day. He was strafing fuel trucks and hangars at the Burlesque Island enemy airfield when his Hellcat was hit either by anti-aircraft fire or by debris from the explosion of his target. Trailing smoke, he nursed the fighter out over the open water, west of the enemy island. He made it 5 miles before he put the fighter into the water. Neel climbed out of the sinking Hellcat but was unable to retrieve his life raft before it sank. His squadronmates spotted him floating in his life jacket and summoned rescue vessels. None showed up in time. Bob Neel was not seen again.

Back aboard *Intrepid*, CAG Phillips was furious about the losses. "Morale suffered," Phillips wrote, "because pilots could not understand why rescue destroyers were not stationed at the area."

———

The next morning, October 30, 1944, should have been another glory day for Alex Vraciu. He and his wingman, Tom Hall, were assigned to the coveted first fighter sweep. In the predawn gloom, Vraciu and Hall were sitting in their cockpits watching the fighters ahead of them roll down *Intrepid*'s deck and merge into the gray sky. For this hop, the Hellcats were making free deck launches—normal takeoffs under their own power—instead of being catapulted.

Vraciu saw Tom Hall's Hellcat taxi up to the launch position. The launch officer was giving him the turn-up signal, rotating his right hand over his head. Hall shoved the throttle up to full power while the Hellcat strained against the brakes.

Following the time-honored choreography of the flight deck launch, the launch officer swung his right arm over his head and pointed ahead: the go signal. Hall released his brakes, and the Hellcat surged forward.

Then something went wrong.

At full power and low airspeed, the high torque of the Hellcat's Pratt and Whitney R-2800 engine caused the airplane to yaw to the left. Pilots had to counteract the yaw with a heavy application of right rudder during takeoff. In the darkness on *Intrepid*'s deck, with no forward reference to guide him, Tom Hall didn't notice soon enough that his fighter was veering to the left. When he did, his left wheel had already dropped over the deck edge.

In the next second, the Hellcat's belly tank, filled with high-octane aviation gasoline, hit the deck edge and exploded. Flaming like a Roman candle, the Hellcat plunged off the bow and hit the water. The orange ball of fire illuminated the sea and the sky for half a minute. Then, as quickly as they had ignited, the flames vanished. The Hellcat was gone.

Vraciu stared at the forward deck. The suddenness of the accident stunned him. It was almost incomprehensible. In the space of a dozen heartbeats, his friend Tom Hall had been snuffed out like a candle.

There was no time to reflect on it. It was his turn to launch. Following the launch officer's signals, Vraciu rolled down the deck and lifted into the dawn sky.

He found no more Zeroes or Bettys in the air. In the official air-craft action report that day, the narrative ended with an unfamiliar comment: "No contact made with enemy planes." The air battle for Kwajalein was mostly over. The ground offensive was beginning.

The strikes continued for two days. On January 31, Marines of the 4th Division, led by Gen. Holland Smith, captured the two small islets flanking Roi and Namur. Then, on the morning of February 1, ten minutes after *Intrepid*'s planes withdrew from pounding the dug-in Japanese positions, the landing ships of the Marine amphibious assault headed for the beaches of Roi and Namur. Simultaneously, at the opposite end of the atoll, a landing force of the U.S. Army 7th Infantry Division was storming the beaches of Kwajalein.

It was a quick and relatively uncostly battle. By the second day the islands had been secured. Almost all the 8,500 Japanese defenders were dead, with a loss of a thousand Marines and Army infantrymen. The Japanese made no air attacks on the U.S. fleet.

To Adm. Raymond Spruance and the commanders of Task Force 58, it meant the tide had turned. The invasion of Kwajalein was the first time the United States possessed an overwhelming superiority in naval forces, airpower, and the number of troops sent ashore. It proved that Japan's ring of island fortresses was vulnerable to a sea-based assault supported by the Navy's fast carrier force.

Before-and-after photos of the islands showed that the palm- and mangrove-covered islands were turned bare by the bombing and shelling by the American forces. Almost nothing was left standing, which gave rise to a couple of new expressions—the "Mitscher shampoo" and the "Spruance haircut."

Aboard *Intrepid* there was elation. Her airmen had tasted combat and performed with distinction. On February 4, 1944, Captain Sprague dropped *Intrepid*'s anchor in the newly captured Majuro Lagoon, 270 miles southeast of Kwajalein, and let his crew take a quick breather.

For *Intrepid*'s young sailors, it was the first taste of liberty on one of the newly captured Pacific atolls. It amounted to a few hours on a shell-covered coral beach. All the vegetation on Majuro had been removed by the recent Spruance haircut. Sailors were each issued two warm beers or Cokes.

And it was hot. Ray Stone remembered how they dealt with it. "With no shade, you soon marched fully clothed into the water, after tucking your wallet and cigarettes into your hat, and sat there submerged up to your chin." Soon, almost all the sailors on the beach were doing it. "It was a ludicrous sight," recalled Stone, "hundreds of heads with white hats barely above the surface."

The liberty in Majuro was brief. Task Force 58's commander was buoyed with the success of the Kwajalein campaign. He had already selected the next candidate for a Spruance haircut.

A shroud of mystery—and myth—surrounded the Japanese complex at Truk. The atoll had a spacious harbor and four airfields, and it was the main anchorage for the Japanese Combined Fleet. It was called the Gibraltar of the Pacific, and for good reason.

Admiral Spruance was taking no chances. Not until Task Force 58 was under way would he even disclose the target. Then he summoned all the air group commanders to a conference aboard *Yorktown*. The assembled CAGs listened to the intelligence briefing, then exchanged wary glances. The strike plan would have the same script as the massive air assault on Kawajalein: wave after wave of carrier-based aircraft roaring over the enemy anchorage, sinking everything in sight.

Truk, briefers told the CAGs, would be one of the most heavily defended Japanese bases in the Pacific. Unlike the Kwajalein campaign, which had been supported by Army Air Force B-24 bombers flying from the island of Apamama in the Gilberts, this operation would be conducted entirely by carrier-based aircraft. Also unlike Kwajalein, no attempt would be made to invade Truk.

The Truk striking force consisted of Task Group 58.1, commanded by Rear Adm. J. W. "Black Jack" Reeves Jr., and including the carriers *Enterprise, Yorktown,* and *Belleau Wood*; TG 58.2, led by Rear Adm. A. E. Montgomery, with *Essex, Intrepid,* and *Cabot*; and TG 58.3, commanded by Rear Adm. F. C. Sherman, consisting of *Bunker Hill, Monterey,* and *Cowpens.* This combined force embarked 276 fighters, 167 bombers, and 126 torpedo bombers.

The intelligence gathered about Truk was skimpy. Some of it, they would later discover, was dead wrong. Briefers told the CAGs they could expect to find aircraft carriers, battleships, and heavy cruisers in the anchorage. And they could expect light aerial opposition. According to estimates, the Japanese had 185 aircraft on Truk's three island airfields.

Task Force 58 arrived at the launch point 90 miles east of Truk before dawn on February 16. *Intrepid's* aircraft lumbered off the darkened flight deck and into the sky. In the lead was Lt. Cdr. John Phillips, *Intrepid's* CAG, flying his F6F-3 Hellcat. As the strike leader Phillips would direct a wave of Hellcats, SBD-5 dive-bombers, and TBM and TBF Avengers on the first strike over the atoll.

CAG Phillips was not a fighter pilot, at least by prior experience. Most of his combat time had been in the lumbering TBM Avenger, and before assuming command of the air group, he'd commanded an Avenger squadron. But CAGs, by tradition, flew every type of airplane in their air group. On this historic first strike on Truk, Phillips intended to lead from the front. That meant flying a Hellcat. A young fighter pilot from Fighting 6, Ens. John Ogg, drew the unenviable job of being the CAG's wingman.

Admiral Spruance's caution paid off. The attack came as a surprise to the Japanese. Not until the Navy planes were almost over the lagoon at 12,000 feet did the anti-aircraft guns open up from below.

But the intelligence estimates turned out to be woefully wrong. Most of the Japanese fighting fleet had left the anchorage. Later intelligence determined that the Japanese commanders, fearing such an attack, had relocated their aircraft carriers, battleships, and heavy cruisers to safer waters in Palau a week before. But the big lagoon still contained targets, mostly freighters and tankers.

And they learned that another pre-strike estimate was badly wrong. The number of Japanese aircraft at Truk was nearly twice what they'd heard in the briefing. For the rest of the day Air Group 18 and its pilots blazed away at the fields on the islets of Moen, Eten, and Param. With F6F Hellcat fighters from all the squadrons of the task force ensuring air superiority, the Japanese Zeroes that managed to get airborne were quickly shot down. Many others were caught on the ground, some still awaiting assembly after having just been off-loaded from ships. Of the estimated 365 Japanese aircraft based on Truk, only a hundred were unscathed after the first day of Operation Hailstone.

Ten Hellcat fighters from *Intrepid* were on the first wave. Alex Vraciu, *Intrepid*'s newly anointed ace, had gotten his wish to be on the first fighter sweep, and this one turned out to be a fighter pilot's dream. A total of seventy-two fighters from the entire task force were launching, with no bombers to escort.

The fighters arrived over Moen, one of the islets in the Truk atoll, at 0805. Vraciu and his new wingman, Ens. Lou Little, were at 13,000 feet, about to roll into their dives on the airfield, when Vraciu spotted bandits high and to their port side.

Vraciu and Little pulled up into a high reversal and slid down on the tail of one of the Zeroes. Vraciu gunned this one down, then another the same way, while Little shot down yet another Zero. When Vraciu spotted a Rufe—a Zero fighter mounted on floats—down close to the water, he shot that down too.

Minutes later, Vraciu glimpsed a Zero ducking into cloud cover. Vraciu positioned himself up sun and waited. When the wary Zero popped out of the clouds, Vraciu was there. He slid into an aft firing position and shot it down. In his report, he "doubted that the Zero pilot ever saw me."

The other pilots of Fighting 6 were having equal luck. The skipper, Lt. Cdr. Harry "Stinky" Harrison, bagged his first and only kill of the war. In their first mission over Truk, *Intrepid*'s fighters shot down seventeen Japanese aircraft.

In all, Task Force 58 lost fewer aircraft than expected. Eight Hellcats were downed, mostly by anti-aircraft fire. One of these was an *Intrepid* pilot, Fighting 6's executive officer, Lt. George Bullard. The big, redheaded Bullard already had four aerial victories and five ground kills. At Truk he destroyed six Betty bombers and four Zeroes on the Moen airfield. Full of a warrior's zeal, Bullard decided to turn his .50-caliber guns on a Japanese light cruiser in the anchorage. It was then that his luck ran out.

An anti-aircraft burst from the cruiser damaged Bullard's engine. With his plane sputtering and trailing smoke, he was forced to ditch close to shore. For several hours Bullard was observed on the surface by his squadronmates. He made it to one of the offshore islets, Alanenkobwe Island, where he carved in the sandy beach "Bull—SOS."

They couldn't help him. He was too close to Japanese forces to be rescued, and by the end of the day, Bullard had been captured. He would spend the rest of the war as a POW.

An Avenger pilot from Torpedo 6, Lt. J. E. Bridges, was too successful in his attack on a Japanese freighter in Eten anchorage. In a shallow dive-bomb attack, he scored a direct hit with his load of four 500-pound bombs. The freighter, which happened to be an ammunition ship, exploded in a blast that soared more than a thousand feet into the sky. Bridges's Avenger and everyone aboard were vaporized in the fiery explosion.

Not until the pilots were returning to *Intrepid* did they realize the strike leader was missing. CAG Phillips had been directing the Dauntless dive-bombers and TBM torpedo bombers from his F6F-3 Hellcat. Somewhere in the swirling tableau of anti-aircraft guns and attacking Zeroes and roiling puffs of flak, Phillips and his wingman, John Ogg, went missing.

More fighters were sent looking for them. They found nothing. There was no trace of either Hellcat. Whether Phillips and Ogg were downed by anti-aircraft fire, Japanese fighters, or freak accident was a mystery. At the end of the day, both were listed as missing in action.

It was a stunning loss to the air group. John Phillips had been in action with Air Group 6 since their time aboard *Enterprise.* Fighting 6's Stinky Harrison, the senior squadron commander, took over the job of CAG.

Another loss was even harder to comprehend. An SBD-5 from

Bombing 6 had spotted a force of enemy heavy ships to the north-west of Truk atoll. The pilot, Lt. Paul TePas, decided to make a message drop on a U.S. ship formation to inform them about the Japanese warships. TePas turned on his IFF—Identification Friend or Foe—which labeled his Dauntless bomber on the surface radars as a "friendly." He then slowed to approach speed, flaps down, and flew along the port side of the battleship *Iowa* to make the drop.

What happened next was the result of a sudden, tragic misjudg-ment. As the Dauntless passed alongside *Iowa,* an orange burst of gunfire erupted from one of her forward batteries. The Dauntless lurched, rolled onto its left wing, and plunged into the sea.

Throughout the day and into the night the attack on Truk con-tinued. Japanese losses were immense: two light cruisers, four de-stroyers, three auxiliary cruisers, two submarine tenders, two sub chasers, an armed trawler, an aircraft ferry, twenty-four merchant ships (five of which were tankers), and several smaller warships would go to the bottom of the lagoon or the waters surrounding Truk.

The task force had lost twenty-five aircraft, most to the intense anti-aircraft fire. Of the downed airmen, sixteen were rescued by submarine or amphibious aircraft. A force of U.S. surface ships and submarines moved into position to guard any possible exit routes from the island's anchorage and to attack any Japanese ships that tried to escape.

The myth of the impregnable Truk Island fortress was shat-tered.

By nightfall, *Intrepid* had recovered her aircraft and was in for-mation with her task group. All the ships in the group were blacked out, cruising slowly so as to leave no telltale wakes. The most seri-ous threat was enemy submarines. A lesser danger, but remotely possible, was the presence of Japanese warplanes.

And then, a few minutes past midnight, sailors on *Intrepid*'s flight deck heard something—a noise that didn't belong.

★ **3** ★

Under Sail

The sound of a Nakajima B5N "Kate" bomber, its nine-cylinder radial engine making a sharp staccato sound in the night, was enough to startle the men on *Intrepid*'s flight deck. To eighteen-year-old Gerald Goguen, at his station on the flight deck behind one of the 5-inch guns, it sounded like "a misfiring lawn mower."

The staccato sound grew louder.

Crewmen standing on the deck would swear that they had seen the torpedo plane. It appeared like a specter in the night, coming from the starboard side. As it swooped in low, its exhaust produced an eerie orange light. The Nakajima skimmed almost directly over *Intrepid*'s forward flight deck.

Later, intelligence officers would speculate about where the plane came from. The best guess was Rabaul, but it could have been Saipan. Whether the Japanese pilot possessed unusual skill or plain luck would be the subject of more speculation. A certain fact was that he had navigated across hundreds of miles of black ocean. It was a bold and unlikely effort by an enemy that had shown little interest in or aptitude for night surface attacks.

On the bridge there was confusion and uncertainty. Was the Japanese pilot taking a potshot, or did he have a specific target? No one knew, not even the radar operators down in the dimly lit CIC. Of the ships in Task Group 58.2, the big carriers *Intrepid* and *Essex* were the obvious targets. CIC had picked up the intruder on radar at 2349 and given it a designation: "Raid Easy." An F6F Hellcat night fighter from *Yorktown* was vectored to intercept the Japanese plane.

Alerted to the danger, the task group commander, Admiral Montgomery, ordered the entire force into an emergency turn to the southwest at a speed of 25 knots. At 0008, CIC reported losing contact with Raid Easy. Montgomery then ordered the task group into a hard turn back to port.

The violent turn was causing *Intrepid* to heel hard to starboard. Her deck was tilted at such an angle that the aircraft on the flight deck would have been swept overboard if they hadn't been firmly chained. It was as hard a turn as a ship displacing nearly 40,000 tons could make.

It wasn't enough. She was still in her turn when the torpedo struck. The explosion reverberated like a thunderclap through every space and passageway. Men were knocked off their feet. Some ricocheted like rag dolls off bulkheads. Others were caught in the passageways and went sprawling headlong.

For those whose battle stations were in the aft starboard section of *Intrepid*, it was the last moment of life. Five were killed instantly by the explosion. Six more were missing and found to have been killed. Another seventeen were injured. Two SBDs on the flight deck were hurled over the side, and two 20-mm gun mounts were carried away with the aft starboard catwalk.

The pulsing gong of general quarters sounded throughout the ship. *Intrepid*'s crew sprinted to their battle stations. A voice blared over the bullhorn: "Damage control parties, lay aft to your stations!"

The 800-kg torpedo had impacted in the aft starboard quarter, 15 feet below the waterline, ripping a gash large enough to admit a flood of seawater. *Intrepid*'s crew was well drilled in damage control; they quickly sealed off the flooded compartments and contained the damage. *Intrepid* was in no danger of sinking, but she wasn't out of trouble. She veered off course, unable to keep her place in the task group. The torpedo had damaged her rudder, jamming it hard to port.

Captain Sprague's voice boomed over the bullhorn: "Men, we have been torpedoed. The ship's rudder is jammed, and we are turning through the task force. Stand by for a possible collision."

In the next minute, it almost happened. The ghostly apparition of *Intrepid*'s sister carrier, USS *Essex,* appeared out of the darkness, bearing down on *Intrepid*'s bow. In a hard-over turn, *Essex* managed to swing away. She passed just behind *Intrepid*'s fantail.

Sprague's seamanship was being put to the test. He found he could keep *Intrepid*'s bow pointed straight ahead only by using asymmetrical thrust—throttling up the port engines while running the starboards at idle.

Later it would be asked why fighters or anti-aircraft guns hadn't tracked the intruding torpedo plane. Reports would indicate that they had. The night fighter pilot from *Yorktown* chased the Nakajima until they were both in range of the task group's anti-aircraft guns. Because of the closeness of the Hellcat, the anti-aircraft director held fire for fear of hitting the U.S. plane. It was also likely that gun directors were ordered *not* to expose the task group's positions by the muzzle flashes of the anti-aircraft guns. The night-flying skills of Japanese torpedo plane pilots were considered inferior and, therefore, a low threat.

Intrepid was out of the fight at Truk. Crippled, she was an easy target for Japanese planes and submarines. Admiral Montgomery ordered her to Majuro, where she'd stopped twelve days before, following the Kwajalein battle. Escorted by a task unit of cruisers, destroyers, and one light carrier, *Cabot,* Sprague headed his ship eastward, powering her with only the port engines.

And then came the wind. It was impossible to maintain course. Despite Sprague's best efforts, *Intrepid*'s bow kept swinging into the relentless 30-knot wind. "She was a like a giant pendulum," Sprague recalled, "swinging back and forth. She had a tendency to weathercock into the wind, turning her bow toward Tokyo. But right then I wasn't interested in going that direction."

It was time for some innovative thinking. The damage control officer, Cdr. Phil Reynolds, huddled with Chief Boatswain's Mate Frank Johnson. Though he couldn't see it, he was sure that *Intrepid*'s rudder had been transformed into something he called a "huge potato chip." The mangled rudder was not only unusable, it made directional control nearly impossible.

The wind was their enemy. It could also be their salvation. Reynolds and Johnson began fabricating a massive sail from everything available—hatch covers, tarpaulins, scrap canvas (the same canvas used to make body bags for burials at sea). They rigged the patchwork sail to the forecastle, the foremost section of the hangar deck, which was open to the wind. In addition, they moved all *Intrepid*'s aircraft to the furthest forward location on the flight deck, which, they hoped, would add even more sail effect to *Intrepid*'s bow. To lower her stern and give her screws more effectiveness, they moved as much cargo as possible to the aft of the ship.

To their astonishment it worked, more or less. In small, wavering increments, *Intrepid*'s bow swung out of the wind. It swayed back and forth, then grudgingly wobbled onto an easterly course, permitting Tom Sprague a small feeling of relief.

Intrepid's orders to Majuro were canceled. She was a casualty, and it was determined that no effective repairs could be made in theater. With her destroyer escorts, she was ordered to make for Pearl Harbor in whatever fashion possible. Her task group was detached, and two destroyers, *Stembel* and *Potter*, were assigned to escort her all the way to Hawaii.

En route, *Intrepid* had to undergo another first. Although a number of Air Group 6 airmen had been lost over Kwajalein and Truk, including the air group commander, CAG Phillips, *Intrepid*'s crew had suffered no casualties. Now that had changed. At noon, on a somber Pacific day while the ship struggled to maintain a course for Hawaii, the crew gathered on the hangar deck with their heads bowed. The ship's two chaplains conducted the memorial service for the eleven lost crewmen. While the Marine honor guard fired a salute, the canvas-wrapped bodies of *Intrepid*'s fallen sailors, weighted with 5-inch gun shells, slid from beneath their American flags and dropped into the sea.

For most of the young sailors of *Intrepid*, it was their first brush with violent death. It would not be the last.

It was *Intrepid*'s most arduous voyage. The slow, erratic course made her a sitting duck for submarines or another aerial attack. A ship's history recalls that the ship's course "looked like a seismograph reading gone wild." Her destroyer escorts, *Stembel* and *Potter*, had no choice except to watch and try to stay out of the way.

"No enemy sub could have ever figured out her zigzag plan," remembered Tom Sprague. "As a matter of fact there was no plan; the pattern was created as we went along, and no one knew for sure how long she'd keep on anything like a straight course."

She kept it long enough to reach Oahu. The sail's co-inventor, Phil Reynolds, remembered the entry into Pearl Harbor. "That sail looked pretty rough. I can't say I was proud of its looks. I wanted to take it off before we came into Pearl Harbor."

"Nothing doing," said Sprague. The sail stayed.

On February 24, 1944, *Intrepid* glided between the rows of warships berthed at Pearl Harbor. Sailors, workmen, gawkers stopped to stare at the spectacle. Even in a base that had seen over two years of both tragic and comic results of battle, this was something new. It would become the stuff of Navy legend and bar stories for the remainder of the war: *No kidding, a carrier sailed into port—I saw it with my own eyes. She had this odd sail rigged on her bow. . . .*

Workmen at the Pearl Harbor Navy Yard did their best to repair the damaged hull and remove the ruined "potato chip" rudder. The idea was to maintain steerage with just her screws long enough to reach San Francisco and the Hunters Point dry dock. On February 29, *Intrepid* was under way again.

It didn't work. Her earlier nemesis, the Pacific wind, struck again. A howling southwest gale buffeted *Intrepid*, shoving her around like a boat on a pond. None of Tom Sprague's efforts at jockeying the two engines would keep *Intrepid* on a straight course. He tried keeping her pointed into the wind. It didn't work. Nor did steering out of the wind. She could make 5 to 8 knots of speed, but her bow would swing as much as 90 degrees in any direction.

The cruiser *Birmingham*, three destroyer escorts, two tugs, and a salvage vessel were ordered out from Pearl Harbor to rescue *Intrepid*. Unlike her triumphant entry under sail five days before, this time *Intrepid* made a slow, ignominious return to Pearl Harbor.

For the next three weeks workmen labored to jury-rig a rudder that would give her adequate steerage. With a cable-operated, movable fin installed in place of her rudder, *Intrepid* again sailed out of Pearl Harbor.

The rig worked, after a fashion. Making a speed of 15 knots, *Intrepid* arrived outside the Golden Gate six days later, on March 22. A tugboat hauled her back to the Hunters Point shipyard, where her canal-damaged bow had been repaired less than three months before.

4

Return to War

March 28, 1944

No one was smiling, not even Capt. Tom Sprague.

Lined up in neat rows on the deck, wearing winter dress blue uniforms, *Intrepid*'s crew listened stoically while their fellow plank owner and commanding officer read his orders. It was a small assemblage, since most of the crew had been given three weeks' leave while the ship was in the Hunters Point dry dock. Those still aboard watched Sprague exchange salutes with his executive officer, Cdr. Dick Gaines, to whom he was turning over command of USS *Intrepid*. It was wartime, and Captain Sprague was moving up. He had been promoted to rear admiral and would be taking command of an escort carrier group.

It was a bittersweet moment. Sprague and *Intrepid* had begun their wartime journey together. Since the day seven months earlier when he stood on the deck and read the orders appointing him as *Intrepid*'s first commanding officer, more than 50,000 miles of ocean had swept beneath them. He had presided over her first strikes against the enemy. He had endured the pain of her first casualties. And like every Navy man who would sail in *Intrepid* over the next forty years, Sprague had a special feeling for the ship. For the rest of his life, *Intrepid* would be a part of him.

To the young sailors, many still in their teens and away from home for the first time, Sprague had been a surrogate father. They would remember his calm, matter-of-fact voice on the bullhorn during the first uncertain minutes off Truk: "Men, we have been torpedoed. The ship's rudder is jammed, and we are turning through the task force. Stand by for a possible collision."

They didn't collide, and it was Sprague who threaded them through dangerous waters, rudderless and under sail. Most of *Intrepid*'s crew, like eighteen-year-old Lou Valenti, would remember that Sprague "was the one who brought us home."

Another change was taking place, and it was almost as disturbing for *Intrepid*'s crew. Their air group, with whom *Intrepid*'s sailors now shared a combat history, was being off-loaded. The legendary Air Group 6, which had seen action from the early days of the war through the attack on Truk in February 1944, would be rotated to shore duty.

There were a few exceptions. One was Lt. (jg) Alex Vraciu, *Intrepid*'s first ace, whose missions over Kwajalein and Truk had brought his total of downed Japanese airplanes to nine. While the ship was in Hawaii, the twenty-four-year-old fighter pilot finagled a transfer to a squadron aboard *Lexington,* just leaving Pearl Harbor for action in the western Pacific. Vraciu's war was just beginning.

Intrepid remained in dry dock, undergoing her repairs, until the end of May. Commander Gaines resumed his role as executive officer when he was relieved by Capt. William Sample. But the game of musical chairs on *Intrepid*'s bridge was not over. Before Captain Sample ever settled into his job on *Intrepid,* he was abruptly yanked away to take command of USS *Lexington,* already at sea and in need of a skipper. Dick Gaines again became the caretaker commander until yet another captain arrived to take *Intrepid*'s helm.

Capt. Joseph Bolger reported aboard on May 30, 1944, and *Intrepid*'s crew quickly took a liking to him. Bolger was a cheerful, round-faced man, different in style and temperament from Tom Sprague. Like most wartime officers of his rank, he was a Naval Academy grad who'd paid his dues in the between-wars, budget-pared Navy. After becoming a naval aviator in 1924, he held a succession of squadron and staff jobs, commanding an observation squadron and serving as aide to an assistant secretary of the Navy.

Like Sprague before him, Bolger had been tagged as an officer on his way up in the wartime Navy.

On June 3, 1944, Captain Bolger headed his ship out of San Francisco Bay for her post-repair sea trials. *Intrepid* not only had a new rudder but had been retrofitted with features that were now standard on the later *Essex*-class carriers. She sported a new paint scheme, a zigzag camouflage of light gray, ocean gray, and black swatches. A second flush deck hydraulic catapult had been installed on her bow.

Two items of original equipment were gone. One was the athwartships hangar deck catapult, which had almost never been used and was viewed with hate and loathing by the airmen. No pilot in his right mind wanted to be launched through an open bay off the *side* of the ship.

Another universally despised item was the forward-rigged arresting cables and barricade and LSO platform, a scheme that was supposed to permit the ship to land aircraft while steaming full astern. It was never used, and it was now removed. The pilots and LSOs all said good riddance.

Intrepid's post-repair sortie not only was a test of the shipyard's work but gave the many new crewmen, including the captain, their first chance to work together. Captain Bolger and his crew hit it off right away. Bolger believed in visiting his men, showing up on the mess decks and at the work stations to ask questions and take an interest in their welfare. It was an age when smoking was a way of life, and the new skipper could be seen in the walkway outside his bridge puffing on a cigar, alarming the fueling and ordnance officers with the trail of sparks flying past the island.

For her next voyage across the Pacific, the mighty warship had been assigned an unglamorous mission: she would be a transport vessel. Every available inch of her decks was covered with airplanes, motorized equipment, passengers, and miscellaneous cargo, all bound for the Pacific. On June 9, 1944, laden with cargo, she again slipped beneath the Golden Gate Bridge and pointed her bow toward Hawaii.

After unloading her burden in Pearl Harbor, she embarked Air Group 19, whose squadrons were only aboard for the ride to Eniwetok Atoll. In *Intrepid*'s absence following the Truk battle and torpedo strike, Eniwetok had been captured by U.S. Marines in February 1944. The atoll was now an important U.S. stepping-stone in the march to the Japanese homeland.

In the company of the destroyers *Smalley* and *Leutze,* which with *Intrepid* formed Task Group 19.7, *Intrepid* departed Pearl Harbor on June 23. A week later, her deck still covered with warplanes, *Intrepid* dropped anchor at Eniwetok.

And then *Intrepid* had another first—a somewhat dubious one. Instead of off-loading the airplanes of her embarked-but-not-flying air group, Captain Bolger watched from his bridge while the Hellcats, Avengers, and Helldivers, one after the other, were catapulted from *Intrepid*'s stationary deck at her anchorage.

Intrepid's transport days weren't over. With her decks now cleared, she embarked hundreds of soldiers, sailors, and Marines, many wounded and on stretchers, to carry back to Hawaii for treatment or transfer. With her two-destroyer escort, *Intrepid* departed the Marshalls on July 4, 1944, bound again for Pearl Harbor.

During most of the next month *Intrepid*'s sailors enjoyed time off in Honolulu and on the beaches of Waikiki. It was a good time to unwind. Hawaii and its balmy, palm-fronded ambience seemed light-years removed from the carnage in the western Pacific. For many of the young Navy men of *Intrepid,* it was the last good time. They would soon be engaged in the greatest sea battle of all time.

The relationship between an aircraft carrier and her embarked air group was not always congenial. When *Intrepid* was joined in Pearl Harbor by Air Group 18, it was not love at first sight. Watching the "airedales" arrive in buses from their shore base in Kaneohe, the *Intrepid* sailors couldn't help feeling a bit condescending. They already had two combat operations—Kwajalein and Truk—under their belts. They'd survived a night torpedo attack, lost crewmates, and gotten their ship across the Pacific without a working rudder.

Unlike Air Group 6, which had fought in almost every battle of the Pacific, Air Group 18 was green. The air group had been commissioned in July 1943 but had spent the war so far on the non-hostile beaches of Hawaii. Their fighting experience, wisecracking *Intrepid* sailors liked to point out, consisted of a few Honolulu bar brawls and mock attacks by their aircraft on practice targets in Oahu.

It was obvious that many of the air group officers and men had never been aboard a ship before. Some didn't know port from starboard. Gazing around at their new steel surroundings, the airedales looked like kids seeing their first big city. For the first few days, *Intrepid* sailors had great fun directing lost airedales to non-existent places on the ship.

For their part, the airedales knew about *Intrepid*'s recent history, and they were making their own wisecracks about the carrier's visits to the dry dock. They were given more material when, on *Intrepid*'s first training sortie with the air group aboard, she developed a vibration that rattled every rivet and bulkhead on the ship. The lubrication system of her power plants had fouled, damaging a main bearing and forcing the ship to limp back to Ford Island for repairs. An air group scribe gleefully wrote that "they had to send out an extra tug to keep the big ship from automatically turning into a dry dock."

Both sides—ship's company and airedales—were finally told by their officers to knock it off. No more dirty tricks, no more wiseass remarks. Sailors being sailors, they nodded and yessirred and went on insulting one another.

The CAG of *Intrepid*'s new air group was Cdr. Bill Ellis, but his pilots had their own name for him: "El Gropo." Ellis was a tall, battle-tested fighter pilot. Like most CAGs and squadron skippers of the time, he was an Academy grad and a regular officer. Except for a sprinkling of experienced pilots in each squadron, most of Air Group 18's aviators were young reserve officers with minimal experience on aircraft carriers. Most were recent graduates of Navy flight training and had never seen combat.

Air Group 18's fighting squadron, VF-18, was equipped with the reliable F6F-3 Hellcat; VB-18, the dive-bombing squadron, was flying the new Curtiss SB2C Helldiver; VT-18, the torpedo/bombing squadron, flew TBF-1 and TBM-1C Avengers (Avengers built in the Grumman factory received the Navy designation TBF, the *F* being the letter assigned to Grumman-built aircraft, while later models built under license by General Motors were designated TBM).

The F6F Hellcat fighter, already established as an air superiority weapon, was evolving into a multi-role warplane. In the coming assaults on Japanese bases, the Hellcat would be assigned every mission—bombing buildings and revetments, strafing Japanese airplanes on the ground, shooting them down if they managed to get into the air. The Hellcat was considered a pilot-friendly airplane, easier to land back aboard than the long-snouted new F4U Corsair.

Like most air groups deployed on the fast carriers, *Intrepid*'s unit had a detachment of night fighters—four F6F-3N Hellcats equipped with the new APS-6 radar mounted in a pod on the fighter's wing.

Intrepid spent the next several days in Hawaiian waters exercising her new air group. El Gropo led his young aviators in simulated attacks, making dozens of practice launches and recoveries back aboard the carrier. By late July, Captain Bolger could report to his superiors that *Intrepid* and her air group were ready to go to war.

But first, they would receive a visit from the commander in chief.

It was July 27, 1944, and white-uniformed sailors lined *Intrepid*'s rails to greet the president. Franklin D. Roosevelt had flown to Pearl Harbor to confer with his two Pacific commanders, Gen. Douglas MacArthur and Adm. Chester Nimitz.

The stepping-stone island campaign was bringing the war ever closer to the Japanese homeland. As the next step toward the eventual invasion of Japan, MacArthur wanted to recapture the Philippines, then take Okinawa. MacArthur's reasoning was both strategic and personal. Before the war he'd been the field marshal of the Philippine Army. When he left the Philippines—on direct orders from President Roosevelt—MacArthur made the promise that would become a mantra and a rallying cry in the Japanese-occupied Philippines: "I shall return."

Nimitz, who held the title of commander in chief, Pacific, had no such sentiments. Bypassing the Philippines made more sense in his view. It would keep the Japanese occupiers bottled up in the Philippines and out of the fight while the United States went directly for Okinawa and then Formosa. From there they would stage invasions of both China and the southern islands of Japan.

President Roosevelt had always been uncomfortable with the arrangement of having two equal-in-rank commanders in one theater. He preferred the idea of a single commander overseeing all the U.S. forces, as Gen. Dwight Eisenhower was doing in Europe. Roosevelt allowed the awkward cocommand in the Pacific because he recognized MacArthur's brilliance, despite the general's towering ego and flair for the dramatic. At the same time, Roosevelt had no wish to diminish the authority of Nimitz, under whose solid leadership the Navy was retaking the Pacific from the Japanese, island by island.

After hearing both officers, Roosevelt sided with MacArthur. The invasion of the Philippines would come next.

MacArthur was taking no chances. Prior to landing his forces in the Philippines, he intended to neutralize the Palau Islands, 500 miles east of the Philippines, which he considered a threat to his right flank. The Japanese-held island group, 1,000 miles west of Truk and 2,000 miles south of Tokyo, had become the Japanese Combined Fleet's new command and logistics headquarters. It had become vitally important to the Imperial Japanese Navy, with its well-developed complex of air and naval bases.

The primary target of the Palau campaign was Peleliu, another of the coral reef islands whose only value to both the United States and Japan was its airfield. Peleliu would prove to be one of the bloodiest island battles of the war, for both the Americans and the Japanese.

It was August 16, and one year had passed since the humid afternoon in the Chesapeake when Tom Sprague read the orders placing *Intrepid* in service. For the occasion, the ship's bakers produced a 782-pound cake, made with 1,080 eggs and topped off with a confectioner's model of *Intrepid*.

The celebration was brief. The cake was devoured, and the crew went to their stations. By late afternoon, *Intrepid* was hauling anchor and threading her way out of the harbor and toward the open sea as part of a multi-carrier task unit, including the carriers *Independence* and *Enterprise*.

Staging out of Eniwetok, *Intrepid* conducted exercises, putting an edge on her crew's gunnery skills and giving the air group more deck practice. Then *Intrepid* received orders. She was headed for the Palau island group as the flagship of Task Group 38.2, a component of Marc Mitscher's powerful Task Force 38. *Intrepid*'s new task group commander, Rear Adm. Gerald Bogan, took up residence on the flag bridge. Bogan was a thick-necked, slope-shouldered man who looked and sounded like the movie tough guy Edward G. Robinson. In his youth Gerry Bogan had been a lightweight boxing champion, and he had the battered face and flat nose to prove it.

One of the islands in the group to which Bogan and the others were headed had an airfield that was vital to the U.S. strategy. And it had a name most of *Intrepid*'s crew couldn't pronounce.

5

Where Are the Fighters?

Babelthuap. After September, the name would be forever stuck in their memory. The island's crushed-coral runway was Air Group 18's first target. Babelthuap would be where *Intrepid*'s young pilots would receive their first taste of combat.

After a dawn fighter sweep on September 6, 1944, that produced no Japanese air opposition, El Gropo led a composite strike of fighters, bombers, and torpedo planes against the air strip at Babelthuap. There were still no Japanese fighters, and even the antiaircraft fire seemed ineffective. The pilots expended their bombs blowing holes in the runway. They couldn't get over the feeling that they were somehow missing the real action.

The next day the air group continued to pound Babelthuap, in preparation for the planned landing on Peleliu, to the south. A Helldiver flown by Andy Anderson took a hit that crippled his bomber, and he ditched it next to *Intrepid*. Later that day, during an attack on an oil dump, Air Group 18 lost its first pilot in combat—but not to enemy fire.

Determined to plant his 2,000-pound bomb squarely on the target, Avenger pilot Dave Savage pressed his attack too low, not releasing the bomb until 1,800 feet. As he pulled out low over his target, the explosion severed the tail of the TBM. The torpedo bomber instantly pitched over and plunged straight into the water, killing all three airmen aboard.

For the next two days *Intrepid*'s Hellcats, Avengers, and Helldivers pounded the Palau Islands, ripping up airfields and neutralizing most of the archipelago's heavy anti-aircraft emplacements and coastal guns. Then the aerial assault withdrew while surface ships moved in to bombard the Japanese entrenchments prior to an amphibious landing by U.S. Marines.

While the invasion of Peleliu was being prepared, *Intrepid* and Task Group 38.2 were ordered west to raid the Japanese airfields on the southernmost Philippine island, Mindanao. MacArthur was concerned that Japanese airpower based on Mindanao might still be potent enough to threaten the Peleliu invasion and the coming landings at Leyte.

The change in venue was good news to *Intrepid*'s pilots. Babelthuap and the islands of the Palaus had been unrewarding targets. For Fighting 18's Hellcat pilots, it had been particularly frustrating, as they kept wondering where the Japanese fighters were.

Striking from within a hundred miles of the coast of Mindanao, *Intrepid*'s warplanes bombed and strafed airfields around the port city of Davao, then torched Davao itself with incendiary bombs. Docks, warehouses, and port facilities were ravaged, sending flames and smoke thousands of feet into the sky.

But they still saw no enemy fighters. Even El Gropo, the CAG, was frustrated. "The Japs," he wrote in his action report, "seem strangely uninterested in combat."

And then on September 13, all that changed.

A pall of cigarette smoke hung over Fighting 18's ready room. The overhead lights glowed through the haze like beacons in a fog. Sprawled in their padded seats, the pilots were smoking, yawning, and scribbling notes on knee boards while they listened to the skipper. In the front of the murky compartment Lt. Cdr. Ed Murphy was briefing them on the morning's target—airfields on the island of Negros.

Murphy had a cordial but distant relationship with his pilots. At thirty-five, he was ten years older than most of them. Before coming to Fighting 18, Murphy had been a dive-bomber pilot, a less-than-glorious credential in the eyes of the young fighter pilots.

Fighting 18's aviators were like most fighter pilots. In their secret hearts they were a cut above other mortals, including those who flew the "Beast" dive-bombers and the "Torpeckers" of the torpedo squadrons. They were *fighter pilots,* a status that in World War II had become a stereotype. In movies, comic books, and newsreels, fighter pilots grinned down from cockpits that displayed rows of swastika and rising sun victory symbols. Fighter pilots were supposed to be flamboyant, cocky, and aggressive both in the air and on the ground.

There were exceptions to the stereotype. One of the exceptions was sitting in the middle row of padded seats in Fighting 18's ready room. Twenty-eight-year-old Lt. Cecil "Cece" Harris was Fighting 18's "quiet man." In a unit rostered with boisterous young men trying to live up to their fighter pilot images, Harris seemed like a mild-mannered schoolteacher, which was exactly what he had been back in South Dakota.

Harris joined the Navy before Pearl Harbor and trained as an aviation cadet. As an F4F Wildcat pilot aboard the escort carrier *Suwannee,* he had participated in the Operation Torch landings in North Africa. By early 1943 he was flying in the Solomons, where, assigned to VF-27, he scored his first two kills. Now, as Fighting 18's flight operations officer, Harris's job was to train the new pilots. One of the new pilots, Lt. (jg) Charlie Mallory, credited Harris with keeping him alive. "He made you think as to why you were there," said Mallory. "He made you appreciate that you were part of a team."

The briefing ended. The pilots strapped on their life vests and parachutes, headed down the passageway, and ascended the ladder to the flight deck. As usual, they were bantering, making raunchy jokes, being typically boisterous fighter pilots. And as usual, the quiet man was with them, smiling and keeping his silence.

A broken cloud layer covered the targets. The targets were the same as on the previous three days—Japanese airfields on the middle Philippine islands of Negros and Cebu. *Intrepid*'s planes were joined by strike aircraft from *Essex, Cabot,* and *Lexington.* Cece Harris and Lt. Jim Neighbors each led a flight of Hellcat fighters escorting the bomb-carrying Helldivers and Avengers.

The Helldiver and Avenger pilots had to look for breaks in the clouds, then push over into their dives, hoping to get a good view of the target before pickling off their bombs. The Hellcats alternated flying high cover for the bombers and diving through the clouds to strafe Japanese airplanes and buildings on the airfields. Two other Hellcat pilots, Charlie Mallory and Lt. Redman "Red" Beatley, had double duty. In addition to flying fighter cover, they carried on-board cameras for photo reconnaissance.

Beneath the clouds, the strike airplanes were having trouble. A TBM flown by Ens. Dan Laner took a hit during a low strafing run on the airfield. Machine-gun fire from the ground pinged into the low-flying Avenger, hitting a vital spot and sending Laner and his two crewmen exploding into the ground.

Next was Jim Neighbors. He was making a shallow diving pass on his target, threading his way through the anti-aircraft fire. As he pulled up, a burst of flak clipped the tail of the Hellcat. Neighbors's fighter pitched over and exploded in a fireball at the edge of the runway.

Above the cloud deck, Cece Harris and his flight had run into a hornet's nest. Thirty-six Japanese fighters in disconnected groups of three and four dove down to attack the bombers. Harris and his flight chased the enemy aircraft down below the clouds, where they were caught up in a deadly, tail-chasing dogfight only a few feet above the ground.

Harris maneuvered in behind one Zero and gunned him down from a 30-degree deflection angle. As he was climbing back above the fight, Harris spotted a Hamp—a clipped-wing variant of the Zero—and shot it out of the sky. Two more Hamps showed up, popping through the clouds. The relentless Harris went after them, killing them both in rapid succession.

It was the first air-to-air engagement of the war for the untested young pilots of Fighting 18. None except Harris had ever seen a Japanese fighter in the air. By the end of the fight, they had shot down nine, losing none to enemy fighters.

Cece Harris had scored four kills in a single day, a rare feat that he would repeat two more times while aboard *Intrepid*. For his valor in the air, the quiet man from South Dakota would be awarded the Navy Cross.

Meanwhile, in the Palaus the amphibious assault on Peleliu was being assembled. Not everyone, including Adm. Bull Halsey, thought it was necessary. Halsey was the overall commander of the Western Pacific Task Force under whom *Intrepid* and Task Group 38.2 were operating. He was surprised at how little aerial resistance the pilots from *Intrepid* and the other carriers were encountering over the Philippines. In early September he sent a message to Nimitz recommending that the Peleliu assault be canceled and, instead, the troops committed to that action be used in the coming invasion of the Philippines. Halsey thought the invasion ought to be commenced as soon as possible.

Nimitz agreed—almost. After consultation with MacArthur, the Joint Chiefs, and the president, it was decided that MacArthur's landing in Leyte could be moved up. But MacArthur insisted that the Peleliu assault go as scheduled. He was taking no chance of leaving his eastern flank exposed.

For the Marines of the 1st Division aboard the transports to the beaches of Peleliu, it was a fateful decision. Peleliu would become one of the bloodiest chapters in their history.

When they stormed ashore at Peleliu on September 15, resistance was lighter than anyone expected. At nearby Ulithi and Angaur islands, where the U.S. Army 81st Infantry Division was landing, they were having the same experience. The landings were unlike the ones they'd lived through on Saipan and Tarawa, where the landing craft met heavy resistance on the beach.

What the U.S. commanders didn't yet know was that the Japanese had changed tactics. Instead of putting up suicidal *banzai* counterattacks on the landing beaches, where they could be decimated by ship and aerial bombardments, the Japanese were holding back, burrowed into the porous terrain of the island. Not until nightfall, while the Americans were still consolidating their beachhead, did they counterattack. They came in focused, deadly forays against the Americans—and withdrew. They were fighting a battle of attrition.

The battle for Peleliu turned bloody for both sides. By the fourth day of the operation, the 1st Marine Division had lost as many Marines as it had during the entire invasion of Saipan. Novelist and Marine Leon Uris called the battle for Peleliu "one of the most savage of the Second World War."

Intrepid and her task group were ordered back to Peleliu. For the next several days her warplanes strafed and bombed the dug-in and mostly invisible enemy, who had fallen back to the thick mangrove swamps. It was harrowing, painstaking duty, firing on smoke-marked targets and camouflaged emplacements, praying there were no friendlies in the zone.

By the second week of fighting on Peleliu, the battle amounted to rooting out the Japanese survivors who were holed up in caves and hidden in the jungle. Meanwhile, *Intrepid* and her air group were on the move again, back to the Philippines.

Charlie Mallory, a week short of his twenty-fourth birthday, had a dilemma. He was a fighter pilot, and a damned good one, in his opinion. He'd already gotten shared credit for shooting down a Zero over Negros in his first air-to-air fight. But he was also a photo pilot, one of a few in Fighting 18 who were trained to fly the camera-equipped F6F-5P fighters. With MacArthur's invasion of the Philippines coming up, the images brought back by photo reconnaissance pilots were vitally important.

It was the morning of September 21. Mallory and three fellow photo pilots were on their way to make a photo sweep over Clark Field, the former American facility near Manila that was now a major Japanese air base.

Sixty miles from their photo target, Mallory spotted something else—five lumbering Betty bombers. Photo mission or not, the Bettys were too tempting to pass up. Mallory signaled his flight to dive on the bombers. "I picked off the one in front," said Mallory, "and the other three guys took the others. We had all four down in five minutes."

Over Clark Field, Mallory dropped down to make a high-speed photo pass down the main runway at 1,000 feet. What he saw on the field shocked him. "It looked like an international airport. Airplanes everywhere."

He was pulling up when he spotted a Japanese Kawasaki Ki-61 "Tony" fighter beneath and in front of him. "I gave him a burp, and he blew up," Mallory said. And then another appeared. Mallory gave him the same treatment. "He blew up too."

By now the sky was full of enemy fighters. Mallory and his wingmen extricated themselves from the melee and returned to the ship. But Mallory wasn't home free. Climbing out of his cockpit back on *Intrepid*'s flight deck, he was met by a yeoman who told him Admiral Mitscher, who was visiting the ship, wanted to hear Mallory's report about the action over Clark.

Mitscher listened with interest to what the young fighter pilot said, then congratulated him for his three kills. Mallory walked out of the flag bridge feeling a warm glow of pride. The warm glow lasted exactly one minute. Waiting for Mallory outside the flag bridge was a messenger from the air group commander: El Gropo wanted to see him, immediately.

The CAG was livid. Mallory had violated a standing order that photo pilots were *not* to engage the enemy for any reason except self-defense. The restriction had come directly from Halsey, who considered the photographs brought back by the reconnaissance pilots to be critical for the upcoming invasion of the Philippines. Photo reconnaissance pilots had even been required to sign a form acknowledging that they understood the order.

Mallory vaguely remembered signing the form. He saw it now on El Gropo's desk.

The tongue-lashing went on. Mallory had better not expect any award for what he did that day. In fact, he was damned lucky he wasn't getting a court-martial. Was that clear?

Mallory mumbled his assurance that it would never happen again and made the quickest departure he could manage. Three hours later he was back in the air.

It happened again.

The skies had cleared over Clark Field, offering an unobstructed view of the airfield below and the sky around them. And again, while Mallory and his flight were gathering images of the targets, a Japanese Tony rolled in on them. The eager Japanese pilot, sensing that these were photo reconnaissance aircraft, overplayed his hand. He overshot his pass on Mallory's Hellcat and pulled up directly in front of his nose.

Mallory considered his options for one or two seconds, then shot the Tony down in flames. Half a minute later, a flight of three more Tonys swept down at them. Mallory shot another one out of the sky.

He flew back to *Intrepid* that afternoon filled with a sense of dread. He'd just had a remarkable day of aerial combat. He decided to plead self-defense—"They attacked me"—and pray that El Gropo would buy it.

To Mallory's great relief, he did. Mallory not only escaped a court-martial but received the first of three Distinguished Flying Crosses. To cap off his spectacular day, he'd just joined an exclusive club: he'd become an ace in a single day.

It took guts to be a dive-bomber pilot. It took even more guts to be the gunner in the backseat, because he was along for the ride. From an altitude of about 12,000 feet, the pilot rolled the Helldiver up on its wing and pulled the nose down until he was diving on a nearly vertical line. He deployed dive brakes—flaps that popped out from the trailing edge of the wings—to keep the speed from building up too quickly, and to give himself time to fix the target in the sights.

As the airspeed increased, so did the noise, swelling to a howl. The target below expanded in his bombsight as in a zoom lens. All his normal references were gone. No horizon, no visual cues, just the howl, a high-pitched vibration, and the target filling up his windshield.

Altitude was critical. Release too high, and the bomb dropped short. Release too low, and either the bomb would kill him or he'd crash into the earth at something over 300 knots. Dive-bomber pilots were subject to a phenomenon called target fixation. Obsessed with keeping the target centered in their bombsight, they sometimes flew straight down and became one with their target.

The U.S. Navy didn't invent dive-bombing, but by the time World War II began, Navy and Marine aviators had taken the technique to an entirely new level. The Navy's bet on dive-bombers paid off in 1942 at the Battle of Midway. Three squadrons of Douglas-built SBD Dauntless dive-bombers sank four Japanese carriers and turned the tide of the Pacific war.

Now the SBD was being replaced with the bigger and more complex Curtiss SB2C Helldiver. Dubbed the "Beast" for its early stability and handling problems, the SB2C was either welcomed or despised. It was faster than the Dauntless and could carry a heavier load, but when the Helldiver first reached the fleet it had such serious maintenance problems and a high accident rate that some air bosses and carrier captains wanted it removed from their decks.

As the Helldiver joined the battles in the Pacific, it began to prove itself as a tough bird that could take hits and get its crew back home. But not always.

At dawn on September 23, Bombing 18's skipper, Mark Eslick Jr., was leading his Helldivers against a Japanese shipping fleet in Coron Bay, part of the Calamian Group, west of Panay and Mindoro. For this mission, Eslick's dive-bombers were carrying auxiliary fuel tanks to reach the target some 350 miles from *Intrepid*. It was one of the longest raids ever conducted by carrier-based Navy planes. They caught the fleet of Japanese ships off guard. *Intrepid*'s bombers and fighters sank seven ships and badly damaged several more.

But not without a heavy price. Three Helldivers didn't make it back. Lt. Walt Madden was last seen diving on an oil tanker when his SB2C was blown out of the sky. Ens. Ross Bunch, on the same attack, was hit and managed to put his Helldiver in the water. He and his gunner were reported rescued by a friendly boat.

Another Helldiver pilot, Ens. Ralph Beatle, planted his first 500-pound bomb directly into the flank of a troop transport. Buoyed with his success, he swung back around to bomb another transport and again scored a hit. But this time, on the pullout, he felt a thunk. An anti-aircraft round had gone through the Helldiver's engine. Smoke and flame were pouring from the cowling.

He and his rear gunner were about to bail out when Beatle looked down at the bay filled with burning and sinking enemy ships. An old attack pilot's adage came to him: *It's a bad idea to bail out over a target you have just bombed.* To hell with bailing out. He pointed the smoking Helldiver's nose toward open water.

With flames licking around the cockpit, Beatle smacked the Helldiver down, skipped once, and sloshed to a stop. He and his gunner, Bud Johnson, clambered out of the sinking airplane and crawled into their raft. With adrenaline-spiked energy, they paddled madly for the shore of the nearest island, where they were picked up by Filipino guerrillas. Not until three months later did they rejoin their squadronmates.

Several *Intrepid* planes had been lost now to anti-aircraft fire, but none to enemy fighters. Only a few Zeroes had come up to engage *Intrepid*'s bombers, and the Hellcat fighters had quickly taken them out.

It seemed too good to last. And it was.

★ 6 ★

Island of No Escape

October 12, 1944

It was a joke, thought the pilots of Bombing 18, and a bad one. They were looking at the map of Formosa that the intelligence officer had provided them. Parts of the map were labeled "unexplored." The grainy old reconnaissance photo had been taken twenty years before.

The truth was, they knew less about Formosa than they did about the Japanese homeland. What they did know was that the Japanese had occupied the island for half a century and considered it a part of their country. To defend Formosa, the Japanese had deployed enough fighters and anti-aircraft guns to intimidate any force that dared attack it.

There was no organized resistance force on Formosa as there was in the Philippines. Any American airman who went down could expect to be killed or captured. Being rescued from Formosa was almost out of the question.

The SB2C Helldiver squadron, Bombing 18, drew the toughest target. Kiirun Harbor was the port of Formosa's major city, Taipei. It had not only the most enticing targets—fat freighters and tankers at anchor—but also the most guns. Kiirun Harbor would be the most heavily defended facility outside the Japanese homeland.

It was still dark when the pilots went to the flight deck to man their aircraft. As usual, the Hellcats were going first. Their job would be to engage the swarms of Japanese fighters that were sure to come.

Bombing 18's skipper, Lt. Cdr. Mark Eslick Jr., would lead the flight of twelve dive-bombers. Behind them would come twelve Avengers, loaded with bombs instead of torpedoes.

The Helldiver crews climbed into their bombers and waited their turn to launch.

Further up the deck, Lt. Cecil Harris was starting the engine of his Hellcat. Up and down the still-darkened flight deck, big round engines were chuffing to life. Harris could smell the sweetish exhaust from the fighter in front of him as orange flame spat from its stacks.

Aircraft handlers were moving among the airplanes, performing their dangerous ballet between the whirling propellers. Harris released the brakes on his Hellcat, following the signals of the director beneath his nose. Each fighter had full fuel tanks and carried a single 500-pound bomb on the center station. Because they were so heavy, they would be catapulted this morning instead of making a deck run takeoff.

Fighting 18 was putting up sixteen Hellcats that morning—four divisions of four fighters each—with skipper Ed Murphy leading the first division. The second division would take station on Murphy's right side, and to his left would be the third division, led by Cecil Harris.

The sixteen Hellcats joined up and climbed through the pale gray sky until they leveled at 15,000 feet. The targets were Shinchiku and Matsuyama airfields. If they were jumped by enemy fighters before reaching the target, the Hellcats would shed their bombs and engage the fighters. In the intel briefing they'd been told to expect aerial opposition over Formosa. The Japanese had at least 350 aircraft on the island, half of them fighters. The pilots hoped, as they always did, that they would have the element of surprise.

They almost did. Even though the fast carrier force reached the launching point southeast of Formosa before sunrise on October 12 without being detected, the initial fighter sweep was picked up on Japanese radars. By the time *Intrepid*'s strike aircraft reached their targets, more than two hundred Japanese aircraft were in the air.

Even before the bombers reached the target, the situation turned grim. In the heavy cloud cover that clung to the 13,000-foot-high mountains of Formosa, the two 6-plane bomber divisions became separated. Worse, clouds obscured their target, Kiirun Harbor, on the north of the island. Then, seeing a hole, Eslick led his division in a dive down through the overcast and emerged directly over the harbor. The Helldivers went roaring across the docks and warehouses, releasing their bombs at low altitude.

As expected, Japanese guns opened up from each side of the harbor. As the Helldivers flashed across the harbor and zoomed for safety, the Japanese gunners sighted on them. The lead Helldiver, flown by Eslick, took a hit and spun into the harbor. Seconds later another Helldiver burst into flames and followed Eslick's plane into the water.

Led by Jack Forsyth, the surviving four Helldivers pulled up at the end of the valley, on the north end of Formosa. Their troubles weren't over. Waiting for them was a swarm of twin-engine Japanese fighters. The Helldivers clustered together, each trying to protect the others as the fighters swept down on them. And then as the fight developed, more bombers appeared from the south— *Intrepid*'s Avengers, just coming off their own target.

The battle dissolved into a chaotic blur of swirling bombers and fighters. The big plodding bombers—Curtiss SB2C "Beasts" and the equally ponderous Grumman TBM "Turkeys"—couldn't maneuver against the agile Japanese fighters, but they could match them in firepower. Each Helldiver and Avenger had not only its own forward-firing guns but gunners firing from the back. When Bob Christofferson, a Helldiver rear-seat gunner, flamed one of the more aggressive fighters, the other Zero pilots backed off.

The bombers finally disengaged and worked their way north to the open ocean, where *Intrepid* waited for them. When the Helldivers landed back aboard, they counted heads. Eleven men were gone, including their skipper, Mark Eslick Jr. Of the twelve airplanes the squadron had put over Formosa that day, a third were still back there, their pieces strewn like chaff in the hills and the harbor. It was the worst day in the squadron's history.

Cecil Harris could see the hangars below on the Shinchiku airfield. Leading the flight of four Hellcats, he rolled into a 60-degree dive. As the target swelled in the reticules of his windshield-mounted gun sight, Harris jabbed the pickle button on the control stick, then felt the thump as his 500-pound bomb released from its rack. Pulling off target, Harris rendezvoused with his flight at 8,000 feet and headed for the Matsuyama airfield, their next target.

Then another opportunity appeared. In the distance Harris spotted a flight of Japanese aircraft—four Kawasaki Ki-48 "Lily" bombers, and one twin-engine Mitsubishi Ki-21 bomber, code-named "Sally"—in the landing pattern at the Taien airfield. Harris and his flight rolled in on the hapless bombers.

The action lasted two minutes. Harris gunned down the Sally bomber and one of the Lilys. His wingmen shot down the other three. But there was no time to celebrate. Dropping from a cloud layer above them were at least fifteen Zeroes. Harris's number three, Lt. (jg) Bill Ziemer, took a barrage of 20-mm hits from a Zero. Trailing smoke from his shattered engine, Ziemer opened his canopy and went over the side. Meanwhile, his wingman, E. J. DiBatista, locked onto the Zero that had shot Ziemer down and destroyed it with his .50-caliber machine guns.

The melee turned into a deadly round-robin dogfight. While DiBatista was still firing at his Zero, another Japanese fighter rolled in on *his* tail and ripped DiBatista's Hellcat with cannon fire. At the same time, Cecil Harris slid in behind the Zero that was still trying to finish off DiBatista, and hammered him with machine-gun fire. The Zero exploded into the trees below.

It was Harris's third kill, and the day wasn't over.

More Zeroes were showing up. With nearly forty Japanese fighters swarming around them, every Hellcat was engaged. Using the Thach weave—a tactic invented by Lt. Cdr. Jimmy Thach when Navy Wildcat fighters were outmatched by Japanese Zeroes—the Hellcats kept crossing one another's tails, leading the Japanese that were chasing them into the guns of their wingmen.

Ens. Art Mollenhaur was a new pilot in the squadron. In the opening round of the fight over Taien, he had shot down one of the Japanese bombers. Now Mollenhaur was in the middle of the fight, attacking one Zero after another, expending more than 1,800 rounds of .50-caliber ammo. In the space of five minutes he downed four Zeroes, becoming an ace on his first combat mission.

He wasn't alone. The Fighting 18 pilots were having a field day. Cecil Harris's wingman, Lt. (jg) F. N. Burley, put down three Zeroes. Lt. F. C. Hearrell downed two Zeroes and one of the bombers. The sky over the Taien airfield was a tableau of fire and smoke and descending parachutes. The combat area encompassed 8 square miles, from 10,000 feet down to the ground. Plumes of fire leaped from the hillside as stricken fighters exploded into the ground.

In their action reports, pilots would grudgingly report that these Japanese fighter pilots, whom they had previously discounted, surprised them with their aggressiveness and skill.

Of the pilots in Harris's flight, only he and Burley were still unscathed. Bill Ziemer was descending in his parachute, steeling himself to meet his Japanese captors. DiBatista, whose Hellcat looked like a sieve from Japanese cannon fire, was still flying, but barely. While Harris was escorting DiBatista out of the battle, yet another Zero pounced on them. Again Harris outmaneuvered the Japanese pilot, sliding in behind and ripping him apart with his .50-caliber Brownings. It was his fourth kill of the day.

Ens. Ben St. John had considered himself lucky—until now. He was number six in a flight of TBM Avengers. A low ceiling and rain obscured the target area, but they'd spotted their target through a hole in the clouds and dropped their bombs. Now they were on their way home, and a swarm of Zeroes had just found them.

With no fighter cover, the Avengers were on their own. They stayed in close formation, using their collective firepower to ward off the Zeroes. It worked. No matter which angle the Japanese fighters attacked from, they met a storm of machine-gun fire from the Avengers. "We got four of them," St. John reported. "And we didn't lose any planes."

But St. John's Avenger took a burst from one of the Zeroes, and the electrical system dropped out. Minutes later, the flight leader took them into a cloud bank, and St. John lost sight of the other airplanes.

Now he was on his own. With no radio or navigation gear, he groped his way through the clouds, then descended to where he thought he'd find the task group. And there they were—guns pointed at him. Without a radio or IFF equipment, St. John prayed they wouldn't shoot while he made a quick "recognition turn." Depending on the day, a recognition turn was a 360-degree turn to the left or right to authenticate one's airplane as friendly.

St. John turned left and prayed again that he was turning the correct way. They didn't shoot. Minutes later he was treated to the most welcome sight he'd ever seen: "There was the *Intrepid*, turning into the wind."

In radio silence, he lowered his landing gear and tailhook and landed back aboard.

Charlie Mallory and his flight were still over Formosa, attacking Shinchiku airfield. Weaving through the intense anti-aircraft fire, Mallory glimpsed four blunt-nosed Nakajima Ki-44 Shoki "Tojo" fighters breaking out of the clouds above. He dove for the ground, shaking the Tojos off his tail, but his wingmen, Red Beatley and Harvey Picken, were in trouble. Mallory pulled back into a steep climb and shot a Tojo off Beatley's tail. The Japanese fighter burst into flame so abruptly that Mallory almost collided with him. He and Beatley then swung in behind the Tojo that had locked onto Pickens's tail, and Beatley sent it down in flames.

The third Tojo was still in the fight. As he swept down on the rejoining Hellcats, Mallory pulled up into a loop, firing on the Tojo coming down the back side of the maneuver. The Tojo disengaged and ran for safety, with the Hellcats in pursuit like hounds after a hare. The chase went on for fifteen minutes at deck level, roaring low over villages, skimming ridges, and following valleys. The Hellcats took turns firing at the Tojo. With only one gun still firing, Mallory finally flamed the Tojo.

Ten miles east of the Formosa coast, they spotted another Tojo and started another hounds-and-hare chase. By now the Hellcats were almost out of ammunition—and gas. Beatley's guns were empty, and Mallory took his place chasing the Tojo. When the Tojo entered a narrow valley, Mallory realized the Japanese pilot would have to pull up to clear a ridge ahead. Mallory climbed—and waited. The Tojo pilot would be forced to pull up.

When he did, Mallory was there. "I fired my one remaining gun and he went down."

It was a costly day for both sides. In after-action reports, pilots reported that during the height of the air battle there was always at least one parachute in the air and at one time five. *Intrepid* airmen shot down forty-six Japanese airplanes, with seven more probables and two destroyed on the ground. Two large Japanese warships had been sunk, and ten more were damaged. Buildings, hangars, warehouses, and a large fuel dump had been razed.

Only twelve of the sixteen Hellcats made it back to *Intrepid*. Three Fighting 18 pilots were dead, and one, Ziemer, was in enemy hands. DiBatista, who nursed his bullet-shattered Hellcat away from Formosa while being protected by Harris, broke his leg when he bailed out over open water and was now aboard a U.S. destroyer.

For Harris, the South Dakota schoolteacher, it was a day of mixed emotions. With the rest of his squadron he was mourning the loss of three pilots. Harris's four victories propelled him into lofty territory. He was now a double ace—and the highest-scoring fighter pilot on the *Intrepid*.

The worst losses of the day were suffered by Bombing 18. Six SB2C Helldivers had been destroyed, and twelve airmen were dead, including squadron skipper Lt. Cdr. Mark Eslick Jr. That evening was a good time, they all figured, for a visit from the friendly flight surgeon.

The flight surgeon was a fixture in every carrier air group, and Air Group 18's was a kindly physician named John W. Fish. What the pilots liked most about Doc Fish was his attitude about medicinal spirits after a grim day of combat losses.

Drinking aboard U.S. Navy ships had been officially banned since 1914, when Secretary of the Navy Josephus Daniels issued General Order 99: "The use or introduction for drinking purposes of alcoholic liquors on board any naval vessel, or within any navy yard or station, is strictly prohibited, and commanding officers will be held directly responsible for the enforcement of this order."

Some rules begged to be broken, of course, and the alcohol prohibition was one of them. Since 1914, Navy sailors had become experts at finding hiding places for their forbidden spirits. Aboard aircraft carriers, junior officers maintained secret caches for the purpose of late-night debriefings and toasts to lost squadronmates. Few commanding officers made an issue of the matter unless someone flaunted it.

But since the early days of carrier aviation, there had been an obscure exception to the prohibition. Flight surgeons, being responsible for the health and fitness of their aviators, were authorized to administer small doses of alcoholic beverages to airmen. Some flight surgeons were stingy about the dosages, and some flatly refused to dispense booze to aviators.

Air Group 18 pilots were lucky. Doc Fish was one of the good guys. Fish would appear at the ready room door with a couple of his corpsmen, each bearing a cardboard box filled with 2-ounce bottles. "Each pilot is entitled to two 2-ounce bottles," he'd say. "I'll let you gentlemen be responsible for distributing it."

It was a responsibility the pilots took seriously. In the toasts that followed, they always raised a glass to their friend Doc Fish.

The strikes on Formosa continued for two more days. Bombing 18 lost two more Helldivers, one to enemy fire and one to an operational water landing. Though the Japanese seemed reluctant to make daytime air attacks on the U.S. fleet, they were sending nightly waves of prowlers, which were fended off by Hellcat night fighters and anti-aircraft gunners from the perimeter ships.

The objective of the Formosa attacks was to decimate Japanese airpower on Formosa that could threaten the coming invasion of the Philippines. To that extent, it succeeded beyond expectations. Five hundred Japanese aircraft were destroyed in the three-day operation, but not without a severe cost: eighty-nine U.S. airplanes were lost, and sixty-four airmen were dead or missing.

On October 20, the first troops of MacArthur's Sixth Army stormed through the surf at Leyte. By the twenty-third, more than 125,000 men and a quarter million tons of equipment were ashore. The landings met only light enemy resistance, but no one had forgotten the lesson of Peleliu. The new Japanese tactic was to wait, picking their moment to counterattack. The Japanese could be expected to put up a ferocious resistance.

What neither the American nor the Japanese ground commanders yet knew was that another battle—the greatest naval engagement in history—was about to commence just beyond their view.

7

The Greatest Battle

Adm. Jisaburo Ozawa was desperate. The tall, charismatic commander of the Mobile Fleet, the Imperial Japanese Navy's carrier task force—or what remained of it—had come under intense pressure. Since early October 1944 it had been clear that the Americans would land in the Philippines. It was also clear, not only to Ozawa but also to every senior officer in the Japanese high command, that losing the Philippines would cost Japan the sea lane to her oil-supplying colonies in the south. The war would spiral down to a suicidal last-ditch defense of the homeland.

What Ozawa wanted—and his superiors demanded—was the classic engagement they were dreamily calling the "Decisive Battle." They wanted to draw the Americans into a massive confrontation in which the remaining forces of the Japanese fleet would deal the Americans a stunning, crippling blow. To accomplish this lofty goal, the planners of the Combined Fleet had come up with a strategy.

Sho-1, or "Victory One," reflected the fatalistic attitude of the Japanese high command. The remaining carriers of Ozawa's fleet were to keep the American carrier force engaged while Adm. Matome Ugaki's surface fleet of fifty-six warships attacked the American fleet guarding MacArthur's landing force. The idea was to lure the American fast carrier force into battle far enough away from the Philippines to allow Ugaki's surface fleet to charge unopposed into the seas around Leyte. Following the destruction of the ships protecting MacArthur, Ugaki's fleet would turn their guns on the transports supporting the invasion. The U.S. troops would be cut off. They would then be decimated by the Japanese Army forces that occupied the Philippines.

It was a brilliantly conceived plan, but it counted on equally brilliant execution. Sho-1 was flawed from the beginning by a scarcity of air cover. American fighter sweeps in the past two weeks had cut deeply into Japanese airpower in the Philippines.

Like every Japanese strategy in 1944, Sho-1 depended on surprise and divine intervention. No one, least of all Admiral Ozawa, had confidence that it would work, but it made no difference. By now *Bushido*—the ancient code of the Japanese warrior—had infected the thinking of even the most pragmatic officers. The honor of the Imperial Japanese Navy was at stake. Fighting to the death with the Americans was as sacred a goal as victory itself.

On October 20, 1944, Ozawa left the inland sea of Japan for the Leyte Gulf aboard his flagship, the carrier *Zuikaku*. With him steamed his fleet—three light carriers and two "hermaphrodites," battleships with short flight decks mounted on their sterns.

For Ozawa, it was an ironic moment. Japanese warplanes had launched from the decks of the mighty *Zuikaku* in December 1941 to humiliate the American fleet at Pearl Harbor. Since then *Zuikaku* had survived the major sea battles of the Pacific. As she sailed to confront more than two hundred warships of Halsey's Third Fleet, her decks were two-thirds empty. Ozawa's entire carrier force had only 108 flyable aircraft embarked, and these were aboard so they could be flown to air bases in the Philippines. Most of Ozawa's pilots were untrained in carrier operations and couldn't land back aboard their ships.

To Ozawa, it didn't matter. His mission was not to attack the enemy fleet but to draw it away from the real battle. Ozawa and his force were being sacrificed for a higher purpose: Bushido.

Intrepid was operating in the Philippine Sea to the west of Leyte. On the morning of October 21, 1944, while MacArthur's troops were still storming ashore on Leyte, *Intrepid*'s bombers and fighters launched strikes against Japanese positions throughout the Leyte Gulf and Visayan Sea. For three days *Intrepid* and Task Group 38.2 hammered Japanese targets while MacArthur's force consolidated its toehold on Leyte.

Guarding the Leyte landings just off the invasion beach were the ships of "MacArthur's Navy," the Seventh Fleet under the command of Adm. Thomas Kincaid. The Seventh Fleet consisted of six battleships, eight heavy and light cruisers, forty-two destroyers and destroyer escorts, thirty-nine PT boats, and several hundred assorted landing craft, transports, and troopships.

Admiral Kincaid's immediate superior was General MacArthur. Admiral Halsey, commander of the Third Fleet, which included the four task groups of the fast carrier force, took his orders directly from Nimitz. This convoluted chain of command was a reflection of the rivalry between MacArthur and Nimitz. In the battle to come, it would have deadly consequences.

Still undetected by the Americans, three separate Japanese fleets were converging on the Philippines. From his base in Brunei Bay, Adm. Takeo Kurita's First Diversionary Striking Force was headed south for the Philippines. At the southern end of Borneo, Kurita's fleet divided, and Adm. Shoji Nishimura turned east with a group of eight battleships, one cruiser, and four destroyers.

A third force, commanded by Vice Adm. Kiyohide Shima, consisting of two heavy cruisers, a light cruiser, and seven destroyers, had sortied from the coast of Formosa to join Kurita's combined fleet.

The plan, which would require exquisite timing, called for all three forces to converge from north and south. Kurita's force would enter the Sibuyan Sea to the north of Leyte, thread the narrow San Bernardino Strait, then charge down the eastern shore of Savo to the Leyte Gulf. At the same time, Nishimura's force would sail into the Surigao Strait, the southern passage to Leyte. Nishimura would be joined by Admiral Shima's force, and together they would race through the Surigao Strait, forming a pincer with Kurita's force.

The key to success lay with Admiral Ozawa, whose carrier force was supposed to lure Halsey and his fast carrier force away from the battle at Leyte. Kincaid's Seventh Fleet—and MacArthur's invasion force—would be trapped.

On the night of October 23, Kurita's force arrived on the western shore of Palawan Island, a long, narrow strip of land that paralleled the Philippine archipelago. His plan depended on reaching the waters of Leyte Gulf before being spotted by the Americans. Soon after midnight, the plan began unraveling. Kurita's force was spotted as they threaded the narrow Palawan Passage. Two American submarines—*Darter* and *Dace*—lay in wait for the Japanese fleet and at dawn put torpedoes into Kurita's flagship, the cruiser *Atago*, as well as the cruiser *Maya*, sinking both. Kurita and most of the crew of *Atago* abandoned ship, and the admiral transferred his flag to the super-battleship *Yamato*.

The presence of the Japanese heavy warships was received with interest—but not alarm—in Admiral Halsey's flag plot aboard the battleship *New Jersey*. What did it mean? Were the Japanese coming out to challenge the American invasion at Leyte? It was difficult to believe the Japanese would be so reckless, particularly since their land-based air cover from the Philippines had been mostly neutralized in the past two weeks. To Halsey's planners, it didn't seem likely.

By dawn on the twenty-fourth, American search planes were combing the seas to the west of Leyte. Helldiver and Hellcat fighter escorts from *Intrepid*'s Bombing 18 and Fighting 18 were assigned quadrants along the Sibuyan Sea, the inner sea of the Philippine archipelago—and a likely route for any intruding Japanese fleet.

At about 0730, Lt. (jg) Max Adams's radarman picked up targets. Adams and his Hellcat escort pilot from Fighting 18, Lt. Don Watts, moved in for a close look. They counted the objects down below. Because of the distance from Halsey's command ship, Adams relayed the sighting to Lt. (jg) Bill Millar, another *Intrepid* pilot.

At 0822 on October 24, Millar's voice crackled over the radio in the flag plot aboard *New Jersey*: "Four battleships. Eight heavy cruisers, and thirteen destroyers, course east, off the southern tip of Mindoro, course zero-five-zero, speed ten to twenty knots."

Adams's count—twenty-five ships—was close. The Japanese force amounted to twenty-eight warships, including five battleships. Aboard Halsey's flagship, there was no longer any doubt about Japanese intentions. The Japanese fleet was steaming into the Sibuyan Sea, a passage that would take them through the San Bernardino Strait and southward to MacArthur's landing forces at Leyte.

The Battle of Leyte Gulf was about to begin. (See map, page 162.)

Led by *Intrepid*'s CAG Bill Ellis—El Gropo—the first wave of warplanes arrived from the east. Ellis had twenty-eight airplanes: eight Avengers, twelve Helldivers, and eight Hellcat fighters also armed with bombs. At the first sighting of the enemy airplanes, Kurita ordered his warships into a defensive formation, with battleships at the center, cruisers surrounding them, and destroyers circling the outer ring. From this formation the ships were able to put up an almost impenetrable wall of flak and fire. It seemed impossible that any attacking airplane could get close to score a hit.

And yet they did, one after the other—Helldivers plunging almost straight down to put their bombs on the evading ships, Avengers coming in low through the flak to launch torpedoes, Hellcat fighters dive-bombing, firing rockets, strafing with .50-caliber guns.

The American pilots stared in awe at a pair of objects they'd only heard about. Both were leaving circular white wakes behind them as they sliced through the Sibuyan Sea.

Speed is life.

It was a torpedo bomber pilot's mantra, and it was playing in Ben St. John's head like a refrain. He was gazing down at the two mightiest warships ever constructed—*Yamato* and *Musashi*. Their guns were filling the sky with a multi-hued curtain of fire and shrapnel.

Speed—the more the better—was what St. John wanted when he skimmed across the water to launch his 2,200-pound Mark 13 aerial torpedo. St. John had never dropped a torpedo in real combat, and now the guns of twenty-eight armored ships were shooting at him. It occurred to him that this was as real as it got.

The Avengers were supposed to dive separately, taking individual targets. In the bomb bay of each Avenger was a Mark 13. When it hit the water, the torpedo ran at a speed of nearly 40 knots. Older torpedoes had to be dropped at very low altitude, 200 feet or less, because the torpedo's motor began running immediately at release and would burn out quickly if it didn't enter the water. The new versions, which *Intrepid*'s Avengers were carrying, had motors that didn't start until they hit the water. They could be released at up to 2,400 feet altitude and at maximum speed.

Every torpedo bomber pilot knew what happened when you went in low and slow. In the Battle of Midway, Torpedo 8's slow-flying Douglas TBD torpedo planes had gone in low and slow to hit the Japanese carriers. None sank a ship, and every torpedo plane in the attack was shot down.

The Avenger's attack profile was supposed to begin with a dive from 12,000 feet, down to a level release altitude of 2,000 feet. One by one the Avengers went into their dives. Each pilot was on his own trajectory now, each "jinking"—flying an erratic, zigzag path, pitching up and down, trying to throw off the aim of the Japanese gunners. The airframes of the big Avengers, traveling at nearly 100 knots over their normal attack speed, were shuddering and vibrating like tuning forks.

Ben St. John picked out the biggest target in sight—*Yamato*. The battleship was slicing through the water in a curving course, almost as fast as St. John's torpedo. Torpedo bomber pilots had an old adage: *Don't try to outguess the ship.* What it meant was that you should launch your torpedo on a course that would intersect with the target. Never mind trying to predict what evasive tactics the ship might take. You were almost always wrong.

St. John yanked the nose of the Avenger around, dodging the bursts of anti-aircraft fire that were blossoming like bright cauliflowers around him. He leveled at 2,000 feet and made the last-second adjustments to send his torpedo after the gray monster looming in his windshield. Bomb bay doors open . . . line up the target . . . make sure the airplane is in absolutely straight flight, no yaw, no skid . . . release. St. John felt a whump as the Avenger shed its 2,200-pound load.

And then he did something inexplicable.

The escape maneuver was supposed to be a hard turn to the left as soon as he released. But in Ben St. John's adrenaline-soaked brain came a subliminal command: *Turn right.*

That saved his life. Anticipating his turn, the Japanese gunners were already laying down a hail of fire to the left. St. John's right turn took him directly over a cruiser whose surprised gunners were too slow to get a fix on the low-flying Avenger.

Then, even more inexplicably, he *continued* the right turn, completing a 270-degree circuit directly over the Japanese cruiser, whose gunners were still trying to fire at the torpedo plane. St. John exited the area in his originally intended direction with gun bursts exploding behind his tail. By a miracle he never understood, he escaped unhit.

St. John's torpedo missed the *Yamato,* but he hadn't wasted the weapon. According to a Helldiver pilot observing from above, St. John's torpedo passed astern the battleship, then continued straight ahead and exploded squarely amidships in a Japanese cruiser.

High above his target, Jack Forsyth rolled his SB2C onto its back, pulled the nose down, and deployed the speed brakes. He too had picked out a battleship, which he thought was *Yamato* (it was *Musashi*).

The Helldiver's airspeed built up. The wind howled over the airframe. The dark gray armor of the battleship grew larger in his windshield. Tracers from the ship's guns seemed to be converging on his airplane. He corkscrewed violently, trying to shake the flashing anti-aircraft fire that was coming straight up at him. It seemed there could be no way to escape the blizzard of shell fire, but it no longer mattered. He hadn't come this close to risk *not* putting his bomb on target.

He put the reticules of his ring sight on the battleship's number two turret. He glanced at the altimeter needle. It was unwinding through 3,000 feet—the release altitude.

He kept diving. To make sure.

Several hundred feet below the minimum altitude he released his bomb and pulled back hard on the stick. The G-meter went to 10.5 Gs—ten and a half times normal gravity. The pilot's 200-pound body weighed a ton. He grunted, trying not to black out from the G forces, trying to regain his vision as the blood left his head. The Helldiver groaned under the high load. Somehow the wings of the Curtiss Beast stayed attached.

He leveled, jinking again to avoid the anti-aircraft guns that were tracking him. From eighteen-year-old Walter Brown, his gunner in the backseat, came a yell: "We got a hit!" Forsyth took a quick glance over his shoulder. Brown was right. A mushrooming black cloud was erupting from the battleship's stern.

Now all they had to do was get out of there alive.

Every ship in Kurita's Central Force had its guns pointed at the attacking aircraft. *Musashi*'s 150 guns alone were pumping out twelve thousand rounds a minute. The surface of the ocean frothed with the splashes of falling munitions and shattered airplanes. The sky filled with the roiling smoke of the anti-aircraft barrage. Some of the shells spewed clouds of white phosphorus, which clung to the wings of the warplanes and continued to burn.

Of the eight SB2C Helldivers from Bombing 18 diving on *Musashi,* two were blown out of the sky. Another Helldiver, flown by Lt. H. E. Johnson, was hit and headed back to the *Intrepid.* Two miles short of the ship, Johnson ditched, and he and his crewman were rescued by a destroyer.

Three Avenger torpedo bombers were caught in the gauntlet of fire and went into the ocean. One, flown by Lt. Ben Riley, managed to ditch, and the crew was picked up by natives in a sailboat. Of the two other Avengers, nothing was ever found.

Even the Japanese ship commanders were shocked at the tenacity and courage of the American pilots. Relentlessly, the Americans dove down through the hailstorm of fire, putting their bombs on target. One Avenger came in so low and close before he released his torpedo, he skimmed directly over *Yamato*'s deck, passing between her bridge and her stacks.

As the attackers withdrew, another wave roared into the battle. And they kept coming. Throughout the day, wave after wave of fighters, bombers, and torpedo planes from six carriers—*Intrepid, Lexington, Cabot, Enterprise, Essex,* and *Franklin*—threw themselves at Kurita's fleet.

A Helldiver pilot put a bomb through the bow of *Yamato,* which was now Kurita's flagship and the pride of the Imperial Japanese Navy. Then two low-flying TBM Avengers put torpedoes into *Yamato*'s sister ship, the mighty *Musashi,* adding to the damage done by *Intrepid*'s dive-bombers. At first the huge battleship appeared to shrug off the blows from the torpedoes. But then observers from her escort ships noticed that her bow was beginning to settle.

Admiral Kurita ordered the battleship to exit the fight and head for a safe haven. For *Musashi,* it was too late. As she limped back to the west, more Avengers and Helldivers swarmed over her like hawks on a rabbit. Bombs from the Helldivers flayed the battleship's decks with shrapnel. The Avengers put ten more torpedoes into *Musashi*'s hull. *Musashi* fought back, not only firing her hundred-plus anti-aircraft guns but using her mighty 18-inch anti-ship guns to fire *sanshiki dan,* or "beehive" shells, which exploded in star-bursts amid the attacking aircraft.

Aboard *Yamato,* Admiral Kurita had seen enough. His urgent request for air support from land bases in the Philippines had gone unanswered. He ordered his force to turn around and steam westward, where they would regroup.

The bombs kept coming. *Musashi* continued limping westward. Then came reports that brought cheers to the ready rooms of Bombing 18 and Torpedo 18. *Musashi* had been observed foundering. Her bow was awash, and she was listing badly to port. The battleship appeared to have been left behind by the Japanese fleet.

By nightfall, it was over. The battleship rolled over, then her stern rose straight up. The once-mighty leviathan slid into the sea, taking more than a thousand men with her, including her captain, Adm. Toshihira Inoguchi.

Aboard *Intrepid*, it was a bittersweet moment. The flak from the Japanese task force had been the heaviest they'd ever seen. Six aircraft—three Helldivers and three Avengers—had been lost to enemy fire. Twelve men were dead or missing. Several crewmen had landed back aboard badly wounded.

They had fought a battle of historic proportions. In a contest of massive surface ships versus U.S. carrier aircraft, the dive-bombers and torpedo planes had won the victory without help from a single American surface ship. "We sank a big ship," Jack Forsyth of *Intrepid*'s Bombing 18 wrote. "A battleship. The biggest battleship the world has ever seen."

In the gathering darkness, American pilots observed the smoking ruins of the Japanese ships. They also reported that the remaining ships of the fleet were now sailing west, away from Leyte. The news was radioed to Halsey's flag plot. "We've stopped 'em!" yelled the officers in Halsey's flag plot. There was no doubt about it, they concluded. The Japanese fleet was withdrawing from the battle.

They were wrong. It was one link in a chain of wrong conclusions—by both sides—that would determine the outcome of the Battle of Leyte Gulf.

Admiral Kurita, in fact, had no intention of withdrawing. He still felt duty-bound to complete his assigned mission—to take his fleet through the San Bernardino Strait at all costs. Even though he'd fallen far behind the timetable, he would still try to rendezvous with Nishimura's and Shima's forces coming from the south.

By now, the timing of the Sho-1 plan had gone badly askew. Even though Kurita was late getting into position, Nishimura wasn't waiting. Like his superior, Nishimura had a fatalistic attitude about the coming battle. His force hadn't been as badly pummeled by air strikes as Kurita's. As duty-bound as his superior, Admiral Nishimura intended to take his force through the Mindanao Sea and into the Surigao Strait, to keep his rendezvous with Kurita at Leyte even though Admiral Shima's force of seven warships, which was supposed to join him in the Surigao Strait, was nowhere to be seen. And no one knew the disposition of Ozawa's decoy carriers, which were supposed to be luring away the American fast carrier force.

On the night of October 24, Admiral Nishimura charged headlong through the Sulu Sea and into the Surigao Strait to do battle with the Americans. He and his fleet, one of his officers wrote later, were steaming "into the jaws of death."

Waiting in the Surigao Strait were the Seventh Fleet's six old battleships. The obsolescence of their hulls was no particular handicap that night. Their big guns would be the decisive weapons in this battle. This time they possessed all the advantages, and for Rear Adm. Jesse Oldendorf, commanding the American warships, it would be a sweet revenge. Five of his six battleships had been salvaged from the wreckage of Pearl Harbor.

Oldendorf had been presented with a naval tactician's dream— "crossing the T." The ships of his horizontal battle line—the upper line of the T—were arrayed stem to stern perpendicularly against Nishimura's row of oncoming ships. Oldendorf's ships could train full broadsides against the enemy, while Nishimura's ships could use only their forward-mounted guns.

Nishimura's force of two battleships, one cruiser, and four destroyers was doomed from the moment they entered the strait. Waiting for him were thirty-nine fast torpedo-firing PT boats, then twenty-eight destroyers with their own arsenal of torpedoes, and then the cruisers firing their 6-inch and 8-inch guns. If any Japanese ships survived this gauntlet, they would then confront Oldendorf's "T"—six battleships all firing 14-inch or 16-inch guns.

Under a low cloud cover, the sea as black as coal, Nishimura sailed into the slaughter. The cloudy sky turned into an orange canopy. Tracers, star shells, and muzzle flashes filled the night. Torpedo wakes slashed across the black water. Firing nonstop, the American warships pumped tons of shells at the oncoming Japanese.

One by one, Nishimura's ships caught fire and plowed to a stop. Two destroyers went down almost immediately. One of the two battleships, *Fuso*, blew apart. Nishimura's flagship, *Yamashiro*, was torpedoed, pounded with shell fire, and set ablaze. Nishimura sent a final message: "You are to proceed and attack all ships." It was his last communication. Minutes later, *Yamashiro* exploded and sank. Nishimura perished with most of his crew.

In the midst of the carnage, another fleet of Japanese ships appeared. These were the two cruisers and four destroyers of Adm. Kiyohide Shima, who was supposed to have joined Nishimura for the charge into Surigao Strait. Because of a lack of communication—Shima and Nishimura disliked each other and resisted coordinating their movements—Shima had arrived late for the party.

The party was almost over. To Shima's astonishment, ships were burning everywhere—and they were all Japanese. As if to add to the weird surreality of the night, Shima's flagship, *Nachi,* collided with one of Nishimura's stricken cruisers, *Mogami.*

Shima considered his options. From his bridge he could hear the pounding of heavy guns—American guns—and he knew they would soon be aimed at him. Nishimura's fleet was doomed. Shima, who had spent most of his career as a staff officer and didn't share Nishimura's sentiments about sacrifice and Bushido, made a pragmatic decision. He turned his ships around and headed for home.

The uncoordinated Japanese effort in the Surigao Strait was a series of blunders. But they were not the only blunders in the Battle of Leyte Gulf. Another commander—this one American—was about to make a classic blunder.

8

The Fog of War

Bull Halsey was the Navy's version of George Patton. The admiral was a tough-talking, damn-the-torpedoes commander who didn't mind breaking a few rules. Enlisted men loved him. Officers either despised him or revered him as a demigod.

By comparison to their Army, Army Air Force, and Marine Corps counterparts, senior Navy officers tended to be bland and low-key. The white-uniformed, stiff-collared gentlemanliness of the Navy was considered a step above the rough-and-tumble mud soldiers and rowdy Air Force pilots. Halsey's immediate superior, Adm. Chester Nimitz, was cut from the traditional mold—a soft-spoken, analytical officer who rarely betrayed his emotions. During the dark days immediately after Pearl Harbor, when Nimitz took command of the Pacific Fleet, he needed commanders who could shore up the Navy's low public image. He wanted a dynamic leader who could show the world the U.S. Navy still knew how to fight.

Bull Halsey was the perfect candidate. The grizzled Halsey looked tough and sounded tougher. In what in modern times would be gross political incorrectness, he put up a billboard for all his sailors to see: ADMIRAL HALSEY SAYS, "KILL JAPS, KILL JAPS, KILL MORE JAPS!"

Halsey missed the turning-point naval battle of the war because he'd been hospitalized with a severe skin rash. Fully recovered, he declared, "Missing the Battle of Midway has been the greatest disappointment of my life, but I'm going back to the Pacific where I intend personally to have a crack at those yellow-bellied sons of bitches and their carriers."

On his flag bridge, he began every day with strong Navy coffee and the first of forty-some Lucky Strikes he'd smoke. Halsey liked to say, at least half seriously, that he didn't trust a man who didn't smoke, drink, and cuss. When ashore he loved bawdy drinking parties, and even in his flag quarters aboard ship he believed in a "medicinal" toddy from the ship's doctor to put him to sleep.

Halsey had graduated from the Naval Academy in 1904, a year after Nimitz. For twenty years he called himself "a destroyer man," but by the 1930s Halsey had caught the whiff of aviation gasoline. At the age of fifty-one, with the rank of captain, he went through flight training in the company of men half his age and earned his wings as a naval aviator. He commanded the aircraft carrier *Saratoga,* then the naval air training station at Pensacola. As a newly promoted flag officer, he led a carrier division, and when war came he commanded the task force that took Jimmy Doolittle's B-25 bombers to within 800 miles of Tokyo in the first attack on Japan.

In October 1942 Halsey was made commander of the South Pacific Forces and South Pacific Area. In June 1944 he assumed command of the Third Fleet and was designated commander of the Western Pacific Task Forces, which included USS *Intrepid* and her sister ships of the fast carrier force.

To Halsey, the destruction wrought on Kurita's and Nishimura's ships removed any immediate threat to the landing force at Leyte. His instinct was to go for the enemy's throat, and to him that meant their carriers. As commander of the Third Fleet, he understood that it was his job to lend strategic support to the landings at Leyte. But MacArthur's landing force had now been ashore for three days and was firmly entrenched. Following the rout of the Japanese in the Sibuyan Sea and the Surigao Strait, there seemed little likelihood the Japanese would again threaten the Leyte beachhead.

Not everyone shared Halsey's optimism. An ominous report had come in from a night search plane off the *Independence* that Kurita's fleet, which had been in full retreat after its mauling in the Sibuyan sea the day before, had turned around. Was it again heading for the San Bernardino Strait?

Halsey didn't think so. In any case, they were too depleted from the previous battle to put up much of a fight. Kincaid's Seventh Fleet and its three task groups of jeep carriers—lightly armored escort carriers converted from merchantmen and fleet oiler hulls—were more than adequate to counter them.

MacArthur and Kincaid thought otherwise. Each was under the impression that the primary mission of Halsey's Third Fleet was to ensure the success of the Philippine invasion. But with the American parallel command structure—Kincaid reporting to MacArthur, Halsey reporting to Nimitz—there was no direct link between the two senior commanders in the western Pacific. Halsey considered it his mandate to attack Japanese forces wherever and whenever he found them.

Now he was obsessed with finding the Japanese carriers. In Halsey's flag plot aboard *New Jersey*, the question was repeated like a drumbeat: *Where are their carriers?* They had to be out there somewhere.

In fact, they *were* out there. The efforts of Admiral Ozawa and his carrier force to have themselves "discovered" by the Americans had so far gone unnoticed. Ozawa had transmitted dozens of telltale messages, unaware that his own radio antenna was broken.

At midday on October 24, he launched seventy-six aircraft with orders to bomb the American carriers, then land at shore bases in the Philippines. If it accomplished nothing else, it would inform the Americans that they had been attacked from a carrier force not far away. Or so Ozawa hoped.

On the afternoon of the twenty-fourth, while reports were still streaming in about the retreat of Kurita's fleet in the Sibuyan Sea, Halsey received electrifying news. A search plane had located the missing enemy fleet off the northern tip of Luzon—one large carrier, three light carriers, two battleships with flight decks, five cruisers, and six destroyers.

It was all Halsey needed to hear. He was on his way, removing his fast carrier force from the vicinity of the San Bernardino Strait. Sailing with them was USS *Intrepid*, still the flagship of Rear Adm. Gerald Bogan's Task Group 38.2.

The "fog of war" was a military cliché, and it aptly described the murk of flawed communications and faulty intelligence that plagued both the Japanese and the Americans. Because of the disconnect between the two chains of command, Kincaid thought that part of Halsey's force was still covering the San Bernardino Strait. Indeed, Halsey had signaled his promise to form a "Task Force 34 if the enemy sorties." Kincaid took this to mean such a force *was* formed and already in position to guard the strait.

Halsey, however, had *not* formed TF 34 and assigned it to protect the strait. Instead, he was making full speed northward with all his ships, including the fast carrier force under Adm. Marc Mitscher. The critical San Bernardino Strait was unguarded.

At dawn on October 25, an anti-submarine search plane from the jeep carrier *Kadashan Bay* reported an ominous discovery: a powerful Japanese fleet was emerging from the San Bernardino Strait. It was already in the Philippine Sea, turning southward along the island of Samar. Only three jeep carrier groups and their handful of escorting destroyers stood between Kurita's fleet and the landing beaches at Leyte.

Halsey's carrier force was closing with Ozawa's fleet to the north. Amassed in Halsey's fleet were sixty-four ships. His carriers embarked more than 780 aircraft—401 fighters, 214 dive-bombers, and 171 torpedo planes. Though he didn't yet know it, his enemy had a total of seventeen ships and twenty-nine remaining aircraft.

That night, October 25, Halsey's search planes lost track of the Japanese fleet. Nonetheless, at dawn the first strikes—180 aircraft—

took to the air. *Intrepid* and Task Group 38.2 joined the attack, led by Cdr. David McCampbell off *Intrepid*'s sister ship, *Essex*.

The search for the enemy fleet took an hour and a half. Finally a Hellcat pilot spotted Ozawa's force—the large carrier *Zuikaku*, the three light carriers *Chitose*, *Chiyoda*, and *Zuiho*, the battleships fitted with carrier decks *Ise* and *Hyuga*, three light cruisers, and eight destroyers.

As the attacking aircraft bore in on the Japanese fleet, the expected hail of anti-aircraft fire filled the sky. Again the flak was of different colors, identifying the source of the shipboard batteries. But to the pilots' surprise, there was little aerial opposition. Only a handful of Japanese fighters climbed up to meet them. The Japanese fighters managed to down one Avenger before they were all shot down or chased away by the Hellcats.

What the pilots from the strike force didn't yet realize—nor did Halsey aboard *New Jersey*—was that the Japanese had almost no fighters. The flight decks of the carriers *Ise* and *Hyuga* were empty. Ozawa's ships were a make-believe fleet. They were bait, but this hadn't yet registered with the commander of the U.S. fleet.

The American warplanes continued to savage the Japanese ships. Wave after wave roared in. Halsey's orders were explicit: *Get the carriers.* They got *Chitose* with multiple bombs and torpedoes, and early in the action she blew up and sank. Then they got Ozawa's flagship, the carrier *Ziukaku*, mauling her with dive-bombers. When she lost communications, Ozawa was forced to move his command to the light cruiser *Oyodo*.

The reports kept streaming back to Halsey. One after the other, his mortal enemies—the Japanese carriers—were going to the bottom. By the third strike of the day, *Zuikaku*, the last of the Japanese carriers that had attacked Pearl Harbor, joined *Chitose* at the bottom of the ocean. Then came news that *Zuiho*, the third and last of Ozawa's carriers, was badly hit and floundering. By the end of the day, it too had settled beneath the waves. For Halsey, this was particularly sweet revenge. *Zuiho* had been involved in the sinking of the *Hornet* at the Battle of Santa Cruz.

But his exhilaration was tempered by disturbing messages from Kincaid: IS TF 34 GUARDING SAN BERNARDINO STRAIT? To which Halsey simply replied, NEGATIVE. He was locked in combat with his target, the Japanese carriers, and still considered Kincaid's fleet to be un-threatened.

Then a more urgent message: OUR CVES [escort carriers] BEING AT-TACKED BY 4 BBS [battleships] 8 CRUISERS PLUS OTHERS REQUEST LEE COVER LEYTE AT TOP SPEED.

Now Halsey was becoming concerned—and perplexed. Vice Adm. Willis "Ching" Lee was in fact the commander of a newly formed Task Force 34, but Halsey had already placed Lee's task force at the front of his attack on Ozawa's fleet, a fact he hadn't bothered to pass on to Admiral Kincaid. Lee and his Task Force 34 were too far north of the San Bernardino Strait to be of any possible help to Kincaid.

Halsey had already dispatched a reserve force, Task Group 38.1, under Vice Adm. John "Slew" McCain. McCain's task group had been en route to Ulithi for crew rest and reprovisioning. Now they'd turned around and were speeding back toward the San Bernardino Strait to protect Kincaid's fleet of escort carriers.

They were too late.

The Japanese guns opened fire.

Led by the big cruisers, Kurita's force bore down on Taffy Three, the northernmost of the three escort carrier groups standing off Samar. The ships were thin-skinned merchant ships converted to escort carriers. Now they were the only American force standing between Kurita's fleet and the landing beaches at Leyte. The air-craft aboard the escort carriers were there to support the landing troops at Leyte. The carriers' only protection, besides their own few guns, was a small screen of destroyers and destroyer escorts.

The big Japanese guns were raking the American ships with merciless fire. The destroyers *Johnston* and *Hoel* and the destroyer escort *Samuel B. Roberts* made gallant last stands against the on-coming behemoths. Each was blown to pieces. The jeep carrier *Gambier Bay* was singled out for the most attention, taking hit after hit, belching fire and smoke from her ruptured hull. While *Gam-*

USS *Intrepid* off Newport News, Virginia, on August 16, 1943,
the day she went into commission.

Crewmen prepare to load a 2,000-pound general-purpose bomb in the bomb bay of a TBM
Avenger aircraft, January 27, 1944. *Intrepid* was then en route to support the invasion of Roi
and Namur Islands, Kwajalein Atoll.

USS *Intrepid* operating in the Philippine Sea in November 1944.

F4U-1D Corsair night fighters aboard *Intrepid*.

F4U-2 night fighters of VF(N)-101 aboard the USS *Intrepid*
during the first Truk strike in February 1944.

Japanese kamikaze suicide plane disintegrates in flames after hitting USS *Intrepid*
during operations off the Philippines on November 25, 1944.

F4U-1D Corsair in the barricade aboard *Intrepid*.

Lt. (jg) Alex Vraciu after downing six Japanese airplanes in one mission.

Lt. (jg) Alex Vraciu after his nineteenth kill, just before returning to the United States on a war bond tour. He would finish the war as the Navy's fourth highest scoring ace.

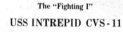

Welcome Aboard the Anti-Submarine Warfare Support Aircraft Carrier
USS *Intrepid*, "The Fighting I" (1962).

In 1968–1969 USS *Intrepid* (CVS-11), "The Fighting I," was operating as an attack
carrier under Captain V. F. Kelley, with Carrier Air Wing 10 aboard.

In 1969–1970 USS *Intrepid* (CVS-11), "The Fighting I," was operating as an
ASW carrier under Captain H. N. Moore Jr.

USS *Independence* (CVA-62), USS *Saratoga* (CVA-60), and USS *Intrepid* (CVA-11) (listed from
bottom to top) under way in 1961, with crewmen paraded on deck in a spell out
commemorating the fiftieth birthday of Naval Aviation.

Zachary and Elizabeth Fisher stand before the Intrepid Museum. Their leadership in saving the veteran ship from the scrap heap has allowed more than 10 million visitors, to date, to walk her decks and learn about her history.

Zachary Fisher shares time with young visitors on the flight deck of the Intrepid Museum. He was thrilled to hear the young lady on his knee wanted to be an astronaut.

SB2C Helldivers flying over *Intrepid*.

bier Bay was capsizing, the Japanese cruiser *Chikuma* pulled nearly alongside and continued pumping shells into the dying carrier.

The besieged carriers managed to get nearly a hundred aircraft—mostly Avengers and obsolete Wildcat fighters—into the air, though most were armed for close air support on the beach, not for attacking heavy ships. They roared in on the Japanese warships, pinging bullets and hundred-pound bombs off the heavy armor plate. They scored hits, and the Avengers actually sank one cruiser, the *Chokai,* with a dive-bomb attack from out of the sun.

With their carriers under attack and trying to escape from the Japanese fleet, most of the aircraft were unable to land back aboard. When their fuel and bombs ran out, they landed at temporary fields newly constructed at Leyte.

On his flagship at Leyte, Kincaid followed the battle with increasing alarm. He sent flurries of urgent messages to Halsey: UNDER ATTACK BY CRUISERS AND BBS . . . REQUEST IMMEDIATE AIR STRIKE . . . ALSO REQUEST SUPPORT BY HEAVY SHIPS . . . LOW IN AMMUNITION.

Even Halsey was concerned by these urgent pleas—but not enough to turn his force around and come to Kincaid's rescue. He had already sent McCain's task group to assist. In any case, his own force, including the controversial Task Force 34, was engaged in destroying the enemy Northern Force. Task Force 34 was only 40 miles from Ozawa's fleet. Before nightfall they would close with them and deliver the coup de grâce with their heavy guns.

Which, at that moment, was precisely what Admiral Kurita was preparing to do to the American escort carriers.

Then came a message from Halsey's superior, Admiral Nimitz: WHERE IS TASK FORCE THIRTY FOUR RR THE WORLD WONDERS. The last part—"the world wonders"—was not part of Nimitz's message but a typical nonsense phrase attached to the end of coded messages. In this case, a young communications officer, either on purpose or by subliminal choice, included words that sent Halsey into a rage. He was convinced that his boss had just rebuked him in the most insulting way.

Halsey then carried out what to him was the most distasteful act of his career: he detached Task Force 34 and Rear Adm. Gerald

Bogan's Task Group 38.2—with USS *Intrepid* in the fore—to steam at top speed back to Leyte. The rest of Halsey's forces would continue to attack what was left of Ozawa's fleet.

"I turned my back on the opportunity I had dreamed of since my days as a cadet," Halsey wrote later. "For me, one of the biggest battles of the war was off."

Both battles, as it turned out, were off. By the next morning, Ozawa had managed to limp away with his much-diminished fleet. Of all the Japanese commanders in the battle, he had come closest to succeeding. He and his sacrificial fleet had accomplished their mission: they had lured Halsey and his great fleet away from the real battle in Leyte.

And by the time *Intrepid* and the ships of Task Group 38.2 and Task Force 34 arrived at the fight off Samar, that battle was off too.

They couldn't believe it. Just when it seemed that the gallant little fleet of escort carriers was about to be shredded, and Kurita's route to the landing beaches was wide open, the Japanese fleet did something that none of the sailors or airmen watching from their battered ships could fathom: it turned around.

From the bridges of the beleaguered escort carriers the Americans stared at the gray shapes of the enemy ships. There was no doubt about it. The Japanese advance ships had stopped firing. They were retiring back to the north. With total victory in his grasp, Admiral Kurita was leaving the fight.

The fog of war had thickened once again. It penetrated not only Halsey's flag bridge but also Kurita's bridge on *Yamato*. The Japanese commander still believed that he was engaged with the American's fast carrier force, not a fleet of undersized jeep carriers, and Kurita decided that his luck had held as long as it possibly could. He knew Nishimura had been wiped out and would not be joining him for an attack on the landing beaches. He also knew that even if he reached his target, the landing transports were empty—the troops had been on the beaches for five days now. Nothing he could do would stop the American invasion of Leyte.

What bothered Kurita most, though, was the thought that the

massed airpower from the fast carrier force would soon descend on him like Furies. Kurita still had four of his five battleships. It was just a matter of hours, perhaps minutes, before American bombers blasted his fleet to eternity.

Kurita steamed back to the San Bernardino Strait, which was *still* unguarded. En route, in a final thickening of the fog of war, the last two ships of his formation were mistakenly attacked by Japanese bombers. On a darkening sea Kurita took his fleet back into the strait and turned west.

Throughout the night, *Intrepid* and Task Group 38.2 steamed at top speed. When they arrived off Samar early on the morning of October 26, the threat to Kincaid's fleet had gone. Kurita's fleet was already through the San Bernardino Strait and was retracing their route away from the Philippines.

At dawn, aircraft from *Intrepid* and *Essex* were over the Sibuyan Sea, again searching for Kurita. They found him at 0834 off the island of Panay, steaming westward. While the Helldivers rolled in from above, once again dodging the now-familiar multi-colored anti-aircraft bursts, the Avengers skimmed in low to launch their torpedoes. The cruiser *Noshiro* took several torpedoes and slowed almost to a stop.

The Helldivers were again giving special attention to *Yamato*, Kurita's flagship. *Yamato* had already survived multiple bombings and torpedoings, saved only by the enormous thickness of the armor on her deck and hull. Three bombs exploded on her forward deck, penetrating watertight compartments and causing her bow to settle ominously. Her captain, remembering the fate of *Yamato*'s behemoth sister ship, *Musashi*, ordered the aft compartments flooded to keep her level. The wounded *Yamato* maintained steerage and continued to dodge the rain of bombs and torpedoes.

By 1000 *Intrepid* and *Essex*'s planes had withdrawn. Losses this time had been light. A Hellcat flown by Ens. Howard Meacham was hit during a strafing pass and plunged straight into the water. Two Avengers and four Helldivers, after being airborne for over five hours, ran out of gas on the way back to *Intrepid* and went into the water. All were rescued except for a single Helldiver radioman.

Back aboard *Intrepid*, there was loud grumbling in the squadron ready rooms. It had been a costly and frustrating day. Despite the efforts of 250 warplanes from two task groups, they had sunk only one light cruiser and one destroyer and forced another destroyer onto the beach at Panay. Worse, they had been snatched out of the battle with the Japanese northern carrier force.

Most blamed the fleet commander. Halsey had sent them on a wild-goose chase, then reversed himself and sent them on another. Neither the northern nor the southern Japanese task force had been wiped out, as they should have been.

Fighting 18 pilot Charlie Mallory summed it up in his diary: "Early this morning we found out too late that the Japanese [Central Force] had slipped out of the best trap that could have been set for them. All of us have been giving the battleship admirals and Halsey hell for not stopping up the straits of San Bernardino."

But Admiral Kurita's ordeal was not over. As he was still escaping to the west, another wave of bombers appeared overhead—land-based Army Air Force B-24s of the 13th Air Force—to deliver their own send-off. As *Yamato* wheeled and weaved to avoid this latest attack, a bomb exploded on her bridge, killing and wounding many on Kurita's staff.

Kurita was unharmed. Like the rest of his staff, he had donned his life jacket, and now he sat staring impassively at this final demonstration of American dominance of the seas. Less than three years had passed since the successful attack on Pearl Harbor. Back then they were calling the Pacific Ocean a Japanese lake. Now it was an American lake.

Yamato survived, and so did Kurita. With the remnants of his shattered fleet, he made it to safer waters, never again to battle an American fleet. His departure from the Leyte Gulf signaled the end of the Imperial Japanese Navy as an effective fighting force. Back in Tokyo, Kurita would be heavily criticized for his precipitous withdrawal from the Battle off Samar, just when the destruction of the American escort carrier fleet was in his grasp.

What would come to be called the Battle of Leyte Gulf was actually four separate engagements—the Battle of the Sibuyan Sea, in which *Intrepid*'s warplanes first joined battle with Kurita's fleet; the Battle of Surigao Strait, wherein Nishimura charged into the jaws of Kincaid's Seventh Fleet; the Battle off Cape Engaño, in which Halsey raced after Ozawa's carriers; and the nearly disastrous Battle off Samar, where Kurita's fleet pounced on the undefended groups of escort carriers.

The battles were a series of miscommunications, blunders, and at least one miracle. Both Kurita and Halsey wrongly assessed their situations. For the Americans, the battle ended in victory, though not as clean and one-sided as it might have been. For the Japanese, it was a defeat from which they could not recover.

In the four days of fighting at Leyte, the Japanese had lost four aircraft carriers, three battleships, ten cruisers, and nine destroyers. More than 11,000 Japanese had been killed. The Americans had suffered too, losing one light aircraft carrier, two escort carriers, two destroyers, and one destroyer escort. American losses amounted to 473 killed and 1,100 missing. The losses had almost no effect on the United States' overwhelming superiority in the Pacific. For the Japanese, it meant the ultimate loss of the Philippines. The outcome of the war was all but certain.

In their final desperation, the Japanese had one weapon left to deploy.

9

Divine Wind

Across the sea, corpses in the water;
Across the mountain, corpses in the field;
I shall die only for the emperor,
I shall never look back.

—Imperial Japanese Navy anthem

Kamikaze. It meant "divine wind," and it echoed the ancient samurai warrior spirit of Japan. It was said to be the name of the wind god who sent a typhoon to repel a fleet of invading Mongol ships in the year 1281. Seven centuries later, the Japanese believed that only another divine wind would save them from the overwhelming might of the United States.

With the defeat in the Leyte Gulf and the relentless march of MacArthur's troops toward Manila, Japanese commanders had become desperate—and fatalistic. Vice Adm. Takijiro Ohnishi had just taken command of the First Air Fleet in the Philippines. What he saw—a depleted and dispirited fighting force—brought him to the brink of despair. Ohnishi knew he had no hope of matching the Americans in numbers of airplanes, ships, or pilots.

The Japanese fighting man, however, possessed one indispensable quality that Ohnishi believed the Americans could never match. He had an unswerving sense of duty to the emperor and to the nation. To die for the emperor was the highest imaginable calling. Ohnishi believed that the Japanese spirit and discipline would prevail over all the material resources the Americans possessed.

What Ohnishi proposed was to launch suicide units against the invading Americans. Each unit would be a *kamikaze tokubetsu kogekitai*—divine wind special attack squad.

Ohnishi put his idea before the pilots of the 201st Air Group (Sentai) at Mabalacat Field, which was an adjunct of Clark Field—an almost daily target for American bombers. One of Ohnishi's officers remembered the pilots' reaction: "In a frenzy of emotion and joy, the arms of every pilot in the assembly went up in a gesture of complete accord." The first twenty-three volunteers were put under the command of Lieutenant Yukio Seki. Seki's unit was named Shimpu—an interpretation of the Japanese characters for *kamikaze.*

Admiral Kurita's fleet was still disengaging from the attack on the Taffy force—the fleet of escort carriers he mistook for Halsey's fast carriers of the Third Fleet—when the first planes of the Shimpu unit took off.

Before takeoff, the pilots drank from a special container presented to them by Ohnishi. While the pilots climbed into the cockpits, those remaining behind sang an old warrior's song: *Ogimi no he ni koso shinane / Nodo niwa shanaji*—"Thus for the emperor I will not die peacefully at home."

One of the first to witness the terrifying new weapon was Rear Adm. Tom Sprague, *Intrepid* plank owner and her first captain. Sprague was now the commander of Taffy One, one of the three escort carrier groups that had just done battle with Kurita's battleships and cruisers. Recently promoted to flag rank and given command of an escort carrier group, Sprague had just ordered his forces to stand down after the battle with Kurita's fleet. Taffy One had been lucky. They'd lost none of their ships to the heavy guns of Kurita's battleships and cruisers. On the morning of October 26, their luck changed.

From out of the low morning sun a lone Japanese Zero appeared. Evading the hurried screen of anti-aircraft fire thrown up at him, the Zero dove on the escort carrier *Santee*, one of Sprague's Taffy One carriers. The Zero pilot opened fire with his 20-mm guns, spraying the deck of the ship. Then, instead of pulling up, egressing in a low, defensive swoop close to the water, he did something unexpected. He crashed into the deck on the port side. The blazing hulk penetrated the 4-inch wooden deck and exploded on *Santee*'s hangar deck, killing sixteen men and wounding many more.

It was a stunning blow, but it appeared to be a singular event. Japanese pilots had often showed a willingness to sacrifice themselves, especially after their aircraft were already damaged.

Minutes later another Zero appeared. Like the one that crashed into *Santee*, this one pulled up, rolled over, and dove into USS *Suwannee*.

The attacks continued: more Zeroes, all of them diving at the escort carriers without bothering to pull up. *Kalinin Bay, Kitkin Bay*, and *White Plains* were all hit. An ominous pattern was appearing.

To the north, a Zero appeared astern of *St. Lo*, flying low and fast. The one was flown by Lieutenant Seki, the young Imperial Navy officer who commanded the new squadron called Shimpu. Seki was a graduate of the Eta Jima naval academy and was recognized as an outstanding young officer with a promising career. Today, Lieutenant Seki intended to die.

When he was still half a mile distant from *St. Lo*, Seki pulled the nose of the Zero up, rolled inverted, and dove straight for the carrier. The Zero crashed through the flight deck and penetrated to a compartment of torpedoes and bombs below. In the next few seconds, *St. Lo* erupted like a volcano. The explosion hurled flaming hunks of the ship a thousand feet into the sky. In fifteen minutes, *St. Lo* was gone, along with most of her crew.

Eleven other pilots of the Shimpu unit dove on ships that day, but none was as successful as Lieutenant Seki, who managed to sink *St. Lo*. It was the final day of the Battle of Leyte Gulf. To the dispirited Japanese high command, the only bright moment of the disastrous battle was the dramatic success of Lieutenant Seki and the special attack squad.

The news was transmitted on Radio Tokyo and sent a thrill of pride through the 201st Air Group. Young pilots clamored to be the next to fly kamikaze missions.

The carriers of the Taffy groups had been the first to experience a new and baffling Japanese tactic. In the next few days, the Japanese attackers would come in greater numbers and with more persistence. Most seemed bent on suicide. In four more days, it would be *Intrepid*'s turn.

★ 10 ★

Gun Tub 10

October 29, 1944

Sweet gray smoke belched from the exhaust stacks. Propeller blades whirled. The Wright Cyclone radial engine coughed, spurted more smoke, then settled down to a deep-throated rumbling idle.

From the cockpit of the TBM, Ens. Ben St. John could see the other Avengers in his flight starting up. He was at the back of the pack, parked nearly on the fantail. Up on the forward deck, the fighters were already launching. The SB2C Helldivers would go behind them. As usual, the Avengers were the last.

St. John and his wingmen were part of the second wave of bombers. The first had gone early, soon after dawn. The target was Luzon, where they'd be hammering the airfields all day long. Japanese airpower in the Philippines was still a formidable force, and the idea was to quash it before MacArthur's invasion of Luzon got under way. That meant going in with Avengers and Helldivers and Hellcats day after day, bombing, strafing, destroying Japanese airplanes wherever they could be found.

Ben St. John liked flying the big, sturdy TBM. Its official name was Avenger, but almost no one called it that. Irreverent pilots had their own names: Turkey, Torpecker, Chuff, Pregnant Beast (the SB2C Helldiver was still *the* Beast), and, to the Royal Navy, Tarpon.

The Avenger lived up to its Ironworks heritage. It was tough, easy to fly, and hard to kill.

The airplanes in front of Ben St. John were moving. One by one they followed the signals from the aircraft handlers to taxi forward. As each Avenger left its place in the pack, the aircraft handler signaled the pilot to spread his wings. When they reached the midsection of the flight deck, they'd be turned over to the launch officer. On his signal they'd run the engines up to full power, release the brakes, and roll down the deck and into the sky. Even with a full bomb load, Avengers usually made free deck takeoffs, which suited the pilots just fine. Making a normal rolling takeoff from the deck was infinitely preferable to a skull-rattling, equipment-breaking hydraulic catapult shot.

It was St. John's turn. He nudged up the throttle, and the heavily loaded Avenger trundled over the teak deck. As he rolled forward, St. John actuated the hydraulic lever to unfold his wings.

That was another innovation on the Avenger. According to legend, Leroy Grumman himself came up with the unique backward-stowing wing fold mechanism by playing with an eraser and paper clips. With a 52-foot wingspan, the Avenger was the largest warplane flying on Navy carriers, but its wings would fold back into a package only 16 feet across. Perched with their wings tucked back, a row of Avengers looked like a flock of sleeping albatrosses.

St. John checked his wings. The left was locked into place. The right wing was only halfway down.

Damn. He refolded the wings, then extended them again. Same result. The right wing wouldn't lock down.

The handler was holding the palms of his hands up: *What's the problem?* St. John shook his head and gave a thumbs-down signal. His Avenger was a no go.

St. John felt a pang of disappointment. He'd gotten up at 0500 to be ready for this mission. He'd fidgeted in his ready room chair, scribbling notes on his knee board, feeling the same sense of excitement he always felt before a combat mission.

The handler was signaling him forward. They wanted the Avenger on the forward elevator so they could drop it down to the hangar deck. St. John refolded the wings and shoved the throttle up again.

He was rolling past the island when he realized that the guns on the port side were blazing away at something. It had been going on all morning. St. John kept his eyes fixed on the aircraft handler beneath his nose. He wanted to get the hell off the flight deck and get down to the hangar deck. It was safer there.

Alonzo Swann Jr. peered into the pale sky. The dusky-colored speck he'd been watching was growing larger. It was another Japanese airplane, probably a Zero. At least twenty had come out from their bases in the Philippines, following *Intrepid*'s strike airplanes back to the ship. Most were chased away or shot down by the CAPs, the combat air patrol fighters.

This one was different. The pilot approached from the starboard side, jinking to miss the hail of anti-aircraft fire that surrounded him. When he passed astern of *Intrepid*, he began to climb, as if he'd had enough and was leaving.

But Swann and his fellow gunners in Gun Tub 10—all but one were African American sailors normally assigned as steward's mates—could see that the Zero wasn't leaving. At the apogee of its climb, the Zero turned, arcing back toward the carrier. It was high, still out of range of their six 20-mm guns. The 5-inchers were blasting away at it, and so were the portside and island-mounted Bofors 40-mm guns.

The gun captain of Swann's crew was twenty-two-year-old Gunner's Mate Third Class Alfonso Chavarrias, a Mexican American whom everyone called "Indian." Chavarrias was the old hand of the crew and the only one with combat experience. Before *Intrepid*, he'd been aboard *Lexington* when she was sunk in the Coral Sea.

Swann kept his eyes on the incoming Zero. He no longer had any doubt. It was coming for *Intrepid*. The sound of the 40-mm guns was now joined by the rattle of the short-range 20-mm weapons. All six of Gun Tub 10's guns were tracking the incoming airplane.

Like all the men on *Intrepid*, Swann had heard about kamikazes. They were a new and vaguely understood phenomenon. To Swann, it was an almost incomprehensible notion, enemy pilots turning their airplanes into human-guided bombs.

But here it was. The Zero was swelling in Swann's view like an apparition from hell. Every gun on *Intrepid*'s port side was firing away. The din of the guns was hammering at Swann's eardrums.

The Zero kept coming.

Signalman Lou Valenti was on his way to the navigation bridge to deliver a message to the captain. Valenti could hear the guns blazing away. Despite *Intrepid*'s torpedoing at Truk last February, her crew considered her a lucky ship. Her gunners had knocked down a succession of incoming Japanese aircraft. Her fighter pilots had accounted for several more. *Intrepid* had never been hit from the air.

The tempo of the anti-aircraft guns seemed to be changing. The sound of the big booming 5-inchers was joined by the frenetic *pom-pom-pom* of the Bofors 40-mm quads. Then came the urgent rattle of the Oerlikon 20-mm short-range guns.

Valenti looked down the port side of the ship. The muzzles of the 20-mm weapons in Gun Tub 10 were all pointed nearly straight up. The gunners were firing at the dusky-colored object diving at them. Their tracers were converging on the object like fiery tentacles, and getting hits—the object was shedding pieces. But it was closer now, still diving at them.

Swann felt a moment of elation. The Zero was hit. He could see the tracers pouring into the diving fighter. In the next moment, the left wing folded back and separated. The Zero went into a spiral, spinning rapidly in the direction of its severed wing.

A bomb dropped from the Zero. Whether it had been knocked off or prematurely released, no one could tell. The bomb hit the water a hundred yards short of *Intrepid.*

The Zero was still coming. The crew of Gun Tub 10 kept pouring fire into the diving airplane, trying to shoot off the Zero's other wing.

The specter of the plummeting Zero filled up Alonzo Swann's

vision. Time seemed to slow to a crawl. Over the breech of his gun he could see the details of the incoming airplane—the cockpit, the stub of the severed wing, the dull red ball on its remaining wing.

The Zero was arcing downward. Swann saw that it would miss *Intrepid*'s flight deck. He knew now with a dreadful certainty where the Zero would hit.

The impact resonated throughout the ship.

Ben St. John heard it while he was still in the cockpit of his Avenger, taxiing to the forward deck. He had been focused on getting his airplane up forward, onto the elevator, and down to the hangar bay, away from the mayhem on the deck. He snapped his head to the left. Behind his port wing, a pillar of flame was leaping from the deck edge, from one of the 20-mm gun tubs.

Signalman Lou Valenti heard it on the navigation bridge. So did Capt. Joe Bolger, *Intrepid*'s skipper, standing next to him. Both men stared at the carnage in Gun Tub 10.

Bolger had already called the ship to general quarters when the inbound bogeys were first spotted on radar. Now a siren was blaring over the PA, followed by the blurted announcement: "Fire! Fire! Fire in the port gun tubs!" Then, more ominously, "Damage control! Corpsmen! Corpsmen!"

On the flight deck smoke and flame were billowing from the port deck edge. Damage control parties were racing across the deck to fight the fire and rescue anyone in the gun tub who might still be alive.

Alonzo Swann Jr. was dazed but conscious. The impact had hurled him against the steel bulkhead of the gun tub. He shook his head trying to focus his eyes. All he could see was orange flame and bodies. His shipmates were still there, still at their guns.

Then he heard screams. His best friend, another steward's mate named Samuel Gant, was entangled in the straps that secured him to his gun mount. Gant was burning to death. Though he was badly burned himself, Swann rushed back into the inferno to try to rescue his shipmate.

He couldn't get the straps free. Swann was reaching for a knife to cut the straps when the burning ammunition in the tub exploded.

The damage control party was there in the next minute. Swann was badly injured. Sam Gant had been killed by the blast. Gently they removed the dead and injured gunners from the gun tub and laid them on the hangar deck, where corpsmen could treat them.

Nine gunners had died at their battle stations. Six were severely wounded. Among the killed was the veteran gun captain, Indian Chavarrias.

For some of *Intrepid*'s crew, it was the first contact with the reality of war. Hector Giannasca was in the island. "When they picked up these bodies, they put them on stretchers. They were bringing them towards the island. And that's the first time really that I saw a dead person."

On the signals bridge, Lou Valenti was staring at the destroyed gun tub. One of the six blackened gun barrels was bent down from the impact of the crash. The other five 20-mm barrels were all pointed nearly vertical. *Sticking straight up like the legs of a dead bird,* Valenti thought. The gunners had stayed at their stations, tracking the Zero right up to the moment of impact.

Swann and the survivors of Gun Tub 10 were put on stretchers and taken down to sick bay. Swann had suffered severe burns, but he would live. He remained on board *Intrepid* and returned to duty.

In a ceremony a few weeks later, Swann and five of his fellow African American gunners were awarded Bronze Stars. Swann quietly accepted his medal, but he insisted that he had been promised a Navy Cross, the second-highest decoration for valor, by *Intrepid*'s captain. The nineteen-year-old sailor made a promise to himself: no matter how long it took, he would receive the award he'd been promised.

He didn't know that it would take forty-nine years.

———

That afternoon, while *Intrepid* was on station 220 miles east of Clark Field, the ship's ensign was lowered to half mast. Men in dress whites assembled on the hangar deck to say farewell to their shipmates. Nine canvas bags, each beneath an American flag, were lined up at the deck edge. They contained the bodies of the gunners from Gun Tub 10.

The chaplain read the service, commending the souls of the fallen sailors to the Almighty. The bugler sounded taps. The Marine honor guard fired a volley. One after the other the canvas bags, each weighted with a 5-inch shell, slipped over the side and vanished in the sea.

·

★ 11 ★

The Expendables

Why is America lucky enough to have such men? They leave this tiny ship and fly against the enemy. Then they must seek the ship, lost somewhere on the sea. And when they find it, they have to land on its pitching deck. Where do we get such men?

— James A. Michener, *The Bridges at Toko-Ri*

Higher is better than lower. It was an old fighter pilot maxim, and it was nagging at Charlie Mallory's brain. He was leading a flight of Hellcats that had launched ahead of St. John and the other bombers. Now they were flying high cover for the Helldivers and Avengers as they rolled in on their targets at Clark Field. But after Mallory took his station at 18,000 feet, something subliminal was bothering him.

On an impulse, he took his flight up to 24,000 feet. As he leveled at the higher altitude, he had a good view of the attacking airplanes down below as they rolled into their dives. And he saw something else.

Japanese fighters were sweeping in from the south at 20,000 feet. Mallory's instinct had been correct. They were outnumbered, but the Hellcats had the advantage of altitude. Mallory led them down after the Zeroes.

The dogfight turned into a hard-turning, energy-depleting melee. One of the Zeroes made a reversal and locked onto Mallory's tail. Mallory yanked the nose of the Hellcat up into an Immelmann—a half loop, rolling out wings level on top—and tried to bring his guns to bear on the Zero.

It didn't work. Coming out of the half loop, Mallory's Hellcat was dangerously low on airspeed. As he kicked the rudders to bring his guns to bear, the Hellcat stalled and spun out of the sky like a shotgunned pigeon. Mallory tumbled downward for 5,000 feet before he could regain control and level off. As he was climbing back up to rejoin the fight, a Zero flashed past his nose, oblivious of the danger. Mallory opened fire and shot him down.

Then came an urgent radio call from his wingman, Lt. Ken Crusoe. He'd been following a Zero down, trying to get a shot, when another Japanese fighter locked onto his tail, peppering him with cannon fire. Three more Zeroes were swarming in for the kill.

Mallory told Crusoe to break left, toward the coast and in a direction where Mallory could help. He caught up with the Zero, then overshot it and pulled up past its nose.

Crusoe was safe, but now it was Mallory who was in trouble. He felt the shuddering impact of 20-mm rounds hammering the airframe of his Hellcat. He heard a swishing sound, then felt the Hellcat abruptly lose speed. His hydraulic system was shot out. One leg of the landing gear had flopped out in the slipstream.

He was a sitting duck. The Zero pilot was about to finish him off. In desperation, Mallory remembered a Japanese tactic. With an enemy close on his tail, a Japanese pilot would split-S—roll his fighter inverted and pull the nose straight down toward the earth.

Which was what Mallory did. He rolled the crippled Hellcat inverted, starting the split-S. Then he hesitated, holding the fighter inverted. As he hoped, the Zero pilot anticipated the escape maneuver. He already had his nose aimed downward to finish killing the Hellcat.

It won Mallory a few precious seconds. The Zero had momentarily lost sight of him. He rolled upright and scooted into a nearby cloud bank. He was shot up but still flying. With one wheel hanging out, the most he could make was 180 knots.

He made it back to the *Intrepid*, but the toughest task of the day was still ahead of him. His tires were flat from the bullet hits. With no hydraulic system, he had to mechanically lock his landing gear down. He had no landing flaps, which meant he would have an excessively high landing speed and a pitched-up attitude, making it difficult to see over the nose.

His first pass at the ship wasn't good. From his platform on the port deck edge, the landing signal officer waved his signal paddles over his head—the order to take it around. *Intrepid*'s air boss came on the radio. Forget landing. Did Mallory want to bail out or ditch in the water?

Neither. Mallory had already diced with death enough for one day. Landing his fighter in the ocean was at the bottom of his wish list. He asked the air boss to allow him one more shot at the deck. If it didn't work, then he'd go into the drink.

The LSO brought Mallory in higher and faster this time, which gave him a better view of the landing deck. The LSO gave the "cut"—the signal to chop the throttle—farther out than normal. The Hellcat sailed over *Intrepid*'s ramp, slammed down hard, then went careening down the deck on its flattened tires. Mallory felt the comforting lurch of the tailhook snagging an arresting wire. The Hellcat lurched to a stop.

When he climbed down from the cockpit and looked at his airplane, he understood clearly why they called the Grumman factory the "Ironworks." The fighter looked like it had been used for target practice. Mallory counted sixty-seven holes in the airframe.

The Hellcat never flew again. After they removed the cameras and guns and radios, they pushed it over the side.

Ben St. John was looking down at the launch officer standing beside the Avenger's nose. The officer was holding up his right thumb. It was a question: *Ready for takeoff?*

It was 1400, and the carnage had been cleared from Gun Tub 10. *Intrepid* was launching the third strike of the day against the Japanese complex at Clark Field. St. John had missed going on the second strike, and now he'd gotten himself assigned to this mission.

He flashed a thumbs-up. *Ready.*

Taking off from a carrier, whether by catapult or free deck launch, was an act of faith. The pilot placed his life in the hands of the launch officer, trusting that all the numbers added up—the wind over the deck, the deck length, the weight of his heavily loaded torpedo bomber.

The launch officer was whirling his right arm over his head. St. John shoved the throttle up, holding the brakes. The engine bellowed and the airframe rattled from the static might of nearly 2,000 horsepower.

The launch officer threw his arm forward and pointed down to the deck. St. John released the brakes. The Avenger surged forward, the big three-bladed propeller biting into the wind.

St. John brought the tail up, giving the airplane less drag as it accelerated. With the deck edge rushing at him, he nudged the stick back and the Avenger clawed into the air. St. John snatched the gear handle up, then dropped the right wing to make a clearing turn.

He was on his way back to the Philippines.

The day hadn't gone well for *Intrepid*'s air group. The previous strikes had run into a hornet's nest over Clark. Two Hellcat pilots, D. A. Naughton and Art Mollenhaur, had been shot down. Naughton was observed ditching just offshore and was presumed captured. Young Ensign Mollenhaur, who'd become an ace on his first combat mission two weeks earlier over Formosa, went down in flames and was presumed dead.

The second strike, which launched just before the kamikaze attack that destroyed the portside gun tub, had also taken casualties. A Helldiver pilot from Bombing 18, Lt. Elmer "Nemo" Namoski, dropped his bombs, then spotted a Zero taking off from the runway below. Filled with an excess of hubris, the young Helldiver pilot went after the Zero.

It was a bad decision. The agile Japanese fighter was more than a match for the plodding Helldiver. The Zero pulled into a tight climbing turn behind Namoski's tail, guns blazing. Namoski went down in his burning Helldiver. His gunner managed to bail out, then was machine-gunned by Japanese troops on the ground.

One of St. John's squadronmates, Joe Rubin, had been hit by anti-aircraft fire over Clark. He made it back to the ship, but he was too badly wounded to land the shot-up airplane aboard. With his radioman helping with the controls, Rubin put the bomber into the water close to *Intrepid*. All three crewmen aboard the Avenger survived and were picked up by a destroyer.

St. John and his squadronmates were climbing westward toward the Philippines, led by Torpedo 18's executive officer, Lt. Cdr. Bud Williams. The bomb bay of each of the six Avengers was loaded with four 500-pound bombs.

The strike went according to plan. As expected, the Japanese put up a hail of anti-aircraft fire, and, also as expected, they sent up a swarm of fighters. The Hellcats of *Intrepid*'s Fighting 18 were in position over the bombers.

While the Avengers and Helldivers dove on their targets at the airfields, the Hellcats tore into the incoming Japanese airplanes. By the time the bombers were exiting the target area, the Hellcats had downed seven Tojo fighters, four Zeroes, and one Nakajima Ki-43 "Oscar" fighter. Lt. Cecil Harris killed four of the Japanese fighters, bringing his count to nineteen. By the end of the war, his total of downed enemy aircraft would reach twenty-four. *Intrepid*'s quiet man would be the second-highest-scoring ace in the Navy.

Pulling off target, Ben St. John felt a sense of relief. They'd been luckier than the pilots on the early strikes. They'd lost none of their flight to either anti-aircraft fire or enemy fighters. There were still Zeroes swarming around, but the Hellcats were keeping them at bay. Now all they had to do was fly 110 miles back to the ship and land. A piece of cake.

The first to spot the danger was Lt. C. A. "Blue" Blouin, the Hellcat flight leader. "You're headed for a heavy squall line," Blouin radioed the controller aboard *Intrepid*. "Suggest you tell them to turn the ship back the other direction to recover aircraft."

The controller aboard *Intrepid* was snippy. He wasn't interested in the pilot's suggestion. He informed Blouin that he should take care of his airplanes and they would take care of the ship.

The ship continued on its course. A few minutes later it plowed straight into the billowing mass of cloud and disappeared from view.

By now all the airmen returning to *Intrepid* could see it—an evil-looking line of rain and clouds that extended from several thousand feet altitude all the way down to the water. The whole task group was steaming directly into the storm.

What the pilots didn't know was that the task group commander, Rear Admiral Bogan, had just made a painful decision. Radar controllers had picked up a large force of Japanese aircraft following the returning strike aircraft back to the task group. Bogan ordered *Intrepid* and her accompanying ships to hide in the rain and fog. If he had to choose between losing airplanes and losing aircraft carriers, he'd save his carriers.

In the number six Avenger returning to *Intrepid*, Ben St. John wasn't worried. He and his flight still had half an hour of fuel. They could make a pass at the ship, and if they didn't get aboard they'd just wait for better visibility.

Not all the returning airplanes had the fuel to wait. Blue Blouin, the Hellcat flight leader, flew into the murk and tried to give the *Intrepid* directions to a clear area. It was too late. The area of bad weather was expanding, enfolding the entire area.

The Hellcats and a few Helldiver pilots finally glimpsed enough of the ship to make it aboard. Others did not. Two Helldivers, low on fuel in near-zero visibility, spotted a friendly destroyer in the fog and ditched next to it. Two Hellcat night fighter pilots, Ens. Jim Hedrick and Lt. Bill Thompson, crashed trying to find the ship and were never seen again.

A Helldiver from the carrier *Hancock*, which was also in the fog, made a spectacular landing aboard *Intrepid*. In the near-zero visibility he missed the arresting wires, careened over the starboard deck edge, and wound up upside down in the horizontal deck edge radio masts, where the aircraft burst into flame. The gunner climbed out of the blazing plane and managed to crawl along one of the masts to safety. The pilot dropped 70 feet into the sea and, by a miracle, was picked up by a destroyer escort.

Ben St. John, who hadn't been worried, was now becoming very worried. He and the other five Avengers had already made a pass directly over *Intrepid,* but none could see well enough to make a landing. Time and daylight were running out. Soon not only would it be impossible to land on the carrier, but a ditching attempt on the black ocean would be fatal. When the big radial engines finally wheezed and quit from fuel starvation, the blunt-nosed Avengers would descend like bricks.

St. John could see Bud Williams in the cockpit of the lead Avenger. Williams was shaking his head. He looked at St. John and pointed his finger downward.

St. John felt his heart sink. They were going to ditch.

The Avengers lined up for a water landing. Williams went in first. St. John saw the Avenger hit the water, skip, then slide to a stop with its tail high in the water. Williams and his two crewmen clambered out and boarded their life raft. Waving the raft paddles, Williams signaled for his wingmen to land alongside.

One after another they splashed down. St. John would be the last. He tightened his straps and told his crew to brace themselves. The bomber was light, almost empty of fuel and armament. He came in as slow as the torpedo bomber would fly, gear up, landing flaps down, and settled onto the water.

It was rougher than he could have imagined. The big Grumman touched the water, skipped, then slammed to a neck-snapping, eyeball-bulging stop. St. John's head barely missed crunching into the glare shield. But the Grumman Ironworks had saved them. The Avenger was still in one piece, though it was sinking fast. It stayed afloat barely long enough for St. John and his radioman and gunner to scramble out and inflate their three-man raft.

As they paddled away to join their squadronmates in their rafts, they looked back. The Avenger was tilting nose downward, almost completely submerged. As they watched, their beautiful torpedo bomber slid beneath the waves and disappeared. The airmen settled into their rafts and waited to be rescued.

And waited. Darkness settled over them. The life rafts were bobbing like corks in a fountain. Each man became violently seasick. In between sessions of barfing, they cursed the weather and the war and the idiots on the ship.

The night wore on. Sometime around midnight, they heard an airplane. St. John hauled out his Smith and Wesson .38, which was loaded with tracer rounds. It was soaking wet, and St. John had no idea if it would fire.

The growl of the airplane came nearer. St. John was about to fire the pistol when someone yelled, "Wait! It doesn't sound like one of ours."

It wasn't. As the airplane passed overhead, they heard the drone of *two* engines. All the U.S. Navy's carrier-based aircraft were single-engine. It had to be a twin-engine Betty bomber.

Another hour passed, and another. The rafts were still bobbing in the tossing sea. The airmen were still retching, even though they had long ago emptied their stomachs. They heard another sound. This time it was the unmistakable growl of a Pratt and Whitney R-2800, which had to belong to a Hellcat night fighter. St. John grabbed the .38 and fired five of his six precious tracers. Each round left a long orange streak against the night sky.

Seconds ticked by, with no response. Then came a glorious sight. The navigation lights of the airplane blinked on, off, on again. Despite their seasickness, the men in the bobbing rafts cheered.

At 0200 the silhouette of a ship emerged from the gloom. It was the destroyer *Halsey Powell* (DD-686), alerted by the Hellcat pilot. Homing in on the dull glow of the airmen's flashlights, the ship eased up to the rafts and hauled the airmen aboard.

The next morning the *Powell* pulled alongside *Intrepid*'s stern to transfer the rescued airmen. One by one, riding a canvas bosun's chair, they returned to their ship. But a certain long-standing protocol still had to be observed. For the return of her crew members, the aircraft carrier was required to pay "ransom." When the last airman had been transferred, the *Intrepid* paid up. A 20-gallon container of ice cream rode the empty chair back to the *Halsey Powell*.

The kamikazes kept coming.

Vice Admiral Ohnishi, who had proposed the idea of a corps of suicide pilots and who organized the first *kamikaze tokubetsu kogekitai,* was buoyed with his success. Since the first day of the Battle of Leyte Gulf, his special attack squads had inflicted more real damage to the American fleet than all the surface ships of the Imperial Navy.

But by the very nature of his strategy, Ohnishi's force was being quickly depleted. He was expending all his available airplanes and pilots on the one-way missions. In November he flew back to Japan to demand more airplanes for the kamikazes. The high command, still skeptical of the idea, finally released 150 planes, most of them salvaged from training bases. With the airplanes came a complement of untrained young volunteers to fly them.

The pilots were sent to Formosa, where they went through a week of training in how to die for the emperor. They spent two days practicing takeoffs, another two days on formation flying, and the last three days learning how to attack a target. With that experience, they were rushed to the Philippines to join the war against the Americans.

On November 6, it was *Lexington*'s turn. A flaming Zero crashed into her flight deck, causing major damage to her island structure. While *Lexington* retired to the newly captured anchorage at Ulithi atoll for repairs, *Intrepid* and Task Group 38.2 continued to attack the kamikaze bases on Luzon.

After more than a month of continuous combat operations, the task group was ordered to turn east toward Ulithi for rest and re-provisioning. En route, they ran into another violent enemy—a typhoon that wreaked havoc with the smaller ships and damaged the flight decks and superstructures of the carriers.

Ulithi was a volcanic atoll surrounded by a wide coral reef. Since its seizure by Marines in late September 1944, it had become the U.S. Navy's principal staging area for the assault on the Philippines. *Intrepid* dropped anchor on November 9. Across the anchorage was her damaged sister ship, *Lexington.* The two *Essex*-class carriers had a shared history. In their short careers, each had taken a Japanese aerial torpedo, and now each had suffered a kamikaze strike.

The stopover in Ulithi was brief. Every able hand aboard *Intrepid,* including the air group crewmen, pitched in to haul provisions aboard. The sailors sweated, griped, and worked hard in the tropical heat. Their brief liberty at the primitive Quonset-hutted facility seemed a million light-years removed from the beaches of Waikiki. At the rocky beach on Mog Mog Island, they drank warm beer, waded in the shallow surf, and swapped stories with the men from a dozen other warships.

After four days, *Intrepid* and her task group were on their way back to war in the Philippines.

★ 12 ★

The Darkest Day

The Hellcat's Pratt and Whitney engine stuttered, belched smoke, stuttered again. Charlie Mallory shook his head. He was poised on *Intrepid*'s flight deck, about to take off. He pulled the throttle back and gave the launch officer a thumbs-down. His fighter had a sick engine.

Seconds later Mallory was riding the aircraft elevator down to the hangar deck, where he would man the ready spare, another Hellcat fueled, armed, and ready to fly. He was in a hurry to catch up with his flight of Hellcats, which had just taken off without him.

Mallory now had eleven aerial victories, which put him in a tie with his buddy and wingman, Harvey Picken. They were still far behind their mentor, Cecil Harris, with his tally of nineteen. But the war was not over yet. There were plenty of Zeroes still waiting out there over Luzon.

It was the morning of November 25, 1944. *Intrepid* and her task group were launching strikes against Japanese ships used to transport troops from Luzon down to join the battle against MacArthur's forces on Leyte. The ships—four cruisers that had survived the Battle of Leyte Gulf—had been spotted off an island in the Sibuyan Sea, south of Manila. At 0640, a strike force of twelve Hellcats, nine SB2C Helldivers, and seven Avengers had launched in the pale dawn to attack the Japanese cruisers and another familiar target, Clark Field, near Manila.

Intrepid was still the flagship of Task Group 38.2, under Rear Adm. Gerald Bogan. In her task group was the fleet carrier *Hancock,* light carriers *Cabot* and *Independence,* battleships *Iowa* and *New Jersey,* light cruisers *Biloxi, Miami,* and *Vincennes,* and seventeen destroyers.

Throughout the morning, "snoopers"—single Japanese intruders—kept appearing on the radars, causing Captain Bolger to order the ship to general quarters. *Intrepid's* first strike returned, and another was launched. A flight of twelve more Hellcats was sent up on combat air patrol duty over the task group, along with two Avengers on an anti-snooper patrol.

At 1215, the bullhorn again blared: "General quarters, all hands man your battle stations." More snoopers, this time a formation of half a dozen. The CAP fighters shot down two, and the rest withdrew. It was becoming routine. From their fields around Manila, the Japanese aircraft would probe the task group's defenses, skirmish with the Hellcats, then pull back.

At 1227 *Intrepid's* third launch of the day was getting airborne—twelve Hellcats, ten Helldivers, and eight Avengers. Again they were going after the Japanese cruisers-turned-transports south of Manila. Now, with Charlie Mallory's Hellcat out of the lineup, they were down to eleven.

On *Intrepid's* bridge, Captain Bolger was receiving the latest report from CIC. At least three Japanese Aichi D3A Val dive-bombers were over the task group.

Again the Klaxon blared. *Intrepid's* crew raced to their battle stations. The launch of the strike aircraft was suspended, and the anti-aircraft batteries opened up. The pilots of the airplanes that hadn't gotten airborne sat in their cockpits on the flight deck feeling exposed and vulnerable. Instead of combatants, they had become unwilling spectators in a sea-air battle.

One of the incoming Vals was caught in the wall of anti-aircraft fire and hit the water in a huge splash off *Intrepid's* starboard beam. A second Val was in its dive, jinking and weaving while the tracers tried to lock onto it.

Steaming side by side with *Intrepid* was *Hancock*, less than a mile away. She too had been launching a strike and, like *Intrepid*, her remaining airplanes were still on deck. Like their counterparts on *Intrepid*, *Hancock*'s pilots were staring up at the flak-pocked sky, wishing they were anywhere on the planet except out there on the exposed flight deck.

The Val was still plummeting downward, somehow evading the blanket of fire. The gunners and the anxious pilots on the flight decks strained to see where the kamikaze was aimed. As they watched, the Val's nose veered to the right. It was slanting down through the flak toward one of the carriers. Which one? In the next few seconds, it became clear.

The kamikaze was going for the *Hancock*.

At the last second, with the Val bearing down on them, *Hancock*'s gunners connected with the diving kamikaze. The Japanese airplane disintegrated in a shower of flame and wreckage. Its bomb came off and hit the water without exploding.

But the flaming hulk of the shattered kamikaze kept coming. It smashed into *Hancock*'s flight deck amid a pair of airplanes waiting to launch. A towering cauldron of flame leaped into the sky. From the deck of *Intrepid*, stunned pilots and gunners watched the flames and smoke rise from *Hancock*'s deck.

By the odds of a coin toss, *Intrepid* had been spared. And now, for the moment, she was out of danger. Bolger turned the carrier back into the wind and resumed launching the strike planes. One by one, the remaining warplanes rumbled down the deck to catch up with the flights that had gotten off before the kamikaze attack.

All but one. Down on the hangar deck, Charlie Mallory was strapping into the spare Hellcat, which was already spotted on the elevator, waiting to be hoisted up to the flight deck. He was in a hurry to get back up to the flight deck and launch.

Following the plane captain's signal, he started the engine. He was ready to ride the elevator topside when, over the rumbling growl of the Pratt and Whitney engine, he heard something else, a deeper, more urgent sound.

Intrepid's anti-aircraft guns. They were firing again.

More kamikazes were inbound. On the flag bridge, Admiral Bogan was assessing the new reports. They had been spotted on radar. Some had apparently gotten past the CAP and were at 8,000 feet, approaching *Intrepid* from astern.

The last of the strike aircraft were still rumbling off *Intrepid*'s bow. Across the water Bogan could see smoke pouring from *Hancock*'s flight deck, but the conflagration had been mostly extinguished. Despite the ominous column of smoke, the flight deck hadn't suffered severe damage. *Hancock* reported that she would be able to recover her own aircraft. As his last strike plane was launching, Bogan ordered *Intrepid* and *Hancock* into a hard evasive turn.

"Raise the damned elevator!" Charlie Mallory yelled over the noise of his idling engine.

No one on the hangar deck seemed interested in getting Mallory's Hellcat lifted up to the flight deck. The chief petty officer standing on Mallory's wing just shook his head and climbed down. Finally Mallory got another petty officer's attention and motioned that he wanted to go topside. The petty officer nodded, then he too walked away.

Mallory stewed in his cockpit. The sound of the anti-aircraft guns topside was increasing in intensity. Then he felt the deck tilting as the carrier heeled over in a hard turn. Through the open hangar bay door he could see the other ships in *Intrepid*'s formation. Their guns were all firing. The sky was filled with roiling black puffs of anti-aircraft fire.

Then he felt the elevator move. Finally, he was going up. Mallory tightened his straps and checked his switches. When the elevator reached the flight deck, Mallory gazed around and saw that the deck was mostly empty. The strike aircraft had all been launched. No one was paying any attention to him because they were preoccupied with incoming kamikazes. Even the launch officer was gone.

Mallory saw that from his position he had a clear run down the deck. He considered his options for a moment, then made up his mind. He shoved the throttle up, and the Hellcat headed down the flight deck.

The problem was that the deck was heeling over at a severe angle because the ship was in a hard turn to starboard. He had to stomp hard on the right rudder to keep the fighter aimed for the bow, which was swinging to the right.

He almost made it to the bow. Skidding and skittering, clawing for speed, the Hellcat drifted toward the left edge of the deck. Seventy feet short of the bow, praying that he had enough airspeed, he yanked the fighter into the air. The Hellcat sailed out over the left deck edge, hovered a few precarious seconds over the open water—then flew away.

Few on *Intrepid*'s deck noticed the unauthorized launch. Nor did they care. Every pair of eyes was now focused aft, on the two dark objects bearing down on *Intrepid*'s stern.

Keep shooting! Come on, kill him!

They sounded like overexcited fight fans. Watching the airplanes hurtling toward *Intrepid*, the men on deck all had the same feeling: *Why don't they shoot him down?*

Signalman Lou Valenti was watching from his station on the starboard wing of the signals bridge. The eighteen-year-old sailor was crouched down, so only his helmet, eyes, and nose were above the steel splinter shield. It occurred to him that he looked like Kilroy, the ubiquitous cartoon character whose image appeared wherever GIs went in World War II.

Valenti's normal battle station was on the bridge, but with Admiral Bogan's staff filling up the signal space, Valenti and his fellow signalman, Odell Cooke, had been told to alternate shifts on Gun Mount 13, a 40-mm anti-aircraft battery on the starboard deck edge, behind the number three aft elevator. Just then it was Cooke's watch in the gun mount. Valenti was hunkered down outside the flag bridge.

He stared at the incoming Japanese airplanes. They were surrounded by bursts of anti-aircraft fire. He saw one take a hit and splash into the sea. The other was still flying. It was headed directly for *Intrepid*.

Valenti whirled and ran into the crowded flag plot area on the bridge, something he would never do under normal circumstances. He found himself face-to-face with Admiral Bogan and his staff. The admiral stared at him as if he'd just landed from space. "Kamikaze!" Valenti blurted.

On the navigation bridge, Quartermaster Hank Scrocca was standing next to Captain Bolger. The ship was in a hard evasive turn to starboard. Scrocca saw the anti-aircraft bursts closing around the first Zero. It exploded 1,500 yards astern of *Intrepid*. Then came a hold-fire order to the aft gunners while a pair of friendly airplanes—an Avenger and a Hellcat—flew across the line of fire. The starboard batteries kept firing at an incoming Zero farther out. It too went into the water, leaving a huge geyser.

The aft gunners resumed firing at the Zero approaching *Intrepid*'s stern. They could see their tracers converging on the Zero. Incredibly, the kamikaze kept flying. Every aft and starboard gun on *Intrepid* was firing at his plane. The collective din of the guns sounded like a chorus from hell. The sky behind *Intrepid* thickened and roiled with the glowing tracers and explosion of gunfire. The sea was frothing with the splashes of the spent ordnance.

Through it all the kamikaze kept coming. A thousand yards from *Intrepid*'s fantail, he abruptly pitched upward to 500 feet. He was hit now, trailing a wake of flame and smoke. The kamikaze pilot rolled up on a wing, then plunged downward toward *Intrepid*'s flight deck.

What happened next was a scene that burned itself into the memory of every crewman who saw it. The Zero and its 550-pound bomb smashed into *Intrepid*'s flight deck behind the island, between the number two and three elevators. A plume of smoke and fire erupted from the deck. The explosion pierced the flight deck, penetrated the gallery deck beneath, then spewed flame and shrapnel into the hangar deck below.

For the thirty-two men in Ready Room 4, death came instantly. The ready room was on the gallery deck, suspended directly beneath the flight deck. Most were radarmen on standby duty waiting to take their turn in the CIC.

The conflagration on the hangar deck spread quickly, fed by fueled and armed airplanes. On the flag bridge, Admiral Bogan ordered the entire task group into a hard starboard turn, trying to spill burning fuel off *Intrepid*'s port side and prevent the blaze from destroying the critical systems in the island.

Damage control crews fought the fires on the flight deck and the hangar deck below. The ship's fire marshal, Lt. Donald DiMarzo, and the crew of Repair One raced to the scene on the hangar deck. DiMarzo was an old pro. He had been a fire chief in California in civilian life, and most of his crew had also been professional firemen. DiMarzo made a quick assessment. It was bad, he reported, but he was sure that he and the crew of Repair One could get it under control.

And they would have, except for what happened five minutes later.

Something caught the attention of Cdr. Lew Schwabe, *Intrepid*'s gunnery officer. Schwabe was at his battle station on the forward air defense platform, above *Intrepid*'s navigation bridge. He had just directed *Intrepid*'s guns onto another target, a kamikaze directly over the battleship *New Jersey*, in formation on *Intrepid*'s starboard side.

The gunners scored a hit. The Japanese airplane went into a tight spin and crashed into the sea.

But Schwabe noticed something else out there. He could barely make it out through the smoke that was gushing from *Intrepid*'s burning deck. *Two more kamikazes.* They were low on the water, coming in fast from the carrier's port quarter, flying beneath most of the anti-aircraft fire being thrown at them.

On the hangar deck below, DiMarzo's firefighters were trying to keep the blaze from spreading. Hearing the increasing tempo of the guns up on the deck, they exchanged wary glances. A few couldn't help peering up at the scorched overhead. They knew they were vulnerable to whatever came crashing through the deck.

Topside, the gunners scored a hit on one of the incoming kamikazes. Shedding pieces, the Zero spun out of control and smacked into the water, leaving a tall geyser.

The other kept coming. For the moment, *Intrepid*'s hard evasive turn to starboard prevented the port guns from training on the target. Still, the Zero was taking hits from the 40-mm Bofors guns and from all the starboard and aft 20-mm short-range guns.

Somehow it kept flying.

The Japanese pilot was possessed of fanatical skill and a hefty dose of luck. A thousand yards from *Intrepid*'s port flank, he executed the classic kamikaze attack maneuver—a sharp pitch up, then a rolling dive back to his target. While plunging toward *Intrepid*'s deck, he released his 550-pound bomb and opened fire with his 20-mm guns. His guns were still firing when he smashed into the already burning teak flight deck.

Most of the Zero's flaming hulk—with its pilot—careened down the flight deck, mowing down every object in its path. The 550-pound bomb, separated from the Zero, punched through *Intrepid*'s flight deck only a few yards aft of where the first kamikaze had struck six minutes earlier. The bomb penetrated the gallery deck, ricocheted off the armored hangar deck, then hurtled forward to where firefighters were battling the blaze from the first kamikaze and exploded.

The devastation was immediate and spectacular. Lieutenant DiMarzo and the crew of Repair One died instantly. Nearly every remaining airplane in the hangar bay burst into flame. The ship rocked with secondary explosions. Fuel and ordnance began detonating like land mines, flinging shrapnel into bulkheads, mowing down the few men still standing.

Thick smoke gushed down passageways and filled compartments above and below the hangar deck. Men were trapped by fire and smoke on the gallery deck. Over the bullhorn came urgent calls for corpsmen. Volunteers qualified in first aid and artificial respiration were told to report to the flight deck.

On the forward air defense platform above the navigation bridge, Lt. Lowell Keagy, USMC, knew better than anyone what grave danger they were in. Keagy was in charge of the anti-aircraft guns on *Intrepid*'s starboard bow quadrant. He realized that the ammunition stores that supplied the ship's anti-aircraft batteries were located almost exactly where the fires were raging on the hangar deck. If the ammunition lit off, *Intrepid* was doomed.

Flames were shooting up through the holes in the flight deck. Radarman Ray Stone was on the deck helping pass a fire hose. Rumors were flying like missiles. Stone heard someone ask if they'd given the order to report to their abandon-ship stations. A few thought they had heard such an order, others insisted they had not. Stone looked around him. Some of the men on deck were looking up at the bridge, shaking their heads negatively. Order or not, they were expressing their sentiments. They wanted to stay with the ship and fight the fires.

Admiral Bogan still had the task group in a starboard turn, spilling burning fuel off *Intrepid*'s port side. The USS *New Jersey,* flagship of Third Fleet commander Admiral Halsey, was on *Intrepid*'s starboard side. *New Jersey* slid in close aboard to help fight the fires.

From the bridge of the battleship, Halsey watched the calamity on *Intrepid*. "An instant after she was hit," the admiral recalled, "she was wrapped in flames. Blazing gasoline cascaded down her sides; explosions rocked her; then oily black smoke, rising thousands of feet, hid everything but her bow."

With more kamikazes reported in the area, *Intrepid* was more vulnerable than ever. The dense smoke pouring over the fantail blinded the aft anti-aircraft gunners. The last kamikaze hit had jammed the ship's sky-search radar. Radarmen were unable to detect any more incoming bandits. Lou Valenti and a party of his fellow signalmen were assigned as lookouts up in the island's forward splinter shield. Human eyeballs had become *Intrepid*'s primary warning system.

Intrepid would be easy to find. The towering cloud of smoke was a beacon for more kamikazes. "For God's sake," said a gunnery officer, "are we the only ship in the ocean?"

They weren't. A report came in that the carrier *Cabot* had just taken a kamikaze hit and was burning. Then they heard that *Intrepid*'s sister ship, *Essex,* had been attacked and set afire. Half a mile away, *Hancock* was still smoking from her own recent hit.

Four ships of the fast carrier force had been struck. It was one the worst days in the history of U.S. naval aviation.

★ 13 ★

The Dry I

Intrepid's pilots still airborne received a sobering message: *Do not return to the ship.* No details were given over the radio, but they could guess. *Intrepid* had been sunk, or damaged so badly she couldn't recover her aircraft.

Intrepid's strike planes had already delivered some payback to the enemy, even though they hadn't yet heard about the kamikaze attacks on their ship. Helldivers from Bombing 18, along with the Avengers and Hellcats, had found the enemy cruisers and destroyers.

Four of the enemy ships had already been sunk in the first bombing strikes of the day. Two destroyers, filled with battle-ready troops, were still afloat in the hidden anchorage, and one after the other, the Helldivers rolled in and hit them with 1,000-pound bombs. After the pummeling from the previous strikes, the Japanese anti-aircraft fire was ineffective. When the smoke and debris had settled, the destroyers were gone, and 1,670 Japanese soldiers and sailors had gone with them.

After his precipitous, sideways takeoff from *Intrepid*, Charlie Mallory couldn't find his flight of Hellcats, so he teamed up with a pair of Intrepid bombers that were busy attacking another Japanese destroyer. Finished with their work, they were headed back to the *Intrepid* when they received the cryptic message not to return to the ship.

Some of the returning aircraft had already landed aboard other carriers. There was no room for any more. Those still in the air were supposed to make their way south to Leyte and land at Tacloban Airfield.

In silence, the *Intrepid* pilots flew across the green expanse of enemy-occupied Luzon, southward over the same sea where a month earlier they'd fought the battleships of Admiral Kurita's fleet. They descended along the coast of Leyte, where MacArthur's troops were still engaged in a fierce battle with the Japanese.

Tacloban Airfield, they discovered, was not really a field. It was a narrow strip of perforated steel planks called Marston mat. It was slippery and treacherous for pilots accustomed to making arrested landings on a hard carrier deck. Sliding off the skimpy steel mat during the landing roll meant digging the wheels into soft sand and flipping the airplane on its back. To underscore the danger, Tacloban's runway was lined with the carcasses of wrecked airplanes.

Each of the airplanes from Intrepid made it down safely. Tacloban, they learned, was also the forward base for Army P-38 fighters, which were supporting the ground war just beyond the ridge to the north. The Army officer who greeted them—with just a hint of sarcasm—handed the Navy men shovels and told them to go dig their own shelters. They were welcome to share whatever luxuries the Army crews had, which meant warm Australian beer, mosquito repellent, and canned rations. *And by the way, gentlemen, welcome to Leyte.*

Later in the afternoon, the reports filtered in about what had happened to *Intrepid*. For the ship's airmen, the reality began to sink in. They wouldn't be landing back aboard their ship. Not for a long time.

The mood aboard *Intrepid* was grim. Damage control crews had the fires on the flight deck extinguished in about fifteen minutes, but three more hours passed before the inferno on the hangar deck could be contained.

For those not already dead on the gallery deck and the spaces adjoining the hangar bays, the greatest danger was smoke. Men were crawling on all fours across decks and passageways looking for air. The lucky ones found ladders to the flight deck, where they emerged coughing and gasping, dragging their semiconscious shipmates with them.

Bodies were stretched out on the still-smoldering deck. Corpsmen and volunteers knelt over fallen men, trying to resuscitate them. The ship's two chaplains were moving among the stretchers, administering comfort to the wounded and last rites to the dying. The ship's doctors were trying to save as many as they could.

One of the doctors wasn't there. The air group's beloved flight surgeon, Dr. John Fish, had been at his battle station near the flight deck. He was one of those killed by the fumes and smoke.

The hangar deck was a scene of horror. Decks and bulkheads were twisted by the intense heat. Aircraft elevator bays were filled with charred debris and foam from the fire extinguishers. Hulks of burned-out airplanes were being pushed over the side. Carnage was everywhere. Bodies were lined up in rows beside the disabled aircraft elevators. Bodies and body parts were still being recovered. Some missing crewmen were never found.

Lou Valenti's fellow signalman, Odell Cooke, who alternated watches with Valenti at a gun position, had been on duty during the first kamikaze attack. Valenti guessed that he had joined the damage control parties fighting the hangar deck fires, but now Cooke was missing. Valenti never saw his friend again.

Later in the afternoon, a message was flashed to all ships in the Third Fleet: "The Nips scored some points today, but they lost the game. Well done on the overall alert and aggressive performance of the Task Force and better luck with the interception next time." It was signed by Admiral Halsey.

By evening, with the fires finally extinguished, haggard crewmen made their way to their quarters. In the enlisted men's berthing areas, entire sections of bunks were empty. The search was still going on for the dead and missing. Sailors lay in their bunks, staring at the overheads, pondering the loss of their shipmates.

"I tried to pray," recalled Ray Stone, "but it was difficult with ghastly distractions flashing through my mind, short-circuiting thoughts. Finally, I did thank God that I was alive and whole, as I have every day since then."

Seaman Ed Coyne, who had come to *Intrepid* as a seventeen-year-old sailor fresh from boot camp, crawled into his bunk. He'd been at his battle station that afternoon with his best buddy, Boatswain's Mate Second Class Ray Rucinski. After the first kamikaze strike, Rucinski had requested permission to go help fight the fires on the hangar deck. Five minutes later, he was dead, along with two other men in Coyne's division.

As Coyne tried to sleep, he heard a mournful sound. It was the ship's organ, located on the gallery deck, not far from Coyne's berthing compartment. Coyne recognized the tune from his childhood: "Where Will We All Be a Hundred Years from Now?"

The ceremony of burial at sea had become a familiar ritual to the men of *Intrepid*. At 1400 the next afternoon, they again gathered to honor their dead. The number of men commemorated at this memorial service exceeded anything they had previously experienced. Rows of canvas body bags covered the deck. Sixty-nine men had died in the kamikaze attacks of the previous day. Another 150 were wounded.

No man on *Intrepid* was untouched by what had happened. Each had a shipmate, colleague, or best buddy in one of the canvas bags. With bowed heads, they listened while the chaplains commended the souls of their fallen comrades to the Almighty. As the mournful notes of taps wafted through the charred hangar bay, many men wept openly. In unison they flinched at each volley of shots fired by the Marine honor guard. One by one the canvas bags were brought to the deck edge. From beneath an American flag, each was tilted downward and slipped into the sea.

Ray Stone was one of the sailors saying goodbye to his comrades. "There was nothing to help you there," he recalled. "Burying sixty-nine shipmates was a numbing experience of both body and mind."

Intrepid was out of action. On November 26, with Task Group 38.2 surrounding her, the wounded carrier set course for Ulithi.

It took three days to reach the huge, heart-shaped lagoon. As the carrier cleared the long coral reef and entered the anchorage, sailors on the deck stared in awe. As far as they could see, warships were moored. The U.S. Navy's overwhelming domination of the Pacific had never been so apparent.

On November 30, Captain Bolger went aboard *Hancock,* the Task Force 38 flagship. Admiral Halsey, who had already decorated Bolger with a Navy Cross for *Intrepid's* actions off Formosa and Japan, presented him with a gold star in lieu of a second Navy Cross. Bolger insisted that everyone, including Halsey, should know that the decoration was symbolic. It should be "in recognition of the outstanding performance of every officer and man of the *Intrepid.*"

Later that morning Bolger returned with Halsey and Adm. John S. McCain, who had relieved Mitscher as Task Force 38 commander. McCain was cut from the same cloth as Halsey, a gaunt, gruff-talking commander who played the horses, drank bourbon and water, and rolled his own cigarettes with one hand. He was called "Slew" by his officers and "Popeye" by the sailors under him. Halsey and McCain followed Bolger through the hangar bay, then up to the flight deck, grimly surveying the aftermath of the kamikaze attacks. Halsey had watched the raging fires from his bridge on the *New Jersey,* but now the tough battle commander was stunned at how severe the damage really was. Tight-lipped, he walked through the blackened compartments.

McCain was already making his case to Halsey that the kamikaze threat required a change in the air defense strategy. McCain wanted to increase the numbers of fighters aboard all the fast carriers of his task force. Earlier, Halsey had dismissed the Japanese suicide pilots as only a minor threat to the U.S. fleet. Now, seeing the carnage aboard *Intrepid,* he agreed with McCain. More Hellcat and Corsair fighters were needed to counter the kamikazes.

Halsey and McCain were in agreement on another matter too:

Intrepid's battle damage was not repairable out here in the Pacific. She would return to the United States. At noon, *Intrepid*'s task group commander, Admiral Bogan, moved his flag to the nearby *Lexington*.

Late that afternoon, crewmen on the *Intrepid* heard a distant drone. The sound swelled to a deep-throated crescendo. From the southeast appeared a huge formation of airplanes—thirty-six in all—swooping down on the lagoon at Ulithi. No anti-aircraft fire filled the sky; the incoming airplanes were friendly.

Pilots like to sleep in their own beds, as the old saying went, and *Intrepid*'s aviators had had enough of Army rations and muddy foxholes. The stranded airmen were coming home.

They'd flown from Leyte across 600 miles of open ocean to the primitive runway at Babelthuap, in the Palaus, where *Intrepid* had supported the Peleliu invasion less than two months before. Refueling, they continued 200 miles up the archipelago to Ulithi. The formation roared across the lagoon, sweeping low over the scorched flight deck of *Intrepid* in a salute to their ship.

What they didn't yet know was that it was a farewell salute. Air Group 18's planes would not be returning to *Intrepid*.

When the pilots had parked their airplanes at the Ulithi air strip and ridden the boat across the anchorage to *Intrepid*, they were stunned. They saw the fire-blackened hull around the hangar bay. In shocked silence, they stared at the charred and twisted wreckage. It was beyond anything they had imagined.

Then they learned the rest of the news. Orders had already been cut. As of the next day, December 1, 1944, the air group would be officially detached. *Intrepid* was returning to the United States.

Air Group 18 was being broken up. The men of Bombing 18 and Torpedo 18 would ride *Intrepid* back to the United States. Fighting 18 was staying behind to augment the fighter squadron aboard *Hancock*.

It was an emotional time, like breaking up a family. They'd come a long way together, *Intrepid* and her air group. Long forgotten were the wisecracks about airedales, the airmen's remarks about the

"Dry I," and the dirty tricks played on one another. Together they had fought in the greatest sea battle in history. They had taken the worst the enemy could give them, and given it back in spades.

In its brief combat history, the "inexperienced" Air Group 18 racked up one of the most glittering records of the war: 187 enemy aircraft destroyed in the air, with 18 probables and 20 damaged; 177 aircraft destroyed on the ground, with 32 probables and 123 damaged. They sank 69 enemy ships, with 27 probably sunk, and damaged 88 more. Their score included the sinking of *Musashi* and severe damage to her sister ship *Yamato*, the largest battleships ever constructed.

But this success was not without a terrible price. Fighting 18 lost thirteen Hellcat pilots. Bombing 18 counted eight pilots and eleven air crewmen gone. Torpedo 18 lost four Avenger pilots and eleven air crewmen. Five pilots and six air crewmen were still missing, either captured or in the hands of resistance fighters.

The night before Fighting 18's pilots left *Intrepid*, their comrades in the bomber and torpedo squadrons threw an impromptu—and unauthorized—shipboard party. The fighters had flown cover for them on every mission the air group had flown. "They'd protected us and risked their lives for us," wrote Helldiver pilot John Forsyth. "We hated to see them go."

Out came the secret stashes of booze. Behind locked doors the aviators toasted one another, their lost squadronmates, their air group, their skippers, their president, their families, and everything else that came to mind. The party went on for hours. The hangovers, according to unofficial accounts, lasted for days.

Intrepid the warship had once again become *Intrepid* the transport. On December 2, 1944, she hoisted her 15-ton anchor and eased out of Ulithi's anchorage, in company with destroyer escorts *Fair* and *Manlove*. She set course for Eniwetok, stopping long enough to pick up a large number of wounded troops, then turned her bow eastward for Pearl Harbor. Among her passengers was a captured Japanese pilot being sent to Pearl Harbor for interrogation.

With no battles to fight, no aircraft to launch, the ship steamed at high speed across the Pacific. For the men of *Intrepid,* it was a time to gaze out at the empty sea and reflect. They felt a peculiar mixture of joy and sadness. They had received an unexpected respite from the war. Many would be joining their families for Christmas. Heavy in their thoughts were the shipmates they had left behind. Images of canvas body bags and honor guards and the lingering echo of taps clung to their minds.

The officers and men of Bombing 18 and Torpedo 18, without their airplanes, were passengers with no shipboard duties. They passed the time sleeping, playing cards, and reflecting on the drama of the past five months. "It was a disturbing passage," wrote Forsyth. "The war sunk in as it never had while we were doing it."

Intrepid stopped for two glorious days in Pearl Harbor. For the crew, it was the first real liberty they'd seen since they departed Hawaii back in August. On the morning of December 16, they again hoisted anchor and continued the voyage to the United States. Four days later she slipped beneath the Golden Gate Bridge and made her way down to the Hunters Point shipyard. To the workers watching the big battle-scarred carrier slide into the dry dock, it was like a homecoming for an old friend. *Intrepid* was back.

★ 14 ★

Return Match

February 15, 1945

Beneath a cloudless California sky, they lined up again in neat rows on her flight deck. Standing in almost the exact spot that he had eleven months earlier, Capt. Joe Bolger said goodbye to his crew. *Intrepid* was getting a new skipper.

It was the military way, this periodic rotation of commanders. Embedded in Navy culture was the belief that no one should be allowed to command anything—ship, squadron, tugboat—for any longer than it took them to get acquainted with the job. Then they moved on, like peripatetic knights, to higher command or to the gray obscurity of a staff job somewhere. This was wartime, and Joe Bolger, like Tom Sprague before him, was moving on. Also like Sprague, he would eventually pin on admiral's stars.

Intrepid's crew wasn't happy about losing Bolger. He had a genial, kindly way about him, gnawing on his cigar, popping into their work spaces to ask questions and pass out attaboys. They remembered Bolger's reassuring voice on the bullhorn when the deck was ablaze and they feared losing their ship. They remembered the praise he gave them for their courage while under attack. Bolger, like Sprague, was a father figure they'd come to trust.

As Bolger exchanged salutes with his relief, irreverent sailors in the ranks couldn't help making wisecracks about the new skipper's name. At five feet six inches, Capt. Giles E. Short stood half a head beneath his predecessor. But Short brought with him impressive credentials. He was an experienced naval aviator and a veteran of the North Atlantic. As captain of the sub-hunting escort carrier USS *Bogue*, Short and his crew had won the Presidential Unit Citation.

Intrepid was not only changing skippers, it was taking on a new air group. Air Group 18, which had covered itself with glory at Leyte Gulf and Formosa, was being rotated ashore and its remaining squadrons reformed. In its place came Air Group 10, led by a tough, seasoned commander named John Hyland.

Hyland had graduated from the Naval Academy in 1934, earned his wings the next year, and gone on to fly almost everything in the Navy. He and his PBY Catalina squadron were caught in the Philippines when the Japanese attacked. In the bloody retreat from the Dutch East Indies, Hyland and his squadron lost most of their airplanes and crews. Hyland had pushed hard to get back into the war, and was handpicked to lead the new Corsair fighter-bomber squadrons of Air Group 10.

Since the Battle of Leyte Gulf, the thinking had changed about carrier air group composition. As McCain and Halsey had already determined, task forces needed more fighters to protect them from the specter of kamikazes. And they needed fighters that could do both jobs—protect the fleet and hit the enemy on the surface.

The composition of *Intrepid*'s air group was a reflection of the new strategy. *Intrepid* embarked a total of sixty-six new F4U-1D Corsair fighters, divided between two squadrons—Fighting 10 and the hybrid Bombing Fighting 10. In addition to their Corsairs, Fighting 10 had six specially outfitted F6F Hellcats—two photo reconnaissance fighters and four radar-equipped night fighters.

With its long, graceful nose and inverted gull-wing design, the Vought Corsair looked fast and sexy. Compared to its contemporaries, the F6F Hellcat and its clunky predecessor, the F4F Wildcat, the Corsair was a leap into the future. It was designed to have the biggest propeller on the most powerful engine ever used on a fighter. The Corsair had long range, could carry an enormous bomb load, and was a good 40 knots faster than the Hellcat.

In its early life, the Corsair had problems. Pilots couldn't see over the long nose during carrier landings. Its nasty stall behavior and the long, stiff-legged landing gear made the Corsair bounce and porpoise wildly when it slammed onto a flight deck. "This will never be a good carrier plane," said the early test pilots, and the Corsair was relegated to land-based duty with the Marines in the Solomon Islands.

Eventually, the carrier landing problems were solved. The landing gear was modified to eliminate the nasty bouncing tendency, and pilots learned to accommodate the long, visibility-hampering nose. A new tailhook was designed to prevent it skipping over the arresting wires. An extended tail wheel strut eliminated most of the porpoising tendency on landing.

The Corsair was a high-performance fighter. Pilots accustomed to the easy-to-fly Grumman Hellcat learned the hard way to respect the new fighter. Vought test pilot Boone Guyton was asked about spinning the Corsair. "Don't," he warned. After a few gyrations, the Corsair tended to wrap up in a violent spin from which most pilots couldn't recover.

The Corsair received nicknames, not all complimentary—"Bent-Wing Bastard," "Hose Nose," "Ensign Eliminator," or just "U-Bird." The Japanese gave it another name, "Whistling Death," because of the high-pitched howl from its wing root air coolers. Marines had more affectionate labels for the fighter that swept over them during amphibious assaults—the "Angel of Okinawa" and "Sweetheart of the Marianas."

In addition to the new Corsairs, the air group still had traditional bombing and torpedo squadrons—VB-10 and VT-10—flying the sturdy Curtiss SB2C Helldiver and TBM Avengers. For the next two weeks *Intrepid* exercised off the West Coast, getting her own crew acquainted with the new air group.

This time there was little of the initial abrasive relationship between the airedales and the ship's sailors. No one felt like making wisecracks about one another's war experience. *Intrepid*'s crew had been bloodied in battle and they had the scars to prove it. Air Group 10, for its part, had fought in almost every major Pacific battle. It was the only air group in the Navy that had flown three full combat deployments aboard carriers.

Fighting 10, nicknamed the Grim Reapers, had one of the most illustrious records in the Navy. The squadron had flown F4F Wildcats in 1942, then moved up to F6F Hellcats in 1943 and 1944. Now the Reapers were flying the ultimate fighter, the Corsair. As part of Air Group 10, Fighting 10 was augmented in size and divided into two squadrons: VF-10, led by Lt. Cdr. Walt Clarke, and a fighter-bomber squadron, VBF-10, commanded by Lt. Cdr. Wilmer Rawie.

The Corsair pilots were going into battle with cutting-edge new equipment and weapons. The pilots had been fitted with anti-blackout G-suits, a new device that squeezed a pilot's legs and torso, preventing "grayout" when blood drained from the head during high-acceleration pullouts.

VBF-10 was also carrying an experimental new weapon—the 11.75-inch Tiny Tim air-to-ground rocket. The Tiny Tim was developed as a heavy ship-killing weapon to replace the slow-moving aerial torpedo. It had a 500-pound bomb as a warhead, and the rocket was driven by a solid-propellant motor that ignited after the weapon was released from the airplane. The idea was that a Corsair could deliver the weapon at high speed, then escape without undue exposure to the kind of close-in anti-aircraft fire that had decimated the torpedo squadrons.

The pilots were skeptical. Even the name, Tiny Tim, seemed like a joke. There was nothing tiny about it. The thing was over 10 feet long, weighed more than half a ton, and looked like a mean-tempered beast that would turn on its owner.

As it turned out, they were right.

One thing they all agreed on later: it was the best send-off they'd ever had.

The morning of February 20, 1945, began like all *Intrepid*'s previous departures. The same crisp wind riffled San Francisco Bay, raising whitecaps on the surface. The crew was lined up at quarters on the flight deck. The ship slid out of Hunters Point and headed across the bay, past the rocky hump of Alcatraz, and as usual the sailors waved goodbye. As always, someone yelled, "So long, Big

Al." It didn't matter that Alcatraz's most famous resident, Al Capone, had long since departed the prison.

Ahead lay the Golden Gate Bridge. As the *Intrepid* approached the span, the sailors on deck noticed something different. Something waving . . . flapping in the breeze. There were people on the bridge.

The ship passed under the bridge, and the sailors saw that the people were *girls.* Dozens of them. They were yelling and blowing kisses. And they were waving things—scarves, brassieres, panties.

The sailors loved it. They yelled, whistled, waved back at the girls. Even the new skipper, Giles Short, who had the best view on the ship, cracked up laughing.

Intrepid entered Pearl Harbor on March 2, 1945, stopping just long enough to load provisions and passengers. Reloaded, she was under way for Ulithi in company with the carriers *Franklin* and *Bataan,* the battle cruiser *Guam,* and eight destroyers—all part of newly formed Task Group 12.2. While zigzagging on their westward course across the Pacific, the task group exercised their air defense systems. *Intrepid* launched her warplanes—thirty-eight Corsairs, six Helldivers, and four Avengers—to run simulated torpedo and dive-bomb attacks on the task group.

At dawn on March 13, *Intrepid* slipped into the anchorage at Ulithi. Most of the crew had been aboard during *Intrepid*'s previous combat deployment, and the coral-reef-enclosed lagoon evoked a flood of memories, some good, some painful. Ulithi was where they'd rested and reprovisioned between battles. It was also where they'd retreated the previous November with their flight deck blackened and smoldering and the smell of death still in the passageways.

By dawn of the next day, they were under way again, part of Task Group 58.4, under Rear Adm. Arthur Radford. In the group were the carriers *Yorktown, Enterprise, Independence,* and *Langley,* with the battleships *Wisconsin* and *Missouri,* plus five cruisers and several destroyers. The task group was part of Marc Mitscher's mighty Task Force 58, bound for an island called Okinawa.

Okinawa lay in the middle of the Ryukyus, a chain of islands that dangled like a stinger from the southern rump of Japan. By March 17, *Intrepid* and TG 58.4 had reached a position to the east of the Ryukyus, where they would support the coming invasion of Okinawa.

The presence of the American ships was no secret to the Japanese. That evening the blips of enemy planes began appearing on the radar. Snoopers were determining the numbers and disposition of the American fleet.

In the darkness before dawn, *Intrepid* launched a flight of Corsairs on a four-hour CAP mission over the task group. In one of the Corsairs was a tall young man from Nebraska, Lt. Bill "Country" Landreth. He had earlier flown with VF-17 in the Solomons, where he'd gotten credit for three and a half Japanese planes downed ("one half" as a result of sharing credit for one kill with another pilot). This morning was Landreth's first mission as a pilot aboard *Intrepid*. It was also the first time he'd flown from a carrier at night.

Gradually the darkness faded as dawn approached. Landreth was watching the first sliver of sun creep over the horizon, bathing the ocean in a pale orange light. He was stunned. "As far as the eye could see," Landreth recalled, "from horizon to horizon, the ocean was covered with the might of the United States Navy. Five task groups, twenty-one aircraft carriers, all their escorts. It was the most magnificent sight I'd ever seen."

That morning, March 18, 1945, *Intrepid* launched her first strike against the Japanese homeland. Thirty-one Corsairs rumbled into the pale gray sky, bound for the Oita airfield on Kyushu. An hour later, a second wave of thirteen Helldivers, eleven Avengers, and twelve more Corsairs departed after them.

Even while the strikes were still assembling and heading for their target, the task group radars were picking up incoming bogies ("bogies" were unidentified; "bandits" were known hostiles). CAPs from the task group carriers began intercepting the targets, which were definitely bandits. The task group's anti-aircraft batteries opened up. One by one the intruders were shot down or turned away.

Except for one. A twin-engine Betty bomber somehow slipped

through the wall of anti-aircraft fire, headed directly for *Intrepid*. It came boring straight in at an altitude of 450 feet, not bothering to jink or avoid the storm of anti-aircraft fire around it.

The gunners aboard *Intrepid* blazed away at the bomber. Men stationed on the deck watched in horrified fascination. It didn't seem possible that it could be happening all over again. Not on their very first day back in battle.

But here he was, another Japanese pilot hell-bent on his own destruction—and on taking their ship with him. He was close enough for the gunners to make out the two round engines, the glass panels of the cockpit, the long tapered wings. The Betty was taking hits, trailing smoke, but the pilot kept flying, just like the last time.

Intrepid's guns blazed away, filling the air with the din of 5-inch, 40-mm, and 20-mm fire. Through it all, as if the kamikaze really *did* have some kind of divine protection, he kept coming. Just when it seemed that the kamikaze would hit *Intrepid* squarely in her flight deck, a 5-inch anti-aircraft shell from one of the starboard batteries clipped the plane's tail.

What happened next took place so fast, no one could agree on what they'd seen, but it was captured on film. The Betty pitched over in a vertical dive, revealing its long slender lines with the ball of the rising sun on the starboard wing. The bomber crashed into the sea 50 feet abeam of *Intrepid*. The explosion hurled a geyser of flame and debris into the carrier's starboard side, torching her side and spewing fire and pieces into the hangar bay.

Flame and smoke billowed from the hangar bay. From other ships, *Intrepid*'s condition looked serious, but damage control crews had the fires extinguished in less than fifteen minutes. The fabric control surfaces of several parked warplanes caught fire, but the airplanes didn't explode. No one was killed by the flame or debris from the kamikaze, but there were casualties. In the frenzy of gunfire directed at the low-flying kamikaze, a ship on *Intrepid*'s port side put a 5-inch shell too close to her fantail. The blast killed one sailor at his battle station and wounded forty-four others.

For *Intrepid*'s pilots and air crewmen, it was their first day of action—and their first losses. Three waves of fighters and bombers swept over the enemy airfields on the Japanese home islands of Kyushu and Shikoku. On the initial nineteen-plane attack, two of VF-10's "nuggets," Ens. Loran Isley and Ens. H. W. Harris, were lost in action. The newly winged aviator Isley had rolled in on a strafing pass, and for reasons no one would ever know—whether he was hit by enemy fire or suffered target fixation—he continued his dive straight into the ground. Harris took a hit in his fuel system and was en route back to the ship when his engine quit from fuel starvation. He was observed ditching and escaping from his downed Corsair, but rescue ships never found a trace of him.

At 1045 that morning, Bill "Country" Landreth launched on his second mission of the day. He and his flight were on a fighter sweep over Shikoku Island, looking for enemy aircraft and targets of opportunity.

They dove down on the airfield at Uwa Jima, strafing buildings and parked airplanes. As he was leaving the target, skimming over an estuary at nearly 400 knots, Landreth spotted a speedboat kicking up a rooster tail of white water. Guessing that the boat contained a target of value, he went for it.

And then he spotted something else. Between the boat and his Corsair was a small island with round tanks and tile-roofed buildings. "I figured I'd give them a squirt on the way to the speed boat," Landreth said. "I gave them one burst, then shifted my attention to the boat."

In the next instant, Bill Landreth's life changed. From the tile-roofed buildings came a red ball of flame and smoke that shot thousands of feet into the sky. Landreth's Corsair plunged through the fireball. The G-forces were so severe, it broke his back. But the worst wasn't over. "I looked down at the little round dial for oil pressure, and it said zero." He knew the big twin-row radial engine wouldn't run for long without oil.

With a sinking heart, he prepared for the inevitable. Landreth managed to glide the Corsair to a water landing. He was able to climb into his raft, where he spent the next three days in a freezing rain. "Everybody saw me go in, and I was in radio contact, but this was an estuary in the home islands of Japan, so you're not there for a Sunday afternoon drive."

He clung to the hope that a boat or an amphibious airplane would come to pick him up. When a boat finally did come, it turned out to be Japanese. Landreth spent the rest of the war as a prisoner.

That evening in "Boys Town"—the junior officers' bunkroom—there was none of the usual hijinks and kidding. For most, it was their first day of war. Ens. Roy "Eric" Erickson was one of the sober young men in the bunkroom. He was a tall, twenty-year-old former art student from Nebraska who now flew as "Tail End Charlie"—number four—in CAG Hyland's four-plane division. Until that day, he had thought flying fighters in combat was the greatest fun he'd ever had. Now he'd just lost three buddies over Japan.

In silence the junior officers gathered up the personal effects of the missing pilots to be shipped back home.

At a few minutes before 0700 the next morning, Plane Capt. Felix Novelli was standing on *Intrepid*'s flight deck watching the Corsair with the big number 5 painted on its side trundle away from its parking spot. The aircraft was armed with the standard full load of .50-caliber ammunition and the new 5-inch high-velocity aerial rocket (HVAR) called "Holy Moses." Keeping the aircraft airworthy and ready for combat was Novelli's job.

As he always did, Novelli stood on the deck and watched the airplanes take off, one after the other, into the gray sky. When the last fighter had rumbled off the deck, Novelli was about to leave when something caught his eye. Up in the broken cloud layer, he glimpsed a silver object. It seemed to be slanting downward. Then it was gone.

The next time he saw it, the anti-aircraft guns were already firing.

15

Floating Chrysanthemum

Twenty miles away, Rear Adm. Gerald Bogan saw the same silver object. Bogan, who had been *Intrepid*'s task group commander at Leyte Gulf, was standing on the bridge of the carrier *Franklin*. He was peering intently at the object descending from the broken cloud layer above the fleet.

Franklin had just launched her strike planes. Crewmen on the flight deck were readying aircraft for the next launch, including Corsairs armed with the new Tiny Tim rockets. In the next few seconds, Bogan heard *Franklin*'s anti-aircraft guns open up. At the same time he could hear the guns of her escorting ships firing.

They were too late. The incoming Asahi D4Y Suise: "Judy" dive-bomber was coming nearly straight down, aimed at *Franklin*. For Bogan, who had just arrived aboard the ship, it was a replay of his previous experience. From *Intrepid*'s flag bridge, he'd witnessed three successive kamikaze hits.

But this Japanese pilot was not a kamikaze. He pickled off two 500-pound bombs, which exploded precisely on *Franklin*'s flight deck, then pulled up hard and vanished back into the clouds.

The results were immediate and catastrophic. "In a very few minutes," wrote Bogan, "the forward part of the ship was an inferno." *Franklin*'s air group, like *Intrepid*'s, was experimenting with the new Tiny Tim rockets. Now the rockets were lighting off, screaming in all directions, through bulkheads and airplanes and personnel. Loaded bombers burst into flame and exploded. Parked warplanes erupted in gushes of flame and debris. Firefighting teams were mowed down by the exploding ordnance.

The carnage went on for hours. The carrier convulsed and heaved with internal explosions. Finally *Franklin*'s skipper, Capt. Les Gehres, ordered most of the crew to abandon ship. He kept 700 men with him to try to save the carrier.

The dense mass of smoke was climbing into the sky, clearly visible 20 miles away on *Intrepid*. Radarman Ray Stone went up to the flight deck. He could see the *Franklin* across the water. "Hearing the numerous, repeated explosions from the fully-armed, about-to-be-launched planes was sickening," he wrote. "You could virtually feel and smell the fire."

While *Franklin* fought for her life, *Intrepid*'s CAG Hyland was leading a ten-Corsair attack on the Kure Air Depot on the Japanese mainland with 500-pound bombs and HVARs. As they were sweeping the airfield with rockets and bombs, the Corsairs were jumped by Japanese fighters. In the ensuing melee, Hyland gunned down a Nakajima A6M2-N "Rufe" floatplane fighter. Two of his wingmen, Lt. Robert "Windy" Hill and Ens. Eric Erickson, became separated from the flight. Engaged by a swarm of Japanese fighters, they teamed up in a Thach weave, killing two Zeroes and a Tojo.

They were followed by another fourteen-Corsair wave from *Intrepid*, led by Grim Reaper skipper Walt Clarke. The Corsairs found a Japanese escort carrier at Inno Shima, to the east of Kure. They attacked with 5-inch HVAR rockets and 500-pound bombs, setting the doomed carrier ablaze.

Another wave of dive-bomber and torpedo planes, escorted by *Intrepid* Corsairs, returned to Kure to pound fuel storage units and an aircraft factory. Two SB2Cs from Bombing 10 took hits and went down offshore. One crew was rescued, and the other was lost. High above the bombers, Fighting 10's Corsairs ran into a flight of Tojo fighters.

The Tojo fighter was a latecomer to the war, and its capabilities still weren't known. "The Tojo could turn inside the F4U-1D easily," wrote Lt. (jg) K. B. Walker in his aircraft action report. "Probably had armor plate behind the pilot and self-sealing gas tanks, as a number of hits were made on the fuselage from the rear and wings without results."

The Tojo was a tough fighter, but not tough enough. Walker and his wingmen shot three of them out of the sky.

When the pilots returned to *Intrepid*, they were stunned by the ominous column of smoke billowing from *Franklin*. *Franklin*'s own warplanes had been sent to other carriers. Some were already landing aboard *Intrepid*.

The fires raged on *Franklin* for the rest of the day. She had already taken on an ominous list to starboard. Finally the fires were extinguished, and she was towed out of range of more Japanese bombers. Under her own power she steamed back to Ulithi. From there she would creep back to Pearl Harbor, then all the way to New York for repairs.

Franklin was out of the war. In all, 774 men died in the attack. Another 265 were wounded, and 1,700 were pulled from the water after abandoning ship. Thirty-five of her airplanes were destroyed, including sixteen precious Corsairs. Those with a superstitious nature were pointing out that the unlucky ship's official designation was CV-13, and the horrendous attack occurred in her thirteenth month of commissioned service.

Franklin wasn't the only victim that day. *Wasp* took a serious bomb hit, and the next day, March 20, it was *Enterprise*'s turn. All three carriers were forced to withdraw to Ulithi. *Intrepid* was the only carrier left still equipped to fire the new Tiny Tim rockets.

The divine wind continued to blow. Kamikaze attacks came in sporadic waves, and each was met with CAP fighters from the task force carriers. On March 21, forty-eight Japanese planes showed up on early-warning radars. They were intercepted by 150 carrier-based fighters and were all shot down or chased away.

But the Navy fighter pilots reported seeing something peculiar attached to the Betty bombers. What they spotted was the latest bizarre development in the kamikaze campaign—the Ohka, meaning "cherry blossom." It was a 20-foot-long manned rocket plane with stubby wooden wings and a ton of explosives. Released from the mother ship, the pilot of the Ohka ignited his rocket motor and dove at almost 600 miles per hour on his target.

U.S. intelligence officers quickly assigned the new rocket plane its own code name—Baka. In Japanese, it meant "stupid."

None of the Ohkas got through to the carriers, but a wave of the tiny rocket planes blazed down on the vulnerable radar picket ships at the perimeter of the fleet. The picket ships had become favorite targets for incoming kamikazes. The average time a picket ship on the northernmost station spent before being hit, according to action reports, was about six hours.

For the next week *Intrepid*'s warplanes flew pre-invasion strikes in Okinawa and into the mainland of Japan. On March 24, the Corsairs of Bombing Fighting 10 put the new Tiny Tim rockets to their first combat test against caves in Okinawa. Of twelve planes in the sweep, eight were carrying the new rockets.

The Tiny Tim wasn't popular, particularly with CAG Hyland. One of his birds, the pristine number five, which was carefully tended by Plane Capt. Felix Novelli, had been the first to fire one of the behemoth rockets. Instead of cleanly separating from the belly of the Corsair before the motor ignited, the rocket took off instantly and flew through the Corsair's propeller, whacking off several inches from the blades and causing a vibration that nearly shook the fighter apart. The pilot nursed the damaged fighter back to the nearest available carrier, USS *Yorktown*, where it was cannibalized for parts.

Hyland's pilots tried the Tiny Tim on several more missions with mixed results. Sometimes the big rockets worked brilliantly, blazing down to the target in a straight, true line. Sometimes they took off on bizarre courses of their own, scaring the hell out of pilots and everyone in the vicinity.

Hyland wasn't impressed. He had no interest in losing valuable Corsairs or pilots to their own rockets. He ordered the Tiny Tims off-loaded. By now, Air Group 10's pilots held Hyland in high regard. Although he was a decade or more older than most of his young aviators, CAG Hyland could hold his own with all of them and flew more missions than anyone. To his young pilots, Hyland was a mentor and father figure.

Operation Iceberg, the long-planned invasion of Okinawa, was the most ambitious island assault of the Pacific war. More than 250 transport ships were assembled for the invasion, protected by an Anglo-American fleet of battleships, cruisers, and carriers. It began on Easter Sunday, April 1, 1945, and by the end of the day, more than 50,000 troops had waded ashore on Okinawa. For the next week *Intrepid* and her air group, along with all the carriers of Task Force 58, devoted their collective assets to supporting the invasion. On April 5 alone, *Intrepid*'s warplanes flew 141 sorties, hitting aircraft and airfield installations at Sakishima Gunto.

Initial resistance to the landings on Okinawa was surprisingly light, the only casualty being a Marine with a broken foot. But the Americans had learned the lessons of Peleliu and Leyte, and no one doubted that the Japanese were picking their moment to fight back. The Japanese considered Okinawa to be part of their homeland. They would commit every resource in their possession to hold it.

The Japanese, in fact, *did* have a strategy to defeat the Americans. They had given it a name, *kikusai*, which meant "floating chrysanthemum." It was an enchanting label for a macabre strategy, inspired by a fourteenth-century Japanese warrior, Masashige Kusunoki, who sacrificed himself and all his men in the legendary Battle of Minatogowa. It was the ultimate expression of Bushido— an unreasoning, suicidal thrust against an implacable enemy.

The overall commander of *kikusai*, Vice Adm. Matome Ugaki, intended to repeat Kusunoki's sacrifice with a withering air and sea kamikaze blitz against the American invaders. Ugaki, who was one of the strategists of the Pearl Harbor attack, had so far led a charmed life. He had been Admiral Yamamoto's chief of staff at the Battle of Midway, then narrowly missed being shot down with Yamamoto in the South Pacific. More recently he had escaped death in the Leyte Gulf when his flagship *Yamato* was bombed and torpedoed by planes from *Intrepid*.

Now Ugaki had three air fleets with a combined strength of 1,815 aircraft, of which he had assigned 540 to kamikaze missions. Ugaki launched his attack on April 6. More than 300 kamikazes and an equal number of conventional warplanes swarmed toward the American fleet. It was the greatest wave of kamikazes the Americans had yet seen. As reports of the large number of inbound kamikazes came in, U.S. commanders ordered their torpedos and dive-bombers stashed belowdecks, ordnance loads removed, and fuel tanks emptied.

Intrepid's Corsairs leaped into the sky, and so did CAPs from every other carrier, vectored by destroyer picket ships stationed at strategic points around the task force perimeter. The melee lasted all day and into the morning of April 7. Fighter pilots were surprised at how little air-to-air resistance the Japanese pilots were putting up. Their tactic seemed to be to remain focused on the targets below and not to engage the interceptors. The Corsairs and Hellcats filled the sky with the trails of blazing Zeroes and Bettys and Tojo fighters. "The primary danger to our pilots," observed one of the pilots in his action report, "was collision or getting in the path of a friendly plane's fire."

Some 288 Japanese planes were gunned out of the sky by Navy and Marine fighters. The few that broke through were hit by shipboard gunners, who shot down thirty-nine more. Still, twenty-two kamikazes made it through the screen of fighters and flak to sink the destroyers *Bush, Colhoun,* and *Emmons.* Two ammunition ships were blown up, and several vessels were damaged beyond repair.

Kikusai, the Japanese counterattack, involved more than suicide pilots. The Bushido ethic was now the mind-set—and the only remaining strategy—of the Japanese high command. In addition to the special attack force of suicide pilots, Admiral Ugaki had assembled a fleet of warships he called the Special Surface Attack Force. Now Ugaki intended to launch a massive coordinated sea-and-air kamikaze assault against the Americans.

In the late afternoon of April 6, while the air battles were still raging over the fleet, two U.S. submarines were lurking outside the entrance to Japan's Inland Sea. The skipper of USS *Hackleback* flashed a report. He had just observed ten warships, including one very large one, passing through the Bungo Strait. They were headed for the open sea.

The large ship was *Intrepid*'s old adversary, the super-battleship *Yamato*. She was coming out to fight.

16

Imperial Sacrifice

From the outset, it was a doomed mission.

The Japanese task force was commanded by Vice Adm. Seiichi Ito. His orders were absurdly unrealistic. Ito and his fleet were supposed to fight their way through the gauntlet of enemy ships and bombard the American troops ashore on Okinawa. The flagship of the Special Surface Attack Force, the magnificent *Yamato,* bore the scars of her mauling at Leyte Gulf, but she was still the most potent battleship on earth. *Yamato*'s massive guns had a longer range than any ship in the U.S. fleet, and she carried over a thousand rounds of the potent 18.1-inch, 3,200-pound shells in her ammunition holds.

In company with *Yamato* was the cruiser *Yahagi* and eight destroyers. The fleet of ten warships, with no air cover, was going up against the collective might of the U.S. Navy's Fifth Fleet, consisting of 40 aircraft carriers, 18 battleships, and 200 destroyers. After emptying *Yamato*'s store of massive shells, Ito intended to beach the giant battleship and send her nearly 3,000-man crew swarming ashore to join Japanese ground forces on Okinawa.

Yamato was on a seaborne kamikaze mission. Like her airborne counterparts, she didn't carry enough fuel for a round trip. It didn't matter to Admiral Ito. As obsessed with Bushido as any samurai warrior, he had no intention of returning to Japan.

With U.S. submarines and scouting planes tracking the Japanese fleet's progress, Vice Adm. Marc Mitscher alerted his fast carriers to ready their strike aircraft. At the same time, Rear Adm. Morton Deyo, who commanded the surface warships off Okinawa, was dispatching his own force of six battleships, seven cruisers, and twenty-one destroyers to go after *Yamato*.

The race to get *Yamato* was on.

Mitscher waited until the Japanese fleet was within 250 miles of the task force, then gave the order to launch strikes. At 1038 *Intrepid* launched her strike aircraft—sixteen Corsairs, fourteen SB2C dive-bombers, and twelve Avenger torpedo planes. At the same time warplanes from every carrier in the task force took to the air.

For *Intrepid*'s aircraft, it would be a 280-mile flight north to *Yamato*'s position. The Corsairs and Helldivers all carried thousand-pound armor-piercing bombs, and the Avengers hauled their trusty Mark 13 torpedoes. Wilmer Rawie, skipper of VBF-10, was designated strike leader for the task group, a total of eighty-three warplanes from *Intrepid, Yorktown,* and *Langley*.

Fighting 10 lost two Corsairs en route to the target, but not to enemy fire. Ens. D. H. Crow radioed his skipper, Walt Clarke, that he thought he spotted a Japanese fighter. Clarke told him to go for it, but when the eager Crow slid under Clarke's airplane to go chase the bogey, he cut it too close. Clarke's propeller chopped through his tail, and Crow's Corsair spun out of control toward the sea. Clarke's had a shattered propeller and an engine shaking off its mount, so he put it into the water beside a destroyer and was rescued. His wingman, Crow, was never found.

Lieutenant Commander Rawie, call sign "Red One," received a radar vector to the *Yamato*, some 25 miles away. The Japanese fleet was beneath a low cloud cover, ducking in and out of rain squalls. Because of the clouds, the dive-bombers were forced to roll in from low altitude, which hurt their accuracy and exposed them to the hail of fire from the Japanese fleet. It also filled the confined airspace with friendly aircraft, which became as much a hazard as enemy fire.

To those who had fought *Yamato* before and failed to sink her, the battle seemed like a rematch. The same multi-colored bursts of anti-aircraft fire were filling the sky. *Yamato* mounted even more firepower now than she had at Leyte Gulf—six 6-inch secondary batteries, twenty-four 5-inch anti-aircraft guns, and 150 machine guns. She had a new type of time-fuse ammunition that exploded into thousands of pieces.

And *Yamato*'s gunners had learned a deadly new trick: they were firing the big 5-inch guns into the water directly in front of the torpedo planes, throwing up huge geysers of water that stopped the Avengers like a concrete wall.

Rawie's Corsairs, diving so low they barely cleared *Yamato*'s superstructure, hurled their thousand-pounders at *Yamato*. One of the Corsair pilots was Eric Erickson, who had been assigned at the last minute to the mission. Now he was dodging flak and darting in and out of the low-hanging clouds. When their bombs were expended, they went back with their machine guns. Erickson could smell the cordite of the tracers. His Corsair was buffeting from the turbulence of the flak bursts.

The first ship to die was the cruiser *Yahagi*, hammered by twelve bomb hits and seven torpedoes. Then went the destroyers— *Isokaze, Hamakaze, Kasumi,* and *Asahimo*—one after the other to the bottom. But the big prize, *Yamato*, was still in the fight.

Just as they had in their first battle with *Yamato* in the Sibuyan Sea, the torpedo-dropping Avengers bored in against merciless anti-aircraft fire. Just as before, several were blown out of the sky. But they were scoring hits. One after another, the Avengers, skimming the ocean at 500 feet, put their Mark 13 torpedoes into *Yamato*'s flanks.

Wave after wave of attacking airplanes threw themselves at the battleship and her escorts. *Yamato* was swerving, trying to evade the swarms of torpedoes that were coming from all directions. Geysers of water and flame leaped from her sides each time a torpedo slammed into her hull. Burning amidships and trailing a slick of oil, she somehow kept up a speed of 20 knots. She was listing to port, which exposed her thinner-plated lower hull to more torpedoes. Seeing the exposed lower hull, one of the Avenger flight leaders instructed his crews to reset their torpedoes to run at a deeper level when they hit water.

Mercilessly the torpedoes slashed into the stricken battleship. The Corsairs and Helldivers, having expended their bombs, continued to strafe the Japanese ship. Flames surged from the top decks of the battleship. The pilots could see Japanese sailors sliding down the sides into the water. From the bowels of the ship came explosions as ammunition stores cooked off. A blast tore through the steel decks and sent a pillar of smoke and fire thousands of feet into the sky.

At 1423 in the afternoon it was over for *Yamato*. Slowly she rolled over and slipped beneath the waves. More than 2,500 Japanese sailors went down with her, including the captain and the fleet commander, Vice Adm. Seiichi Ito. Fewer than 300 of *Yamato*'s crew survived. The world's greatest battleship was gone. And so, for all practical purposes, was the Japanese Imperial Navy.

When *Intrepid*'s exhausted airmen returned to their carrier, they had been in the air for more than five hours. It was a triumphant and emotionally draining day. While they had been destroying the Japanese ships, two kamikazes had dived on *Hancock,* setting her ablaze and killing seventy sailors. Ten task force planes and twelve airmen had been lost in the attack on *Yamato*. Every air group had joined in the battle, and each was claiming credit for having sunk the world's greatest battleship.

The question would continue to be asked throughout the fleet: who really deserved credit for sinking the *Yamato?*

"Our guys," insisted Plane Capt. Felix Novelli, whose Corsair flown by Eric Erickson had made it back safely to *Intrepid.* "They get at least fifty percent credit." The young sailor was biased, because the day of the battleship's sinking happened to coincide with his birthday. For the rest of his life Novelli would insist that *Yamato* had been his twentieth-birthday present.

The kamikazes kept coming, and the fighters kept shooting them down. Wave after wave of *kikusai* mass raids flew toward the task force. The easiest targets were the picket ships, which the kamikazes hit almost daily. So many picket ships had been hit, a sailor on one of them had put up a sign with a big arrow: THAT WAY TO THE CARRIERS.

CAPs from *Intrepid* were assigned stations overhead the picket ships. To the Corsair pilots, it was evident that the kamikazes were mostly untrained aviators. Their evasive tactics were rudimentary, amounting to little more than skids and abrupt turns, usually away from one another, which made them easy pickings for the eager fighter pilots.

"My target pulled out to left in a sharp turn," wrote Lt. R. E. Goetter of Fighting 10 in a typical action report. "I followed and opened fire and his plane began to burn after a five second burst." Goetter's wingman, Ens. T. J. Boucher, had a similar experience: "I overtook the Tony [Kawasaki Ki-61 fighter] easily in a slight climb. He did not try to turn away or use any evasive action. About a two second burst blew him up."

Intrepid's night fighters—F6F-5N Hellcats equipped with radar—were having equally good results. Night after night they intercepted Japanese intruders either snooping or trying to make torpedo runs on the fleet. Fighter directors aboard *Intrepid* had become skilled at vectoring the night fighters to the bogeys. Twenty-year-old Ray Stone was one of the radarmen in *Intrepid*'s CIC. "You had a sense of the hunted and the hunter," wrote Stone, "as you watched the gap between the pips quickly closing on the scope. Hearing a pilot's resounding 'Tally ho!'—followed by 'Splash one bogey!' was a beautiful, exhilarating, soul-satisfying sound."

In action on April 12, twelve Corsairs from Fighting 10 intercepted a flight of sixty-six incoming Japanese aircraft. Every pilot in the flight shot down at least one enemy airplane. By the end of the swirling dogfight, the Corsairs had killed twenty-two enemy airplanes, including thirteen Val kamikaze dive-bombers.

Four of the pilots in the flight were Marines, reassigned from squadrons aboard the *Wasp* to augment the pilot strength of VF-10. Marine 1st Lt. W. A. Nickerson had already flamed three Japanese airplanes when a Judy bomber's rear gunner put a 7.7-mm burst through his engine's oil system. Almost blind because of the oil on his windshield, Nickerson managed to splash his Corsair into the water next to a destroyer and was picked up.

His fellow Marine, 1st Lt. F. M. Jackson, had already shot down one Zero and was in hot pursuit of another with only one of his six guns firing. Too late, he spotted a four-plane Wildcat flight making a pass at the same Zero. On a collision course, Jackson clipped one of the Wildcats, lost control of his Corsair, and was forced to bail out. Minutes later, he joined his Marine wingman, Nickerson, on the same rescue destroyer.

It was a big scoring day for *Intrepid*'s fighter pilots, but it wasn't their biggest. That came four days later, the day of *Intrepid*'s last battle at Okinawa.

Later, they would all say the same thing: April 16, 1945, was a hell of a day.

It began at dawn when Fighting 10 skipper Walt Clarke took a twelve-plane flight to their CAP stations over the northern radar pickets. A division of four, led by Lt. Phil Kirkwood, was vectored to intercept an incoming swarm of kamikaze dive-bombers. Kirkwood split his division, sending Ens. Horace Heath and Ens. Alfred Lerch above the cloud deck while he and his wingman, Cdr. Norwald Quiel, stayed beneath.

Phil Kirkwood was one of Fighting 10's old hands. He'd already flown one combat tour in Hellcats aboard *Enterprise*, where he'd been credited with four downed Japanese aircraft. Since coming to *Intrepid*, he'd scored two more. Now he and Quiel received an urgent call from a picket ship, which was under attack by twenty kamikazes. Racing to the rescue, Kirkwood blasted six Japanese airplanes out of the sky, while Quiel put down four more. The brief action propelled Kirkwood into double ace status, making him *Intrepid*'s top gun and one of the war's highest-scoring aces.

Meanwhile, the two nugget fighter pilots, Heath and Lerch, who lacked Kirkwood's gunfighting experience, were endowed with something else: incredible luck. At 7,000 feet, the pair ran into a flight of Japanese aircraft and in a quick fight gunned down four of them. Minutes later they were vectored by radar controllers behind a flight of thirty old Nakajima Ki-27 "Nate" and Aichi D3A "Val" fixed-gear warplanes. Within minutes Heath and Lerch picked off five of the slow-moving Nates. In a single sortie the baby-faced Alfred Lerch had shot down seven enemy airplanes, a record shared by only four other American fighter pilots in history.

In a skirmish to the south, skipper Walt Clarke was busy shooting down three enemy planes while his wingman, Lt. (jg) C. D. Farmer, killed four more. In all, Clarke's flight of twelve Corsairs accounted for twenty-nine downed enemy airplanes, with a loss of none.

And it was just the beginning. Later in the morning, a CAP led by Lt. G. T. Weems ran into Zeroes over a picket ship and in a fifteen-minute dogfight blasted four of them out of the air. CAG Hyland led a twelve-plane flight of Corsairs against targets on the Kokubu airfield, dropping 500-pound bombs and firing rockets. Spotting Zeroes above them, Hyland and his flight pulled up to engage them. Again, the enemy airplanes were kamikazes, focused more on reaching their targets than dogfighting with enemy airplanes. In the space of a few minutes, the Corsairs shot down five and scattered the rest. But when Hyland's flight rejoined at their rendezvous point, one of the new pilots, Ens. E. M. Bailey, who had last been seen diving on the hangars at Kokubu, was missing. He was presumed shot down and not seen again.

In a separate strike mission, a flight of VBF-10 Corsairs on a CAP station over the fleet engaged an incoming flight of Japanese fighters. Three more junior officers, Ensigns R. V. Lanier, L. L. McDonald, and R. W. Sweet, took out four of them.

Intrepid's fighter pilots had shot down forty-two enemy aircraft, and the day was only half over. But the enemy hadn't given up. Another *kikusai*—a wave of kamikazes—was on its way.

The guns were firing again. At his radar scope in CIC, Ray Stone could hear them. And he could see what they were shooting at. On his fluorescent screen, the blips of incoming bogeys were moving like glowworms toward *Intrepid*.

On the flight deck Felix Novelli heard them, and he could see the oily black puffs dotting the sky. The kamikazes were coming in waves of four and five at a time. It was nerve-racking, thought Novelli, and fascinating.

At 1330 a dozen Fighting 10 Corsairs launched on another CAP mission. At almost the same time, a fresh wave of five kamikazes made it through the screen of anti-aircraft fire, diving on the task group. Captain Short ordered the ship to general quarters. The anti-aircraft guns opened up.

For the men belowdecks, it was a replay of a now-familiar scene—staring at the steel overhead, listening to the distinctive sequence of the anti-aircraft guns. They had learned to tune out—almost—the deep-throated blast of the long-range 5-inch guns. It meant something was out there, but still a distant threat. Every ship in the task group was firing at it.

But now they heard the stuttering *pom-pom-pom* of the 40-mm guns, and they paid attention. It was impossible *not* to pay attention. It meant a kamikaze had gotten close enough to pick his target.

Then they heard the urgent rattle of the 20-mm guns. Every man froze. The enemy was close. *Close enough to hit with a beer can,* thought Ray Stone, hunkered down in his compartment, which was lit by the red glow of emergency lights. After the previous attacks in which he'd lost twenty-nine of his fellow radarmen, Stone didn't have a good feeling about his battle station. "If the flight deck had a target painted on it, the meatball in the center would be right over CIC. The wooden flight deck and thin steel ceiling above us wouldn't stop much. One day, I thought, one of these bastards is going to hit the bull's eye and that will be it."

The U.S. Navy's aircraft carriers had been built with wooden flight decks, unlike the British Royal Navy's. The carrier HMS *Indefatigable* was part of the British task force that had joined the American fleet at Okinawa. When a kamikaze crashed into *Indefatigable's* steel deck, the damage amounted to little more than a 3-inch dent in the armor plating, a fact noted with interest by U.S. carrier and task group commanders who had been watching kamikazes plunge straight through their wooden decks.

Aboard *Intrepid*, whose deck had already absorbed the fury of four kamikaze strikes, the gunners blazed away at the incoming planes. The bogeys were low on the water. As they neared *Intrepid*, they split into two groups, approaching their target like predators, closing in from ahead and behind. For a couple of miles around *Intrepid*, the sea leaped and convulsed with the geysers of exploding ammunition and crashing airplanes. The sky was a roiling tableau of yellow tracers and angry black clouds and bursts of fire and shrapnel. The collective thunder of the guns resonated like hammers of hell through the steel compartments of USS *Intrepid*.

Eighteen-year-old Ed Coyne was watching from his battle station. "How did they get this close?" he recalled wondering. "There were other ships out there. In your mind, you'd be blaming the destroyers. Why didn't they get them? And the battleships—can't they hit anything? What's wrong with the cruisers?"

A Tony fighter was boring in from dead ahead, and *Intrepid*'s 40-mm gunners caught it just in time. The Tony splashed into the sea just off *Intrepid*'s starboard bow. Then a Zero, zooming in just behind him, was caught in the barrage from the entire task group and hit the water off the port quarter. Another Zero came in low from astern, pitched up to make his dive, then changed course and dove on the battleship *Missouri*. The big ship's guns tore him apart, and the Zero's burning hulk fell into the water. It was three for three. *Intrepid*'s luck was holding.

There was a lull of a few minutes, then they came again. From astern, two kamikazes roared toward *Intrepid*, somehow threading a path through the hailstorm of gunfire. The nearest took a hit, burst into flame, and cartwheeled into the sea. Then the second was hit. Spewing flame and smoke, he kept flying, sweeping closer and closer to *Intrepid*'s fantail. When he was almost directly over the ship, he dove straight down toward *Intrepid*'s flight deck.

It seemed like a replay of the attack off Luzon the previous November. The engine and fuselage of the kamikaze plane punched through the wooden deck into the hangar bay below. As before, the 550-pound semi-armor-piercing bomb ricocheted off the hangar deck and exploded farther forward in the bay, opening a 5-by-5-foot hole in the armored deck.

The results were horrific. Fueled and armed airplanes exploded. Fires ignited everywhere in the crowded hangar bay. Again, the gallery deck was shattered and filled with deadly smoke. A 12-by-14-foot gash had been ripped in the flight deck, and the deck directly above the bomb explosion was pushed a foot upward by the concussion. The impact of the Zero was so great, the imprint of its wings was embedded in the wooden deck.

Eight men were killed in the attack. Another would die of his wounds later. Nearly a hundred had been injured. Forty of *Intrepid*'s airplanes were destroyed. The number three elevator, freshly rebuilt during the last session at the Hunters Point shipyard, was again ruined.

By now *Intrepid*'s crew were experts at damage control. Her firefighters attacked the blazes in the hangar and gallery decks as aggressively as her gunners fired at kamikazes. In a record fifty-one minutes, they had the fires contained.

But the enemy wasn't finished. While damage control crews were still battling the flames, two more Zeroes came sweeping in low over the water. One released a bomb, which exploded in the water 75 yards short of *Intrepid*'s starboard quarter. The Japanese pilot, either not a committed kamikaze or one who'd lost his nerve, was pulling up to escape when *Intrepid*'s gunners blew him out of the sky. A second Zero dove close enough to put his bomb into the water alongside *Intrepid*'s port bow. Like his fellow Zero pilot, he was blown apart as he tried to escape.

Capt. Giles Short, watching the drama from *Intrepid*'s bridge, had another problem. His pilots from the last strike were still up there. Now they needed a deck to land on. Short issued an order to his damage control officer: patch the hole in *Intrepid*'s deck, and do it quickly.

In a display of heroism and skill under pressure, carpenters and welders and damage control crews went to work. With guns blazing away on either side of them, they jury-rigged a steel plate over the gaping hole in the flight deck.

At 1615, less than three hours after the kamikaze pilot wrecked the flight deck, *Intrepid*'s exhausted pilots were landing back aboard their ship.

★ 17 ★

Endgame

She was crippled but still operational.

The next day *Intrepid* was ordered to the fueling area, away from the immediate battle zone, to evaluate her damage. To no one's surprise, the naval logistics group that surveyed the damage declared that further combat operations weren't possible, not until she'd been repaired. That afternoon, in company with the destroyers *McDermut* and *Kalk, Intrepid* headed for the anchorage at Ulithi.

While under way, *Intrepid*'s crew lined up on the number two elevator for a familiar ritual. Standing in front of eight flag-covered canvas bags, the chaplain commended the souls of *Intrepid*'s fallen crewmen to the Almighty. The bugler played taps. The Marine honor guard fired a salute. The canvas bags with their 5-inch-shell weights slid from beneath the American flags and into the Pacific Ocean.

The next day one of the badly wounded sailors died, and the ritual was repeated.

Intrepid pulled into her berth in Ulithi lagoon, where she was joined by the repair ship USS *Ajax*. Her days were spent loading ammunition and stores so she could return to combat. Meanwhile, repairmen went to work trying to get her back into combat condition. With her number three elevator damaged beyond repair, they figured the ship might be at best 80 percent capable.

And then another problem arose: the number two elevator was out of alignment and needed a major repair. That was it. From the commander in chief, Pacific, came the order: *Intrepid* would return to Hunters Point for repairs to her war damage.

There were cheers from most of the crew—and a few moans. Yes, it would be nice to go home, if only briefly. But after their last repairs, they'd been in the war less than a month. Still, it didn't matter, most thought. The war wasn't over. It would go on, everyone figured, at least through 1946.

Forty-eight of *Intrepid*'s airplanes were catapulted off to join other air groups. Again, while crossing the Pacific, the carrier would become a transport. She embarked another load of U.S.-bound passengers, including the pilots from the carrier *San Jacinto*.

On May 4 *Intrepid* slipped out of Ulithi lagoon, bound for Pearl Harbor. Escorted by the destroyer USS *Gregory*, she set course for Eniwetok, then onward to Pearl Harbor. Soon after crossing the international date line on May 8, the crew of *Intrepid* received the news that Germany had surrendered. The war in Europe was over.

There was cheering and back-slapping and, for those with stashed spirits, a few clandestine celebrations. Ray Stone, working in CIC, was one of the first to get the news. "Yippee!" he heard someone shout. "Now they'll be able to send more troops and ships and stuff to help. Our war will end sooner." How much sooner? No one knew. The best guess was another year. The invasion of Japan would be the last battle of the war and, everyone agreed, the bloodiest.

In a repeat of her voyage of six months earlier, *Intrepid* pulled into Pearl Harbor on May 11 and slid through the channel to Ford Island. Waiting on the dock to greet the delighted sailors was a twenty-piece band, hula girls, and a women's glee club. After the unloading of ammunition and war stores, reprovisioning, and taking on passengers for the homeward voyage, *Intrepid* was under way again on the fourteenth.

Five days later, the crew heard on the bullhorn, "Golden Gate in sight." With the memory of their last westward departure still fresh in their minds, sailors swarmed over the deck, staking out the highest perches they could find. As before, the bridge was covered with well-wishers to see the carrier back, including the girls. Again they waved and blew kisses to the cheering and whistling sailors below.

Intrepid crossed the bay and put into Hunters Point, where she was dry-docked for repairs. The crew was given leave, but it would be short. *Intrepid* had to get back into the war, and the shipyard was wasting no time. A sign went up alongside the dry-docked carrier: THIS FIGHTING LADY HAS A DATE IN TOKYO. DON'T MAKE HER LATE!

It took a month. And then, on June 29, 1945, there was another departure from Hunters Point, another whistling and waving passage past Alcatraz, through the Golden Gate, and into the open sea. As *Intrepid* sped westward for her date in Tokyo, there was time for more reflection.

She was back in fighting shape, her flight deck resurfaced and her damaged aircraft elevators rebuilt and fully functional. She wore the same paint scheme that had been applied during her refit the previous January—sea blue hull from the waterline to the main deck, ocean gray above. Someone in the Navy hierarchy had decided against any more zigzag camouflage swatches.

Her captain was still Giles Short, whose irreverent sailors still made wisecracks about his stature. Her resident airedales were still Air Group 10, and their CAG was still the formidable John Hyland. Each squadron had lost airmen during the deadly battles over Okinawa, and now they were augmented with fresh pilots and air crewmen.

After pulling into Pearl Harbor on July 5, *Intrepid* took on provisions, then spent the rest of July exercising in Hawaiian waters. On liberty in Honolulu, *Intrepid*'s crew dealt with the various nicknames their ship had picked up. The one they liked was the one she'd been given early in her career—"Fighting I." But now that *Intrepid* had the distinction of being the most-hit carrier in the fleet, she was being called "Evil I"—an insult guaranteed to provoke brawls in Honolulu bars. Because of her sojourns in the Hunters Point dry dock, she had acquired some other inflammatory names: "Dry I," "Yard Queen," and "Decrepit Intrepid."

A new nickname was the one they heard the Japanese had given their carrier—"Ghost Ship." *Intrepid*'s sailors liked that one. *Intrepid*—the ship that kept coming back from the dead.

While *Intrepid* was laid up in dry dock, the bloody battle for Okinawa ground to a conclusion. The island was now a U.S. launch point for strikes against the Japanese homeland. Bull Halsey's Third Fleet was pounding the coastline of Japan, ravaging ports and airfields, sinking ships at their anchorages, setting entire cities ablaze. The war was in its endgame, and *Intrepid* was scheduled to be one of the players.

Intrepid and her two escorting destroyers, USS *Cotten* and USS *Ross,* left Pearl Harbor for Eniwetok on July 30, 1945. On the way, she would engage in what had almost become a ritual for ships and bombers heading for the West Pacific: conducting a day-long strike against the Japanese-occupied island of Wake.

On the evening of August 5, *Intrepid* arrived off Wake Island. The next morning would be their first combat action since the day off Okinawa when they'd shot down forty-two Japanese airplanes—and nearly lost their ship.

From the cockpit of his new F4U-4 Corsair, CAG Hyland gazed down at the horseshoe-shaped atoll. A few puffs of anti-aircraft fire were already floating up from the gun emplacements that ringed the atoll. Combat air patrols were in place, but Hyland didn't expect any Japanese fighters. He could see the runways—what remained of them—at the southeast corner of the atoll. They had been cratered so many times by passing bombers that nothing could fly off them. In any case, any airplanes the Japanese once had on Wake had long ago been reduced to scrap.

Wake Island had no strategic importance. Stranded in mid-Pacific, 2,000 miles west of Hawaii, its target value was purely symbolic. Following the attack on Pearl Harbor, Wake Island had been defended by a garrison of U.S. Marines, who held off a Japanese invasion force for more than two weeks before they were overwhelmed. "Remember Wake Island" became a rallying cry and an effective recruiting slogan throughout World War II. The story of Wake Island, like the Alamo, was seared into American memories.

In the island-hopping campaign across the Pacific, MacArthur and Nimitz decided to bypass Wake. Instead of expending resources on an invasion, they chose to blockade the island with submarines. For the past three and a half years, the Japanese garrison had been slowly starving, reduced to eating the atoll's sizeable rat population. Wake became a practice target for every bomber and carrier task force en route to the western Pacific.

And that's what troubled Hyland now. He hated the idea of risking precious pilots and planes on what he considered a training exercise. "If there is anything that sounds unreasonable to a pilot," he wrote in his action report, "it is the idea that he should practice encountering fire from an anti-aircraft gun."

Thirty-eight Corsairs armed with HVARs had launched from *Intrepid*'s deck at dawn, followed by fourteen bomb-loaded Avengers and fourteen SB2C Helldivers. *Intrepid* now had the latest model of the Corsair, the F4U-4, which was the best fighter-bomber to serve in World War II. With a massive four-blade prop and Pratt and Whitney R-2800-18W engine, the new Corsair could haul 4,000 pounds of ordnance on its centerline and pylon racks.

As expected, there was no air opposition, and even the anti-aircraft fire seemed dispirited and ineffective. More waves of *Intrepid* warplanes followed the first, and the attacks continued for most of the day. In all, *Intrepid* launched 193 sorties, including 18 combat air patrols and anti-submarine patrols. The targets were the gun emplacements that ringed the island, power plants, a water distillation plant, and a bridge on the island. During the day's action, they dumped 42 tons of bombs on the atoll and fired 490 HVAR 5-inch rockets. The only serious threat was the towering summer cumulonimbus that swelled over the atoll during the afternoon. It forced the bombers to dive from low altitude, giving them more exposure to Japanese guns.

None was hit, and by the end of the day Hyland was breathing easier. His only losses were two Helldivers, one with an engine failure and one with an uncontrollable propeller. Each ditched alongside a destroyer, and their crews were rescued. By evening all his pilots were back in their ready rooms.

Wake Island was supposed to be a warm-up for the real battles ahead. But what Hyland didn't yet know was that while his airplanes were still bombarding Wake, another warplane—a lone U.S. Army Air Force B-29—was over its target in Japan. Its single bomb incinerated the city of Hiroshima. The end game was coming more quickly than Hyland or anyone aboard *Intrepid* had imagined.

Intrepid and her small task unit turned southwestward, covering the 530 miles to Eniwetok in fewer than twenty-four hours. She dropped anchor just before nightfall in the coral-reef-enclosed lagoon to await developments.

The news came two days later. A second atomic bomb had been dropped, this one on the city of Nagasaki.

More days were spent waiting. It was a nervous, frustrating time for *Intrepid*'s crew. They remained at the anchorage while the ship loaded ammunition and fuel. Questions flew like the wind among the anchored ships at Eniwetok. Would Japan surrender? Would there be a final, climactic battle? Where were they going next?

At 1100 on August 15 came the message that President Truman had announced the surrender of Japan. At the same time *Intrepid* received the order from Admiral Nimitz, commander in chief, Pacific: "Cease offensive operations against Japanese forces."

It was over. Throughout the ship—up and down passageways, in every compartment—there was cheering and celebration. A collective din of sirens and horns and cheering resounded over the Eniwetok anchorage. It was a time for celebration.

It was also a time for reflection. No one aboard *Intrepid* had been untouched by the drama of the past two years. All had memories of deck-edge ceremonies, the flag-covered canvas bags, Marine honor guards, the bodies of their shipmates dropping into the sea. For young men barely out of their teens, it was a confusing, poignant time.

The enormous impact of the war was still not comprehended by the young warriors. The cost in human life was too immense for them to grasp. More than 50 million people were dead. The political geography of the world had been torn asunder. Entire nations had seen their economies wiped out. In just a few years of war, military technology had advanced in quantum leaps. The development of nuclear weapons raised the stakes of global war to an unthinkable level.

The next day, August 16, was the occasion for another celebration. It was *Intrepid*'s second birthday, time for another gargantuan cake from the ship's bakery. It was also an appropriate time for tallying up her combat record. *Intrepid* had taken the worst punishment the enemy could give—five kamikaze attacks and one torpedoing—and each time had returned to the fight. She had delivered far more devastation than she received. *Intrepid*'s aircraft had destroyed 301 Japanese airplanes and helped sink 122 enemy ships, including shared credit for the super-battleships *Yamato* and *Mushashi*.

On August 21, *Intrepid* received new orders. She was to lead a task group consisting of the carriers *Antietam* and *Cabot* and a collection of destroyers to Okinawa, where they would join the victorious armada that would preside over the occupation of Japan. The warrior was about to become the enforcer of the peace.

By the terms of the peace agreement, Japanese ships and planes were forbidden to operate in the Yellow Sea, and it would be *Intrepid*'s job to police the region. After refueling in Buckner Bay, Okinawa, on August 31, *Intrepid* and her task group headed into the Yellow Sea off the coast of China. Their mission was to put on a show of strength for the benefit of America's allies as well as her former enemy. Neither Japan nor any of the formerly occupied countries must doubt that U.S. and Allied forces had total dominion over the sea and the sky.

Massed formations of warplanes from *Intrepid, Antietam*, and *Cabot* roared low over the formerly Japanese-occupied city of Shanghai. The next day *Intrepid* launched 140 sorties on another muscle-flexing exercise over Keijo and Jinsen in southwest Korea. The displays continued, sending formations of warplanes over Dairen and Port Arthur in Manchuria. Back in the Yellow Sea, *Intrepid* sent waves of warplanes over Tientsin, Taku, and Peiping in mainland China.

It was legalized buzzing, and the young airmen loved it. One division of Corsairs after another would swoop down over the towns, each flying lower than the previous group.

While *Intrepid*'s task group was busy displaying American might, another show of strength was being conducted in Tokyo Bay. Douglas MacArthur, Chester Nimitz, Bull Halsey, and the senior commanders of the U.S. Pacific forces stood on the deck of the battleship *Missouri*. It was Sunday, September 2, and they were there to accept the unconditional surrender of the Japanese Empire.

At almost the same moment the signatures were affixed to the documents of surrender at 0925, the sun broke through the clouds. A deep rumbling rose from the distance. An armada of warplanes thundered over Tokyo Bay—waves of B-29 bombers, Mustang and Thunderbolt fighters, and more than 400 Navy Hellcats, Avengers, Helldivers, and Corsairs.

It was the ultimate show of strength. To those watching from the surface, it left no doubt that the war was truly ended.

But another potential enemy was making its intentions known. On August 8, after the first atomic bomb had destroyed Hiroshima and the fall of Japan seemed all but certain, the Soviet Union declared war on Japan. During the last week of the war, Soviet forces surged into Manchuria, Sakhalin, and the Kurile Islands.

During *Intrepid*'s flag-showing foray into the Yellow Sea, a flight of Corsairs on CAP station was vectored to intercept a flight of ten bogeys. The unidentified warplanes turned out to be not Japanese but Russian. They were Catalina patrol planes, donated to the Soviet Union by the United States. The warplanes were now attached to the Soviet forces that had just invaded Manchuria.

No gunfire was exchanged, and all aircraft returned to their respective bases, but it was a portentous encounter. It was *Intrepid*'s first brush with the adversary that would challenge the United States for the next forty-four years.

Intrepid and her task group returned to Okinawa on September 13 for two weeks of rest and replenishment. Then it was more of the same: back to the China coast, showing the flag and enforcing the new peace. At the end of September, *Intrepid*'s planes were providing reconnaissance and air cover for the Marine 3rd Amphibious Corps, which had gone ashore near Taku on the coast of China. A week later, *Intrepid* covered another Marine force advancing from Tientsin to Peking. Another hazard for *Intrepid* and her escorts was the thousands of Japanese mines that still floated in the waters outside the formerly occupied ports.

Finished with flag-showing on the China coast, *Intrepid* headed for Saipan on October 8. There she said goodbye to Air Group 10. In their brief combat tours aboard *Intrepid,* the air group had blazed a name for themselves in naval aviation history. Their two fighting squadrons had shot down a hundred enemy airplanes and destroyed another eighty-six on the ground. Their warplanes sank eleven ships, with two probably sunk and forty-one damaged. They had lost eighty-eight of their own airplanes. Twelve pilots and three aircrew members were dead or missing.

Several of Air Group 10's officers would become well known in later years. CAG John Hyland, who had distinguished himself as a combat leader, would rise in the Navy to wear four stars and become commander in chief, Pacific Forces. The air group administrative officer, Lt. Cdr. William P. Rogers, would return to civilian life to eventually became U.S. attorney general and, in the Nixon administration, secretary of state.

There was no time for sentimental farewells. In three hours, Hyland and his air group were gone, and their replacement, Air Group 14, was aboard. Air Group 14 was another seasoned unit that had fought in the Sibuyan Sea battle and in every other major engagement until the end of the war.

Intrepid spent a week in Guam, which was still recovering from successive invasions by Japanese and American troops and a steady barrage of bombing. Then *Intrepid* headed for Tokyo.

It was a strange and exotic experience, liberty in the home of their former enemy. The young sailors stepped off the boats warily on October 25, 1945, not knowing what to expect. Everywhere they looked, they saw devastation. Scarcely a large building was standing. They could only imagine the horror of the firebombings from the B-29s.

To most of *Intrepid*'s crew, many still in their teens, it was their first time in a foreign city. For many Japanese, it was their first encounter with a Westerner. They eyed one another with curiosity and suspicion. The Navy men, to their surprise, met little hostility. The defeated Japanese, young and old, men and women, were respectful and in most instances friendly. It was hard to imagine that this same society had spawned kamikazes and fight-to-the-death soldiers and armies that plundered and raped the countries they invaded.

Intrepid operated out of Yokosuka, on the western bank of Tokyo Bay, for the rest of November 1945, conducting training exercises with her sister ship *Lexington* and their task group. Finally, on December 1, the orders came that the men of *Intrepid*—and their families—had been praying for. They were going home.

After embarking 2,000 Army troops for the ride back to the United States, *Intrepid*, in company with *Lexington*, pointed her bow toward California. It was the longest nonstop voyage of her career. The great-circle route to San Francisco took her into the North Pacific, a thousand miles above Hawaii. After nearly two weeks at sea, *Intrepid* moored at her berth in Alameda on December 15.

Never in *Intrepid*'s history would there be a sweeter or more triumphant moment. Her crew had fought a fanatical enemy in the most momentous war in history. With victory in their grasp, they were coming home to the adulation of their countrymen. Their young lives were filled with the promise of peace and prosperity. Christmas was ten days away, and their families awaited them with unbounded joy.

On December 18, *Intrepid* and her skeleton crew resumed their transport duties, embarking 1,100 servicemen for an overnight passage to Long Beach, California. For six weeks she remained in southern California while most of her crew took holiday leave.

In a flight deck ceremony in early February, Captain Short passed command of *Intrepid* to her new skipper, Capt. R. E. Blick. For Blick, it was a short posting, long enough to take the carrier back to San Francisco, where on April 11, 1946, he was relieved by Capt. H. G. Sanchez, *Intrepid*'s seventh commanding officer.

Both officers were caretaker skippers. No air group was embarked, and *Intrepid* was not headed back to sea. Her operational days were over, at least for now. On August 15, 1946, she received the designation "in commission, in reserve," which in Navy bureaucratese meant she was available for duty but not needed. She remained in this vague condition until March 22, 1947, when her status changed to something more precise.

Intrepid was officially decommissioned. After three and a half years of duty, most of it in wartime, her services were no longer required. With armament and machinery weatherproofed, *Intrepid* entered her deep sleep.

It would last five years.

PART TWO

Metamorphosis

Where are the carriers?
—Asked by every U.S. president
since Franklin D. Roosevelt

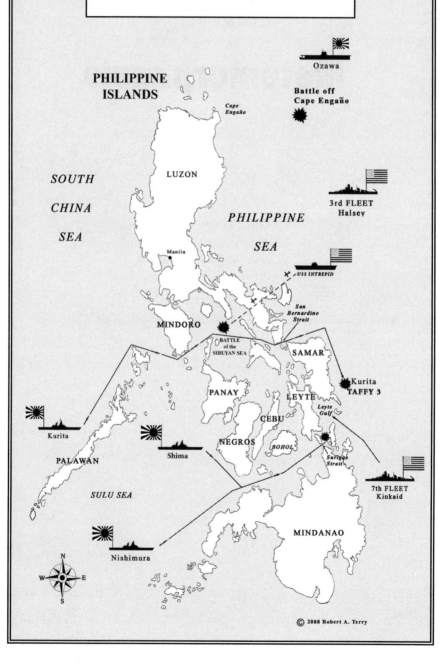

THE BATTLE OF LEYTE GULF
October 24–25, 1944

Ozawa

Battle off
Cape Engaño

PHILIPPINE
ISLANDS

Cape
Engaño

SOUTH

CHINA

SEA

LUZON

PHILIPPINE

SEA

3rd FLEET
Halsey

Manila

USS INTREPID

San
Bernardino
Strait

MINDORO

BATTLE
of the
SIBUYAN SEA

SAMAR

Kurita
TAFFY 3

PANAY

LEYTE

Leyte
Gulf

CEBU

Kurita

NEGROS

BOHOL

PALAWAN

Shima

Surigao
Strait

7th FLEET
Kinkaid

SULU SEA

MINDANAO

N

W   E

S

Nishimura

© 2008 Robert A. Terry

Intrepid Resurgent

Hunters Point Naval Shipyard, San Francisco
February 9, 1952

Standing on the flight deck, Tom Sprague took in the scene around him. The place had the look and feel of a graveyard. Warships were moored fore and aft, side by side, all in varying states of decay. Each had been weatherproofed, gun barrels sealed, closed off to the world, but nothing had stopped the rust that was eating at them like orange cancer.

The assemblage of old ships had an official name—the Pacific Reserve Fleet—but everyone knew it as the Mothball Fleet. For most of the aging residents, this was the end of the line. This was where ships came to die.

It was where *Intrepid* had dwelled since 1947.

Tom Sprague was older now, his hair gone mostly white, a pattern of fine wrinkles fanning out from his eyes. It had been nine years since he stood in nearly the same spot and read the orders placing *Intrepid* into service. Both he and *Intrepid* had traveled a long way since then. He was Vice Admiral Sprague now, commander of all the naval air forces of the Pacific Fleet. He had come here to see his old ship return to service.

The band was swinging into another brisk Sousa march. Sprague couldn't help remembering the glow of pride he'd felt back when he first took command of the ship. He and his young crew—plank owners like himself—had gone to war for the first time at Kwajalein, suffered their first losses from an enemy torpedo, made their way home with the help of a jury-rigged sail.

Since then, the world had undergone seismic changes. Most of the mothballed ships moored alongside *Intrepid* had become dinosaurs. The world had left them behind. Their World War II armament and technology were hopelessly outdated, and they were headed for the scrap yard. By a quirk of history *Intrepid* would be spared.

She wasn't going back on active duty, at least not directly. She was being transferred from the Mothball Fleet back to "in commission, in reserve" status, which meant that she was being commissioned just long enough to make the voyage to the East Coast, whereupon she would again be decommissioned to undergo extensive modernization.

Still, it was a day for celebration. The Boy Scouts of San Francisco had named their training ship *Intrepid,* and they were there to present the carrier with a liberty bell "from one *Intrepid* to another." The commander of the San Francisco Group of the Pacific Reserve Fleet, Capt. A. M. Cohan, had come to place the ship back in commission and hand her over to her new skipper, Capt. Benjamin Lovett. Tom Sprague, *Intrepid*'s first captain, was there mostly in the role of a doting godfather.

He wasn't the only old *Intrepid* hand present. The carrier's new executive officer was Cdr. Lloyd Van Antwerp, the old Avenger pilot who had commanded Torpedo Squadron 18 through the historic battles of Leyte Gulf.

The ceremony followed the script of all commissionings. When it came his turn, Tom Sprague took the podium and told the assembled guests and crew that *Intrepid* had a glorious future ahead of her, just as she had already had a glorious past. With his voice betraying just a touch of emotion, he told them how proud he was to have been part of *Intrepid*'s life.

The traditional salutes were exchanged. The ship's bell rang, and the ensign was run up the mast. Captain Lovett gave the order to post the watch. The ritual was complete. *Intrepid* had come back from the dead again.

During the five years *Intrepid* languished in the Mothball Fleet, science and geopolitics had altered the nature of warfare. The Soviet Union and its surrogates were challenging the United States and its allies, and the specter of nuclear warfare had become the driving force behind military technology. To counter the Soviet nuclear threat, the United States was building fleets of long-range bombers—huge six-engine B-36s and all-jet B-47 Stratofortresses, with the B-52 on the way.

The Navy was campaigning for an equal share of the strategic weapons mission. To support its own bombers, the Navy needed new carriers and new technology. A supercarrier had been authorized, the USS *United States.* Her keel had already been laid, and she was the U.S. Navy's placeholder in the nuclear weapons mission.

There was one major obstacle to the Navy's plans. It changed names and uniforms over the years, but it was the same obstacle the Navy had confronted since the 1920s. It was called the U.S. Air Force.

The blood feud between the two services dated back to when Army Brig. Gen. Billy Mitchell, an early airpower advocate, enraged the U.S. Navy by declaring *all* the navies of the world obsolete. To make his point, he and his fliers, against orders, bombed and sank a target ship, the captured German battleship *Ostfriesland.* The incident ignited a thirty-year simmering hostility between the services. For his impertinence, Mitchell was court-martialed and removed from high command, but his disciples in the Army Air Corps, and later the U.S. Air Force, never forgave or forgot Mitchell's treatment.

The interservice rivalry reached a flash point in 1949 during a battle for new weapons appropriations. The Air Force believed the nation's defense against the Soviet threat should be built around the

B-36 long-range bomber, carrying a load of thermonuclear weapons. The Navy argued that the nation would be best defended by supersized aircraft carriers launching fast attack jets loaded with atomic bombs.

In the tight postwar budget, there was not enough funding for both. To the zealots of the two warring services, it was a zero-sum game: equip the Air Force with heavy bombers and get rid of the useless aircraft carriers, or scrap the big, vulnerable six-engine B-36s (which enemy fighters could shoot down like fat geese) and deploy supercarriers with squadrons of fast attack airplanes.

One day in 1949, Defense Secretary Louis Johnson announced that he was canceling the Navy's dream carrier, the *United States*. To the Navy's top brass, it was a sneak attack worse than Pearl Harbor.

What happened next went down in military history as the "Revolt of the Admirals." The admirals included Rear Adm. Dan Gallery and Vice Adm. Gerald Bogan, who had been *Intrepid*'s task group commander at Leyte Gulf. They wrote letters and articles lambasting the decision to scuttle the *United States* and deriding the Air Force's notion that strategic bombers were the United States' best defense.

For most of the admirals, it was a career-ending move. Adm. Louis Denfield, the chief of naval operations, was a casualty. So were Bogan, Gallery, and a number of other senior officers. Naval aviation appeared headed for oblivion.

And then on July 25, 1950, everything changed. War broke out on the Korean peninsula, and the Navy had to cobble together a carrier task force from its few still-active *Essex*-class carriers. For three years the overtasked carriers distinguished themselves as they launched thousands of combat sorties over Korea.

The debate about the obsolescence of carriers was over. The Navy received authorization for its first new supercarrier, but instead of a strategic platform like the canceled *United States,* it would be an all-mission carrier to support a new generation of tactical jets. She was called *Forrestal,* first of a class of ships that would be the model for every carrier of the next fifty years.

But it would take decades—and billions of dollars—to build a fleet of *Forrestal*-class supercarriers, and the Navy needed carriers immediately. The solution was to recall and modernize the mothballed *Ticonderoga*- and *Essex*-class carriers.

For *Intrepid* and her sisters, it meant deliverance.

The ship was a mess.

Capt. Ben Lovett sniffed at the dank air in the passageways. She smelled of mildew and rust and neglect. He peered into a long-sealed compartment, ran his hand over the rust-coated bulkhead, scuffed the soles of his brown shoes on the flaking deck. *Intrepid* might have been back in commission, but she definitely wasn't seaworthy. Her engines hadn't run in five years. None of her electronic gear worked.

For most of a month Lovett's crew labored to make the carrier ready to leave San Francisco. They removed weatherproofing, did their best to make radios and navigation gear and radar functional, and swabbed and freshened the spaces they'd be occupying for the next several weeks. Most important, they brought her four big Babcock and Wilcox superheat boilers and Westinghouse geared turbines back to life.

The flight deck equipment—catapults and arresting gear—they didn't bother with. For this trip, *Intrepid* wouldn't be launching or recovering airplanes. A convoy of one, she would retrace the voyage she took in 1943 when she first left her Virginia birthplace for San Francisco.

On March 12, 1952, Lovett eased *Intrepid* out of Hunters Point and into San Francisco Bay. It was her first passage in half a decade past the jutting rock of Alcatraz, beneath the two massive bridges, down the coast to Panama.

Lovett knew about Panama. The collision with the steep bank of the Gaillard Cut in 1943 was a part of *Intrepid*'s history, and Lovett had no intention of adding another chapter to the story. With painstaking care, he threaded the channels and turns and locks of the canal without a scratch, completing the seventeen-day voyage and docking at Pier 4 of the Norfolk Naval Operating Base on April 9, 1952. His job as caretaker skipper was completed. *Intrepid* was decommissioned for the second time in her life, and Lovett crossed the naval base to take command of an operational aircraft carrier, USS *Antietam*.

Intrepid's modernization took two years and two months. The program had a classically convoluted Navy designation, SCB-27C, which stood for Ship's Characterization Board Number Twenty-Seven. The *C* referred to the second phase of the program, which would come later—the addition of the new angled landing deck.

Intrepid was refitted with new aircraft elevators with more lifting capacity, a reinforced flight deck, modern radar and electronics gear, a streamlined island superstructure with the gun mounts removed, and a relocated primary flight control bridge that gave the air boss a better view of his flight deck. The number three elevator, centered in the flight deck aft of the island, was moved to the starboard deck edge so that airplanes could be shuttled more easily during flight operations. She received a longer "clipper" bow—the exposed fore-castle below the flight deck—to accommodate two new 3-inch 50-caliber gun mounts.

Some of the changes came from bloody lessons learned in the Pacific. The squadron ready rooms were relocated from the gallery deck, which was suspended directly beneath the flight deck and had taken horrific damage from kamikazes, down to the more secure main deck. An escalator was installed to transport airmen to the flight deck. The hangar deck, which had been ravaged by fires after bomb and kamikaze hits, was fitted with massive doors to seal off the separate hangar bays.

Some of the improvements reflected the new Cold War mission. *Intrepid* was fitted with heavily shielded spaces deep belowdecks to store and handle nuclear weapons. Her aircraft fueling system was expanded to handle fuel for jets—aircraft that didn't exist when she was last in service.

Two postwar advances in technology—the steam catapult and the angled landing deck—had changed the way aircraft carriers operated. Significantly, neither was invented in the United States.

Unlike propeller-driven aircraft, jets could not launch from an aircraft carrier without a catapult. By the end of World War II, hydraulic catapults had nearly reached the limit of their potential. The new jets needed something more powerful.

The solution was the steam catapult, which had been developed in Great Britain. *Intrepid*'s two old hydraulic catapults were replaced with the radically new C-11 Mod-1 steam catapults. Though other *Essex*-class carriers had already been fitted with British-built catapults, *Intrepid* had the first American-built models.

It was June 18, 1954, and the late spring sun shone down on *Intrepid*'s new teak flight deck. The ship gleamed in her fresh coat of haze-gray paint. The shuttles of the two new steam catapults jutted from their tracks like rabbits poised to race.

It was the day of *Intrepid*'s third commissioning ceremony, and the script hadn't changed. Again a band played, more speeches were delivered, and a new captain, William T. Easton, stood on *Intrepid*'s deck and read the orders placing the carrier back in service.

Bill Easton was a handsome man with a slender, athletic build. He was a 1929 Naval Academy graduate and had been a naval aviator since 1931. He'd been a fighter pilot, torpedo bomber pilot, and photo reconnaissance airman, and he'd led a dive-bomber squadron in the Pacific. In the postwar years he'd commanded the Naval Air Station Sanford and was skipper of a seaplane tender, USS *Valcour*. Today was the high point of Bill Easton's career—his first major seagoing command.

In a variation on an old theme, a giant cake was baked for the occasion, and helping slice the cake was an old *Intrepid* friend, Mrs. John H. Hoover, who, as the wife of a vice admiral and *Intrepid*'s sponsor, had smashed a bottle of champagne on the carrier's prow at her launching in 1943.

In the autumn of 1954, *Intrepid*'s new captain took her to sea off the Virginia shore on Project Steam II—the operational testing of the new American-manufactured steam catapults. Representatives from the Naval Air Test Center, the Bureau of Aeronautics, various aircraft manufacturers, and the staffs of every major command were all on board to observe the tests.

They launched examples of every type of new airplane in the Navy's inventory with the new catapults, including the radically advanced, twin-tailed Chance Vought F7U Cutlass. They launched the workhorse jets of the 1950s, the McDonnell F2H-2P and the F2H-4 Banshee, and the North American FJ-3 Fury, as well as the propeller-driven Douglas AD-5 Skyraider and the Navy's nuclear bomber, the North American AJ Savage. The Savage was the first carrier-based bomber built specifically to carry nuclear weapons. Developed during the transition between high-performance reciprocating engines and pure jets, the Savage was a hybrid, driven by two 2,400-horsepower Pratt and Whitney R-2800-RW engines, plus a J-33 jet engine in the aft fuselage.

The tests of the new steam catapult were a huge success. It proved that fully armed and fueled fighters and long-range bombers could be launched at heavier gross weights than had ever before been possible. In its ongoing rivalry with the Air Force, the Navy had just acquired a powerful new tool.

To go with *Intrepid*'s new look, *Intrepid*'s skipper wanted a new name for the ship's newspaper. He ran a contest, offering a prize of $15 for the best name. The winner was one of the ship's youngest sailors, a seaman apprentice, who came up with the name that remained with the ship for the rest of her life: *The Ketcher,* taken from *Intrepid*'s namesake, the wooden fighting ketch that won glory in the battles of Tripoli.

The warplanes on *Intrepid*'s deck were a reflection of the Navy's mission in the mid-1950s. The fighters were venerable McDonnell F2H-4 Banshees and swept-wing North American FJ-3 Furies, the Navy's version of the U.S. Air Force F-86 Sabre jet. Also embarked were the nuke-carrying Savage as well as AD fighter-bombers, propeller-driven attack planes that had their origins in World War II and had been the Navy's best air-to-ground attack plane in Korea.

The whine of jets wasn't the only new sound aboard *Intrepid*. The *whop-whop* of helicopter blades had now joined the cacophony of flight deck noise. "Angel" helos hovered off the ship's starboard quarter, ready to snatch downed airmen from the water. Helicopters were also logistics vehicles for "vertical replenishment," or VERTREP, shuttling personnel, supplies, and mail between vessels.

After nearly a year of evaluations, exercises, and one shakedown cruise to Guantánamo Bay, Cuba, *Intrepid* was ready for her first operational deployment since returning from Japan in 1945. As the new flagship of Carrier Division 6, she steamed out of Norfolk on May 28, 1955, headed for the Mediterranean.

★ 19 ★

The Middle Sea

It was still an age of innocence.

Dwight D. Eisenhower was in his first term as president, presiding like a rumpled uncle over the bumptious young nation. Americans had not yet tasted the bitterness of Vietnam, the assassination of a president, the debacle of Watergate. The crewmen of *Intrepid*, in the bloom of youth and high spirits and typical of their generation, were welcomed by their European hosts.

At *Intrepid*'s ports of call—Naples, Livorno, Genoa, the French cities of Cannes and Marseilles, the Spanish ports of Barcelona and Palma, the eastern Mediterranean ports of Athens, Istanbul, Beirut, and the islands of Cyprus and Crete—it was easy for the young sailors to feel as if they had been sent on an immersion course in foreign culture and history. A day after launching and recovering warplanes in a multi-ship NATO exercise, *Intrepid* sailors could be skiing in the Alps, wandering through a souk in Istanbul, or downing beers in a Spanish pub. Hundreds of white-uniformed young Americans swarmed ashore to roam ancient streets, snap photographs, and flirt with dark-eyed Mediterranean beauties.

Intrepid's first Mediterranean idyll, in 1955, lasted six months. She returned to the United States in time for Christmas, and then, after ninety-eight days at home, was back in the Mediterranean.

It was the same old story: the Navy was short of carriers. Most of *Intrepid*'s sister ships were in shipyards undergoing their own SCB-27C modernization, and the available carrier force was stretched to the breaking point. Of the coming generation of supercarriers, only *Forrestal* had joined the fleet. The next in line, USS *Saratoga*, would not be ready for operational duty for another year.

It meant another summer of intense at-sea operations, interspersed with port calls in southern Europe. *Intrepid*'s sailors watched bullfights in Cadiz, bought clothes for wives and girl-friends in Livorno, toured the ruins of Rome and Pompeii and Athens. A select group of *Intrepid* men attended the wedding of Grace Kelly to Prince Rainier of Monaco. Another group participated in a pilgrimage to the religious shrine of Lourdes, in France. During a port call in Italy, the ship hosted a head of state, Italian president Giovanni Gronchi. Later that summer, Secretary of the Navy Charles Thomas came aboard to observe flight operations on *Intrepid*.

In the balmy Mediterranean, it was easy for young Navy men to forget the real reason for being there. The Cold War seemed an abstract concept, like an ongoing drill for a fire that never happened.

And then at sea they'd get a glimpse of reality. They'd see the ominous silhouettes of Russian ships shadowing the carrier. Sonar-men would report the presence of Soviet submarines. Sometimes, high overhead, sailors glimpsed the long swept wings of Russian reconnaissance bombers. The enemy was out there. He was rehearsing the same abstract war that they were.

On August 28, 1956, *Intrepid* "chopped"—Navy shorthand for "change of operational control"—out of the Mediterranean. Eight days later she was back in Norfolk, and instead of turning around and heading back to the Mediterranean, she was on her way to the shipyard.

Intrepid was about to become a modern attack carrier.

It was the "C" phase of the SCB-27C retrofit—the angled deck. By now, the advantage of the angled landing deck on aircraft carriers had been proven beyond doubt. The supercarriers *Forrestal* and *Saratoga* had been constructed with the angled deck, and so would all future carriers. Now it was *Intrepid*'s turn.

At the end of September 1956, she entered the New York Naval Shipyard in Brooklyn, where she dwelled for the next eight months. In addition to the angled deck, the modernization program added a "hurricane" bow—a streamlined forward structure that enclosed the open forecastle beneath the forward flight deck. She received the latest shipboard radar, and she shed most of the old gun mounts, a reflection of the new reality of naval warfare. To a greater extent than ever, aircraft carriers would be protected by their own fighters and by warships of their battle groups.

The simple geometry of the angled landing deck changed everything about the way Navy pilots landed on carriers. Instead of making flat, turning approaches to the ramp of the ship, the pilot flew a straight, descending final glide path all the way to touchdown on the angled deck. No longer did he take his cues from the stripe-suited, paddle-waving landing signal officer. Guidance came from the "mirror"—another British invention—mounted at the port edge of the landing deck. A high-intensity light was shined against the mirror and reflected upward at the precise angle of the glide slope. A set of green reference lights was rigged midway up the mirror, serving as a datum—an "on glide slope" reference. A pilot making his approach would see the reflected light on the mirror as a ball, and its position above or below the datum lights would tell him he was high or low on the glide slope. "Flying the ball" was the pilot's ticket to a precise landing.

Instead of the previous fourteen or more arresting cables in the landing area, they now needed only four. The arresting wires stretched across *Intrepid*'s deck were actually 1.375-inch-thick steel cables, suspended 5.5 inches above the deck. Each cable ran to its respective "engine"—a giant hydraulic cylinder that worked like a shock absorber. When an airplane's tailhook snagged one of the cables, the cable pulled a piston in its hydraulic cylinder, absorbing the energy of the arriving airplane and bringing it to a stop on the deck.

With the angled deck, an airplane could "bolter"—land without snagging an arresting wire—and take off again. It also meant that pilots could practice touch-and-goes, landing with their tailhook retracted and taking off again. Without the necessity of a barrier between the landing deck and the forward deck, a carrier could now recover airplanes while it was launching them at the same time.

The LSO no longer waved his paddles, but he still had the final word. From his platform at the aft port deck edge, the LSO monitored every landing. Instead of communicating with body language, he used the radio. Each LSO had his own cajoling, reassuring style on the radio—"sugar talk," the airmen called it. It was the voice he used to coax stressed-out pilots down to the wires. "Pow-werrrr," the LSO might call on the radio, urging the pilot to add throttle. Or "Eeeee-zzzeee," meaning not to overcontrol the throttle.

Because of the Navy's habit of retaining anachronistic labels, the LSO was still called "Paddles," but instead of paddles he used a microphone and a light switch. The LSO could still wave off the incoming plane, but he did it by flashing an array of red lights atop the mirror. A wave-off was still a direct order, never to be disobeyed.

When the ship was recovering airplanes, everyone on and off the ship—pilots, the air boss, even the captain—deferred to Paddles. As they had in World War II, LSOs still tended to be outrageous characters, often given to wild costumes and personal habits. Sometimes they clenched cigars in their teeth, and a few affected a Zen-like demeanor when they were on the LSO platform.

In James Michener's *The Bridges at Toko-Ri,* his fictional LSO was a big-bellied Texan called "Beer Barrel." The pilots placed a special trust in their LSO. "Beer Barrel is my shepherd," they would intone, "I shall not crash."

Intrepid's sailors loved New York. For the seven months that *Intrepid* was in the shipyard, the sailors of *Intrepid* immersed themselves in the ambience of the city. They walked the streets, explored the boroughs, rode the subways. It was the beginning of a lifelong relationship between *Intrepid* and the city of New York. The crew thought themselves so fortunate, they gave their ship yet another nickname: "Lucky 'Leven."

During the last weeks of April 1957, *Intrepid* moved from the Brooklyn Navy Yard to Bayonne, New Jersey, for the finishing touches of her modernization. On May 7, her refitting complete, she steamed past the Statue of Liberty and headed south to Norfolk. Lucky 'Leven's New York sojourn was finished—for now.

By May 20, she was bound for Guantánamo Bay with a deck load of fighters and attack planes to begin learning the nuances of angled deck carrier operations. "Gitmo," as Guantánamo was known to Navy men, had the distinction of being the only U.S. naval base within a Communist country. Since 1903, when it was leased from the new Cuban government after the Spanish-American War, it had been used by the U.S. Navy. Though the Castro government had long since repudiated the agreement giving the United States the right to use the territory, the Navy maintained a steadfast presence in Gitmo. Balmy weather and unfettered target ranges made it an ideal training base for East Coast carriers and air groups.

In September, her air group aboard, *Intrepid* headed across the North Atlantic to join Operation Strikeback, a massive NATO exercise involving the forces of five countries. *Intrepid*'s crew, still wearing tans from the Caribbean, rode their liberty boats ashore in Bangor, Ireland, and then in Brest, France, where many climbed on buses for a four-day tour to Paris.

Back in the United States, *Intrepid* spent the last months of 1957 on a project called Operation Crosswind—the first scientific study to determine the effects of adverse winds on aircraft carrier flight operations. The idea was to determine how far a carrier could deviate from a direct headwind and still safely launch airplanes.

The results were an eye-opener. With the powerful new catapults, carriers such as *Intrepid* didn't require a headwind to catapult airplanes. They could launch their aircraft with a substantial crosswind, and even while steaming downwind.

For carrier group commanders, it was a godsend. It meant that in confined bodies of water such as the Mediterranean and the Persian Gulf, they could launch airplanes without being forced to turn their carriers into the wind.

In September, she received another new skipper, Capt. Joseph Kuhl, a 1932 Naval Academy graduate and experienced naval aviator. For the rest of the year and into the first half of 1958, *Intrepid* operated close to home port. By now the crew had settled on another nickname: "Mighty I." The bad old days of World War II and the uncomplimentary nicknames *Intrepid* had received were mostly forgotten—but not entirely. The ship's softball team reprised one of *Intrepid*'s wartime names—one that had provoked more than a few brawls in Honolulu bars—and stenciled it on their uniforms: the Evil Eyes.

By the end of summer *Intrepid* was operating again on the East Coast of the United States. That fall, in keeping with the Navy's habit of rotating a commanding officer as soon as he had learned his job, Capt. Paul Masterton relieved Captain Kuhl, becoming *Intrepid*'s sixth commanding officer since her return to active duty.

On March 1, 1959, in company with USS *Franklin D. Roosevelt,* *Intrepid* embarked on another seven-month deployment to the Mediterranean. The lineup of aircraft was the latest of the Navy's sleek fighters and attack planes. In addition to the venerable Douglas AD-6 Skyraider, called the "Spad" in a reference to the clunky World War I fighter, the air group now had the hot little delta-wing A4D-2 Skyhawk and two supersonic fighters, the bat-wing Douglas F4D Skyray and the Grumman F11F Tiger. Also aboard were the "cats and dogs," the detachments of F9F photo reconnaissance jets, radar-equipped AD-5N and AD-5W Guppy early-warning aircraft, and twin-rotor Piasecki HUP-2 Retriever helicopters.

For the men of the *Intrepid,* it was another idyllic cruise. The Mediterranean in summer was a balmy, haze-covered lake. Weather was seldom a factor, and daytime operations for the pilots were great fun. They launched and recovered on *Intrepid*'s sturdy deck with almost flawless precision.

Night operations were another matter. By darkness the Mediterranean Sea and the sky could merge together into a horizonless, vertigo-inducing milk bowl. Pilots having trouble getting aboard were sent to a waiting tanker, an *Intrepid* A4D Skyhawk carrying an external "buddy store," or they were given a "bingo" signal—the order to land at a nearby shore base.

On August 9, 1959, *Intrepid* was relieved at her anchorage in Pollensa Bay, on the Spanish island of Mallorca, by her sister ship *Essex*. Twelve days later she was home again in Norfolk. After her heavy-duty schedule, *Intrepid* was due for another overhaul. In October, she entered the Norfolk Navy Yard for a four-month, $4.5 million renovation that included replacement of aging sea valves, props, rudder, and shaft; renovation of her engineering plant; major alterations to her hangar deck and flight deck; and a spanking new exterior paint job.

And while she was at it, she took on yet another skipper, one who was no stranger to *Intrepid*.

★ 20 ★

Tigers to Guppies

As his name suggested, Edward Cobb Outlaw was a character. A gruff, flamboyant, and sometimes obtuse skipper, Ed Outlaw's career included wartime command of a fighter squadron and air group. His reputation was made as skipper of the famous "Outlaw's Bandits"—VF-32 aboard *Langley* in 1944. Outlaw himself gunned down six Japanese aircraft, and his squadron accounted for forty-four kills. For years after the war, whenever old Navy fighter pilots convened for reunions, the subject of Outlaw and his bandits always came up.

And so on August 30, 1959, when Ed Outlaw arrived on *Intrepid* as her new skipper, it was like a homecoming. As operations officer of Rear Adm. Gerald Bogan's Task Group 38.2, he had served aboard *Intrepid* during the climactic battles of Leyte Gulf, and from her bridge he had witnessed the deadly kamikaze attacks in the Philippine Sea.

Following *Intrepid*'s overhaul, Outlaw took his new ship to Gitmo in January 1960 on a shakedown and training cruise. Her old nickname, "Mighty I," had been usurped by the new 80,000-ton supercarrier *Independence*, which had moved into the berth next to *Intrepid*'s spot at Pier 12 in Norfolk. Outlaw came up with a new name—one that would stay with *Intrepid* the rest of her career: "Fighting I." To go with the new name, the crew fashioned a banner that no one aboard the carrier next door could miss: THE FIGHTING I: THE OLDEST AND THE BEST.

Intrepid stayed busy in 1960. In the spring she was off the Virginia capes conducting carrier suitability tests for the Navy's newest and hottest fighter, the F4H Phantom II. The tests were successful, after a fashion. What they proved was that big twin-engine fighters such as the Phantom weren't a good fit on small-deck carriers such as *Intrepid*.

But if *Intrepid*'s size and age were a handicap, she didn't show it. That summer she broke her own record and set a new fleet record by launching eleven jets in eight minutes and thirty-two seconds on a single catapult. The same year her air operations department won the Battle Efficiency "E," making it, officially, the best in the fleet. *Intrepid* also established the best safety record of all the attack carriers in the Atlantic Fleet, and her Skyraider outfit, VA-65, won its own "E" as best overall squadron.

It had been a good year. With these laurels in hand, *Intrepid* sailed out of Norfolk in August, bound again for the Mediterranean.

Music—a new sound aboard a carrier at sea, and it was Outlaw's idea.

During replenishing or refueling under way, or sometimes at noon during normal operations in the hangar bay, the crew heard it. Outlaw had managed to embark the seventeen-man Naval Air Force Atlantic band for the Mediterranean deployment. They played everything—jazz, hymns, military music, rock and roll.

"We have two primary missions," Outlaw told his crew. "Combat readiness and building goodwill." The band, in Outlaw's view, was part of the goodwill mission. The air group and the ship's crew would take care of the combat readiness.

During the first air operations as they entered the Mediterranean, Lt. Bob Rasmussen of VF-33 notched three important records. Flying an F11F Tiger, he made his 100th carrier landing while also logging his 1,000th hour of flight time. By luck and some careful finagling, Rasmussen's landing also happened to be *Intrepid*'s 42,000th landing since her recommissioning in 1954. Of course, it was a cause for celebration. A 16-foot-long, 700-pound cake was baked for the occasion and completely devoured in thirty minutes. Rasmussen, around whom the ceremony revolved, was already on his way to greater things. From flying F11F Tigers aboard *Intrepid*, he moved on to the famous Blue Angels demonstration team.

Another pilot in *Intrepid*'s air wing who moved on to greater things was a young lieutenant (jg) named John Sidney McCain. McCain was a Skyraider pilot in the "E"-winning squadron VA-65. Except for being the son and grandson of four-star admirals, McCain seemed to have little else going for him. None of his squadronmates would have predicted that the rambunctious young officer would become a prominent senator and presidential candidate. His grandfather, Adm. John S. "Slew" McCain, had commanded the mighty carrier Task Force 38 in World War II, which included USS *Intrepid*. McCain's father, a former submariner, would also become an admiral and commander in chief, Pacific. The two elder McCains were the first father-and-son four-star admirals in Navy history.

The youngest McCain graduated from the Naval Academy in 1958 and earned his wings a year and a half later. *Intrepid* was his first ship, and he liked it. "We were a tightly knit group," he remembered. "When we were in the Mediterranean, we thought we were on the front line of defense."

After his squadron tour aboard *Intrepid*, McCain was assigned as an instructor in the Training Command, then went to an A-4 Skyhawk squadron. On Yankee Station off North Vietnam, he narrowly escaped death aboard *Forrestal* when a horrific fire triggered by a Zuni rocket turned the flight deck into a hellish conflagration that killed 134 men. With *Forrestal* out of action, McCain requested transfer to another A-4 squadron aboard *Oriskany*. On October 26, 1967, he was shot down over Hanoi and spent five and a half years as a prisoner of war.

In September *Intrepid* pulled into Rome's port of Fiumicino. For Ed Outlaw it was a bittersweet time. "I hate to say farewell," the old fighter pilot told his crew in a flight deck ceremony. He exchanged salutes with his relief, Capt. Charles S. Minter Jr., and left for his next assignment and a promotion to rear admiral.

Autumn became winter, and the benign weather of the Mediterranean changed. Gone were the hazy days and the milk bowl nights. In their place came howling storms that blew down from the southern Alps, churning the sea and causing the ship's deck to pitch up and down like a yo-yo. Snow flurries sometimes not only obscured the ship but socked in the critical divert fields ashore.

But weather, a pitching deck, and howling winds weren't the worst things about winter ops in the Med. What the pilots who flew off carriers hated the most was the poopy suit.

It was one of those unbending Navy rules. When the sea temperature dipped below 65 degrees Fahrenheit, carrier pilots had to wear a rubberized, unventilated anti-exposure suit with tight seals around the wrist and neck. They called it the "poopy suit," and wearing the thing for a two-hour flight caused them to sweat off 5 pounds or more of body weight. The purpose was to protect the pilot from hypothermia if he went into the frigid water. After a winter of poopy suits, pilots swore that they preferred hypothermia.

Intrepid spent Christmas 1960 at anchor in Genoa, Italy, while her crew listened to carols played by the band that Ed Outlaw brought aboard. When the ship finally headed for home after seven and a half months deployed, she received a visit—and praise—from Sixth Fleet commander Vice Adm. George Anderson (soon to be chief of naval operations). "You can go home with a great feeling of accomplishment," Anderson told *Intrepid*'s crew. "Each one of you has been important in the part that has been played in making this ship a great ship, and in making your operations over here successful."

It was true. More than 40,000 miles of ocean had passed beneath her hull. Of her 185 days away from home, 121 were at sea, and *Intrepid* had not missed a single commitment. She was still the best in the fleet.

It was May 24, 1961, a splendid spring day in Norfolk. Capt. J. Lloyd "Doc" Abbot Jr. was standing at the podium on *Intrepid*'s flight deck. Assembled on the deck were the guests, including his father, a retired Navy captain, and his two sons, who would soon follow their father and grandfather to the Naval Academy. The Abbots were a Navy family. His brother was a Navy chaplain, and his sister was a lieutenant commander in the naval reserve.

Abbot was forty-three, prematurely bald, with a trim, athletic build. He had a quick grin, and was known for his fondness for telling stories. Abbot also knew when to shut up, and today, he decided, was one of those occasions. "I have been to many change of command ceremonies," he told the crowd. "The ones I like best are those where the new man says, 'I am happy to be aboard,' and reads his orders."

Abbot read his orders, then turned to Captain Minter. "I relieve you, sir." Thus began Doc Abbot's lifelong love affair with USS *Intrepid*.

During the early weeks of summer, *Intrepid* operated in the Caribbean and along the East Coast. On August 3, 1961, she departed Norfolk, once again bound for the waters of the Mediterranean.

Embarked was Air Group 6, led by a slim, soft-spoken fighter pilot named Jim Holbrook. Holbrook had been skipper of an F11F Tiger squadron before getting his air group, and now his mount of choice aboard *Intrepid* was the Tiger's replacement, the Chance Vought F8U Crusader.

The Crusader was the newest and hottest operational fighter in the fleet. The last fighter designed with guns as its primary weapon, the Crusader was a superb dogfighter and a match for any fighter in the world in a turning, tail-chasing gunfight. It was big for a carrier airplane—54 feet long—and was powered by a Pratt and Whitney J-57, which in afterburner mode kicked out 18,000 pounds of thrust and could propel the Crusader to Mach 1.85—nearly twice the speed of sound. The Crusader was a tricky airplane to land aboard an *Essex*-class carrier and suffered a higher-than-average accident rate. Its high-mounted, variable-incidence wing pivoted up 7 degrees from the fuselage for takeoff and landing, which kept the fuselage in a level attitude approaching the ship.

The Crusader wasn't the only tricky jet to land on the ship. Another was the "Ford"—the bat-wing F4D Skyray. Just how tricky became evident on *Intrepid*'s first night of flight operations in the Mediterranean.

It was one of those classic Mediterranean summer nights with no horizon, sea and sky merging together in a murky soup. *Intrepid* had just entered the Mediterranean, relieving USS *Roosevelt* on station. The first day of flight operations had gone well enough. Then came nightfall.

Up in pri-fly, the glass-paned command post high in the island, CAG Jim Holbrook was talking to the air boss, Cdr. "Pinky" Joslin. They could see the lights of the incoming fighter. It was a Ford—an F4D Skyray—and the pilot was having trouble. Holbrook knew the pilot, Lt. (jg) Bill Stratton from VF-162.

The Ford was supposed to be the fleet's night and all-weather interceptor. It had an advanced radar intercept system that allowed it to shoot incoming enemies without ever seeing them. The problem was, the Ford was a notoriously troublesome fighter to land back aboard the carrier. Its safety record was one of the worst of all the Navy's embarked fighters.

Now CAG Holbrook was seeing why. As the Ford in the groove behind *Intrepid* came closer, Holbrook was beginning to make out the pancake-shaped silhouette. Unlike other jets, the Ford had no landing flaps, which caused it to approach the ship in a cocked-up, nose-high attitude. The Ford also had no tail, just a single vertical fin, and at landing speed it looked like a wallowing bat.

The Ford was going low.

"Pow-werrrrr," called the LSO from his platform at the left deck edge. He was using his best sugar talk, coaxing the pilot to add throttle and get back up on the glide path.

The Ford was still low. And closer.

"Power! Power!" No more sugar talk. The LSO's voice had an urgent edge to it.

The pilot added power. It wasn't enough. The big pancake shape of the Ford was nearly over the aft end of the ship, and it was still sinking.

"Wave off! Wave off!" the LSO yelled, and he hit the flashing red wave-off lights. It was an order. The pilot had to go around.

A torch of yellow flame spat from the Ford's tailpipe as the pilot hit the jet's afterburner. The Ford looked like a rocket lifting from its pad.

Too late. Up in the darkened pri-fly compartment, Holbrook felt his gut tighten. He'd been around carrier aviation long enough to know what would happen next.

The Ford almost made it. The jet was nose high, pulling up, when its belly slammed into the ramp of the flight deck. The explosion illuminated *Intrepid*'s flight deck in a harsh yellow glow. Still climbing, the flaming hulk of the Ford soared like a comet up into the night sky, then arced off to the right and hit the sea a mile abeam of *Intrepid*'s starboard bow. For several seconds the flames danced like a witch's cauldron on the surface, then sputtered and extinguished.

On *Intrepid*'s navigation bridge, Captain Abbot was watching the spectacle when something else caught his eye. It was the plane guard destroyer on station on *Intrepid*'s port side, barely visible except for its stern light. Abbot saw something that made his blood chill—the destroyer's red *starboard* running light. The destroyer was heading for the crash site, cutting directly across the path of the onrushing aircraft carrier.

Abbot grabbed the microphone of his radio and yelled at the destroyer: "Continue the right turn, full rudder, and pass down my port side."

The destroyer skipper obeyed. The destroyer kept turning, nearly grazing *Intrepid*'s port side, passing at a closure speed of 50 knots.

On the bridge of *Intrepid*, there was a stunned silence. In the space of a few heartbeats, they had watched a man's life snuffed out like a candle, followed by what was almost a horrific collision of ships.

When the destroyer arrived at the spot where the jet hit the water, they found only an oil slick and pieces of flotsam. The pilot and the Skyray fighter were gone.

It was a tough first night.

As it turned out, the second wasn't any better. There was the same horizonless sea and sky melded together like the inside of an ink bottle, and CAG Holbrook was in pri-fly again, watching his jets come aboard. Another Ford was having trouble, this one flown by a young ensign named Fred Gayer. He'd made several passes at the ship, none of them steady enough to land. Twice he'd boltered— landed on the deck but missed the arresting wires—and taken off again. The next pass was erratic, and the LSO waved him off.

Now the Ford was downwind, flying abeam the ship at 600 feet above the black sea, setting up for another pass. The air boss was concerned about the jet's fuel state. When he was down to the minimum required to divert to an emergency field ashore—what they called "bingo" fuel—he'd order him to head for the divert field.

Someone radioed the pilot, asking his fuel state.

"Stand by," Gayer replied from the cockpit of the fighter.

Seconds ticked by while they waited for the pilot's answer. It was a bad feature of the Ford. The fuel quantity gauge was located in the lower right well of the cockpit, which meant the pilot had to take his eyes off his instruments while he peered down at the fuel quantity gauge.

They could see the lights of the jet in the darkness. While they watched, waiting to hear Gayer's fuel state, the lights abruptly vanished. An orange fireball flared in the darkness, briefly casting an eerie glow over the sea. Then it was gone.

The fighter had flown into the water.

Peering into the darkness from pri-fly, Jim Holbrook couldn't believe what he'd seen. *Two in a row.* This time the destroyer didn't charge into the path of the carrier. When it reached the crash site, they found the same results: an oil slick, pieces of the destroyed Ford still smoking, floating on the sea. The pilot and the rest of the crashed plane were gone. They would never know exactly what happened, but the likely cause was that the jet had descended into the water while the pilot was peering at his fuel gauge.

A grimness settled through the ready rooms of *Intrepid,* and it was felt most of all in the VF-62 ready room. The closely knit fighter squadron had just lost two of their own. CAG Holbrook worried that the squadron's morale would hit the skids.

It didn't. In a textbook display of leadership, VF-62 skipper Cdr. Thad Taylor rallied his pilots behind him, reviving their spirit. For the rest of the deployment, the squadron flew the bat-wing, temperamental Fords with remarkable precision, losing not one more airplane or pilot.

Summer slipped into autumn. When the sea temperature chilled to the cutoff of 65 degrees Fahrenheit, the pilots grudgingly pulled on the hated poopy suits, which they would have to wear for the rest of the cruise. The tempo of flight operations continued at full tilt. *Intrepid* joined a series of NATO exercises called Checkmate, with *Intrepid*'s attack squadrons swooping in to hit simulated targets in the high, rugged mountains of Greece and Turkey.

For the first portion of *Intrepid*'s Mediterranean deployment, her Sixth Fleet sister carrier was USS *Independence*. Between *Intrepid*'s captain, Doc Abbot, and *Independence*'s skipper, Capt. Pete Aurane, was an old friendship—and a rivalry—that went back to their Naval Academy days. Often the two ships would be steaming in company, launching aircraft side by side, and that was when it turned into a contest.

"In spite of having only two catapults to *Independence*'s four," Abbot remembered, "*Intrepid* would get the launch into the air almost as soon as *Independence*—and occasionally *sooner!*"

In midwinter, a bilateral French-U.S. exercise called Big Game sent waves of attack planes from *Intrepid* and the newly arrived Sixth Fleet carrier *Saratoga* on low-level strikes into the French interior. The mission profiles had been designed to resemble the real nuclear weapon delivery missions the pilots would fly to targets in the Eastern Bloc countries. French Mystère fighters came up to challenge the Navy warplanes and to simulate their own attacks on the fleet.

Intrepid's days in the Mediterranean were not all spent at sea. In keeping with the Sixth Fleet flag-showing mission, she made frequent port calls to places such as Barcelona, Cannes, and Livorno, then cruised into the eastern Mediterranean, where she pulled into Corfu, Rhodes, and Athens. On December 18, 1961, she dropped anchor in Naples, on the southern part of Italy's boot, where the men of *Intrepid* spent the Christmas holiday. The next day she was at sea again for a three-day flight ops session, then back to Naples to celebrate the New Year.

On a hazy January day off the coast of Spain, the VA-76 executive officer, Lt. Cdr. Jim Peddy, catapulted off the bow in his A-4 Skyhawk. Instead of climbing straight ahead as usual, the A-4 gradually descended, crashing into the sea ahead of the ship. Peddy and the Skyhawk sank to the floor of the Mediterranean.

It was an unexplained and troubling accident. Unlike the two pilots lost in the first month of the cruise, Peddy was a highly experienced carrier aviator. Whether he'd been incapacitated or experienced an airplane malfunction was never learned. For the young airmen flying off *Intrepid* in the Mediterranean, it was another sobering reminder that readiness for war could be as costly as war itself.

Intrepid returned to her berth at Pier 12 in Norfolk on March 1, 1962, for another joyous homecoming. And a triumphant one—it wasn't yet official, but the word was out that in the competition for this year's Battle "E," *Intrepid* had beaten out all the four-catapult, big-deck supercarriers. She was, officially, the best attack carrier in the fleet.

The award seemed like a cruel joke, however, because the word was also out that even though *Intrepid* had proven her excellence as an attack carrier, effective March 31, 1962, her designation would change from CVA-11 to CVS-11. Like most of her *Essex*-class sister ships, *Intrepid* would become an anti-submarine carrier.

The change in mission caused no joy aboard *Intrepid*. Sure, the anti-submarine mission was critical. And certainly the new ASW—anti-submarine warfare—airplanes and weapons were at the cutting edge of technology. But the mission lacked the visceral, hardball edge of the attack carrier role. No more would they hear the thunder of afterburners on *Intrepid*'s catapults. Gone was the howl of jet engines. From now on they'd hear the mellow growl of reciprocating engines, the pulsing beat of rotor blades.

Hunting submarines, by definition, was warfare in slow motion. Success was hard to measure because you never actually got to *kill* the enemy, just to try to keep track of him and, sometimes, give him a rude reminder that you *could* have killed him. Sometimes— more often than anyone liked to admit—it worked the other way. The enemy let *you* know that he could have tagged you before the sub slipped away in the murky depths.

Intrepid's Air Group 6 airedales were replaced with Anti-Submarine Warfare Air Wing 56. Instead of sexy, pointy-nosed fighters, the airplanes were plodding, two-engine Grumman S2F (S-2 in the new designation system) Trackers and HSS-2 (SH-3A) Sea King helicopters.

With its bulbous nose and blunt, unstreamlined features, the S-2 looked like a flying truck. It could carry homing torpedoes or a load of depth charges in its bomb bay, and it had stations on the wings for more torpedoes, or rockets. In its aft engine nacelles it carried thirty-two sonobuoys.

Helicopters were an integral part of an anti-submarine warfare air group. The SH-3A Sea King was a big, twin-engine, turbine-powered helo that carried almost the same arsenal as the S-2. In addition, the Sea King carried a dipping sonar that it deployed from a hover to track subs. For fleet missile defense, the Sea King was equipped with a chaff pod from which it could deploy clouds of radar-deflecting foil.

Also gone were the AD-6 (A-1H) Skyraider attack planes of the old air group. Aboard now were Guppies, AD-5W (EA-1E) variants of the Skyraider with bulging radomes and large "greenhouse" cabins that accommodated a crew of electronic warfare specialists.

For her conversion from CVA to CVS carrier, *Intrepid* went back to the shipyard at Portsmouth, Virginia. The modifications, in fact, were minor. "Essentially," said Doc Abbot, "they erased the 'A' and painted in an 'S.' "

Same ship, different mission. But before *Intrepid* went off to hunt submarines, she had an appointment with an astronaut.

★ 21 ★

Aurora

Doc Abbot was peering straight up into the Caribbean sky when he had a sudden troubling thought. *What if the first thing we see is the capsule coming down from directly overhead?*

Intrepid was 200 miles east of Turks Island, at a spot called Recovery Station 9. It was where a Mercury spacecraft was supposed to splash down after a three-orbit flight around the earth. On board was a horde of camera-and-microphone-toting newsmen to record the pickup and flash it back to the world. Also on board were technical support people from the contractors supporting the Mercury Project. A flag officer, Adm. John L. Chew, commander of the Project Mercury rescue forces, was ensconced on *Intrepid*'s bridge.

Still looking up into the empty sky, Abbot made a decision. He would have all eight of *Intrepid*'s boilers on line, just in case. If the space capsule was somehow precisely on target, *Intrepid* was going to get the hell out of the way.

They had left Norfolk on May 5, 1962. On the flight deck were the aircraft that matched *Intrepid*'s new sub-hunting job description—S-2 Trackers and SH-3A helicopters, as well as a complement of Marine Corps H-34 helos. Before they reached the recovery area they got the word that the launch was delayed. Abbot took *Intrepid* into the Virgin Islands port of St. Thomas for a three-day break, then headed back out for the recovery area. Then came another two-day delay, which *Intrepid*'s helicopter crews used to practice hauling a dummy Mercury capsule from the sea.

Finally, on May 24, came the word from Cape Canaveral. The Atlas rocket with its Mercury capsule, *Aurora 7,* would launch a few minutes before eight in the morning. And the whole world would be watching.

Lt. Cdr. Scott Carpenter was a Navy man and a test pilot, but he was different from his fellow astronauts. For one thing, he wasn't a fighter jock like the other six Mercury astronauts. Carpenter came from the patrol plane community, which meant he'd spent most of his flying time in big, long-range anti-submarine and surveillance aircraft.

He was different in another way too. Unlike most test pilots, including Al Shepard, Virgil I. "Gus" Grissom, and even John Glenn, his best friend in the astronaut corps and for whom he'd served as backup pilot on the first orbital mission, Carpenter had an intense curiosity about things *outside* his airplane. He preferred to think of himself not so much as a test pilot sent to do scientific work as a bona fide scientist who happened to be flying a spaceship.

Carpenter was an athletic, good-looking young man who'd studied engineering at the University of Colorado, then abandoned college just short of graduation to be a Navy pilot. During the Korean War he'd flown Far East patrol missions in the Lockheed P2V. He was chosen for test pilot training in 1954, and was then assigned to the Electronic Test Division at the Navy Flight Test Center at Patuxent River, Maryland. After his test pilot stint, he went to the Navy's air intelligence school, then was assigned as air intelligence officer on the USS *Hornet*.

In 1959 he was astonished to find his name among the selectees for something called Project Mercury. The seven chosen airmen, all military test pilots, would be called "astronauts" and might actually ride into space someday in American-built spacecraft that didn't yet exist. For the next three years Carpenter trained with his fellow astronauts down in the sand flats of the Cape, for the day when they would actually sit atop a fiery rocket and launch into space.

For Scott Carpenter, that day came sooner than he expected. Following the suborbital flights of Alan Shepard and Gus Grissom, John Glenn had achieved everlasting fame by becoming America's first man into orbit. The second orbital flight was to be flown by USAF pilot Deke Slayton. But then a squiggle on Slayton's EKG— idiopathic atrial fibrillation, it was called—caused NASA to scratch Slayton.

Scott Carpenter was named to be the next American to orbit the earth.

The great Atlas engines fired at 0745. Smoke, flame, steam, and dirt billowed in a dense cloud from beneath the rocket. The earth shook as the tall, slender rocket rose from its pad. Americans stared at their televisions, holding their breath as one of their own headed into space.

In the capsule of *Aurora 7,* Scott Carpenter tensed himself against the acceleration. The G forces—each G being a unit of earth's gravity—gradually built up until he was feeling eight Gs. He could feel the vibration from the mighty Rocketdyne engines and, perched up at the tip of the vehicle, he could feel the rocket swaying slightly. He knew this was all normal. This part of the flight—the launch sequence—had been experienced by three astronauts before him. The last one, the flight of John Glenn, had been the first orbital flight by an American astronaut.

At five minutes and nine seconds into the flight, Carpenter radioed, "I am *weightless!*" He sounded exhilarated, and he was. The capsule was beginning the first of three planned orbits of the earth, and Carpenter was busy. The flight plan called for a continuous series of scientific experiments as well as taking multiple photographs. All this required him to maneuver the capsule continually, changing its attitude with the hydrogen-peroxide-fueled thrusters.

Carpenter's exhilaration—the thrill of weightlessness, the spectacle of the continents rolling beneath him, sunrise followed by sunset followed by sunrise—continued into the second orbit. Then mission control noticed something disturbing. Carpenter was using up thruster fuel at an alarming rate. If he didn't conserve fuel, he would be unable to position the capsule at the correct angle, heat shield forward, for reentry after the third orbit. *Aurora 7* stood a good chance of becoming space toast.

Part of the problem was the ship's automatic control system. It was supposed to scan for a horizon, then keep the ship oriented in a stable attitude, but the system was malfunctioning. Carpenter was told to let the capsule drift—turn in any attitude it wanted to so as not to use any of the precious thruster fuel. So for a while he did that, floating weightlessly as the capsule drifted in its orbit.

But then his insatiable curiosity took over again. Through the window he noticed a cloud of the mysterious "fireflies" that John Glenn had reported during his flight. This, he decided, deserved some scientific attention. Carpenter began maneuvering the capsule again in order to better observe the fireflies.

By the third orbit, the fuel situation was critical. It was time to prepare for reentry, and Carpenter was behind in his checklist. Because of the failed automatic system, he had to position the capsule for reentry by fly-by-wire—manual thruster control. He would fire the retrorockets manually on command from the ground.

Back on earth, America was listening to its favorite journalist, Walter Cronkite, describe the flight of *Aurora 7*. The avuncular Cronkite, the "most trusted man in America" according to polls, had made himself the dean of space reporters with his coverage of Glenn's flight. Now Cronkite was telling viewers about Carpenter's fuel problem.

Just beyond the outer layer of earth's atmosphere, Scott Carpenter was trying to get *Aurora 7* into something close to a correct reentry attitude. He was having trouble. His supply of maneuvering fuel was nearly exhausted. The automatic control system, which was supposed to orient the capsule at a 34-degree nose-down tilt and a zero-degree yaw angle, had failed utterly. He was aligning the capsule with the fly-by-wire manual system, peering out the tiny window and using references on the ground.

Alan Shepard, the controller for the final leg of the last orbit, gave the countdown for the retrofire. When he called "Fire one!"

the angle of the capsule was still off about 9 degrees in pitch and 25 degrees in yaw axis. And Carpenter was a few seconds late hitting the switch, which, at 17,500 mph, would cause a gross overshoot in the intended splashdown point.

The retrorockets fired and the capsule headed downward into the atmosphere. Carpenter spent what thruster fuel he had left to keep the capsule oriented in its reentry attitude. The capsule was buffeting and oscillating as it literally dropped out of the sky. As the heat intensified, reaching nearly 4,000 degrees at the heat shield, an orange glow surrounded *Aurora 7.* The phenomenon was already known and, as expected, it caused a long period of radio blackout.

At the cape, there was silence. Mission controllers feared the worst. It seemed likely that *Aurora 7* had plunged into the concrete-thick air of earth's atmosphere at a bad angle and burned up. NASA executives were already thinking about how far back this was going to set the Mercury program.

Americans watched their televisions in stricken silence. Cronkite had been keeping them informed about Carpenter's fuel problem. Now his voice took on a new seriousness. They'd lost contact with the astronaut. It was possible that he'd begun the reentry at an improper angle.

Minutes ticked by. They still didn't know where Carpenter was. Cronkite delivered the bad news. "I'm afraid that . . ." His eyes filled with tears as he struggled to go on. "I'm afraid . . . we may have . . . lost an astronaut."

Meanwhile, Scott Carpenter, not lost at all, was descending through 50,000 feet. The oscillations were getting worse. The capsule was rocking like a cork in a waterfall. He pulled his drogue chute to steady the capsule. At 10,000 feet, the main chute deployed. Carpenter could see the water now—and nothing else. No ships, no helicopters, no waiting vessels. He knew he'd missed the landing point by a good margin.

The splashdown was not hard. Carpenter decided to exit the capsule. He climbed out the nose hatch and settled into his life raft. With legs crossed, hands clasped behind his head, the astronaut waited for his rescuers to show up.

———

At Recovery Station 9, Doc Abbot was no longer worried. He'd just been informed that the capsule was coming down 250 miles away. Now he had other things to worry about.

Instead of recovering the astronaut and the capsule with the assigned Marine helicopters and surface ships, they'd dispatch a pair of fast, turbine-powered Sikorsky SH-3A helicopters from *Intrepid*'s helicopter anti-submarine squadron. Speed was now essential, and the Sea King was the current holder of the world's helicopter speed record.

But there was another problem. The pilot of the lead helo, squadron skipper Cdr. John Wondergem, informed Captain Abbot that the round trip was several miles beyond the Sea King's maximum range. Not to worry, Abbot told him. He had *Intrepid* steaming "balls to the wall." *Intrepid* would be well within his range by the time he made the return trip.

Meanwhile, as the Sea Kings raced across the Caribbean, homing on the radio beacon in the astronaut's life raft, Carpenter was receiving other visitors. A Navy Lockheed P2V Neptune flew overhead and radioed the news that the astronaut was alive and well. Then appeared an Air Force C-54, and Carpenter watched in amazement as two frogmen parachuted down to him. They brought their own rafts, which they quickly tethered to his. A flotation collar dropped out of the sky, which one of the frogmen attached to the capsule.

Then another Air Force airplane—a Grumman Albatross amphibian—arrived. The pilot requested permission to land and recover the astronaut. No, said Mercury Control, who wanted no part of an Air Force–Navy feud over rescue rights. They would stick to the game plan and *Intrepid*'s helos would pick up Carpenter.

Which took ninety more minutes. The Sea Kings arrived with more divers, photographers, and a medic. Hovering over Carpenter's raft, the helo crew lowered a rescue collar. As he'd trained to do, Carpenter slid the collar under his arms and gave the sign to hoist him.

Up he went. Then down again. A gust of wind or a malfunctioning winch—Carpenter never found out—dunked him back into the ocean. Despite his effort to save his precious camera film, half was ruined by the seawater.

Aboard the rescue helicopter was a NASA flight surgeon who inquired how Carpenter felt. "Fine," the astronaut reported. In fact, he had never felt better. He spent most of the hour-and-twenty-minute flight to the USS *Intrepid* talking about his incredible adventure. Meanwhile, his spacecraft, *Aurora 7*, was being hauled aboard by the first Navy vessel on the scene, the destroyer USS *Pierce*, which had raced at flank speed to reach the capsule.

While the lead helo was making the flight back to *Intrepid*, squadron skipper John Wondergem glanced back to see how his passenger was doing. His heart almost stopped. Carpenter was leaning on the bottom half of the cabin door, sightseeing out the open top half. The door was hinged at the bottom. If the catch was not securely fastened, the man who had just survived an 80,000-mile journey would fly back into space—200 feet to the ocean. Wondergem bolted from his seat, grabbed Carpenter, and unceremoniously stuffed him into a seat.

The Sea King alighted on *Intrepid*'s deck to a tumultuous welcome. Waiting for the astronaut was Rear Admiral Chew, Captain Abbot, senior Air Force and Marine Corps officers, NASA officials, technical reps, and a swarm of reporters and cameramen. In the background was a crowd of *Intrepid* crewmen, eager to get a glimpse of the astronaut. No one could remember seeing a lieutenant commander receive such a welcome aboard an aircraft carrier.

Carpenter underwent a physical exam, took a shower, and donned a starched, clean flight suit. At the captain's dining table, he bowed his head while Captain Abbot offered a prayer of thanks for his safe recovery.

Three weeks later came the day that Doc Abbot had been dreading. He stood in his dress whites gazing across the flight deck at his crew. His year as skipper of the *Intrepid* had passed in what seemed to be the space of a heartbeat.

They had come a long way together, he and *Intrepid*—an eventful

Mediterranean deployment, the pickup of astronaut Scott Carpenter after the flight of *Aurora 7*, presiding over *Intrepid*'s conversion to an anti-submarine warrior. And, of course, winning the "E." Of all their accomplishments, that was the one that made him proudest—and proudest of his superb crew. Their little *Essex*-class carrier with two catapults had taken on the big-deck supercarriers and kicked all their butts.

"I'm standing up here as one of you," Abbott said, "and telling you that *Intrepid* has a soul herself—independent of her officers and men. There are at least sixteen people who understand—my sixteen predecessors."

Having said that, Abbot stood at attention and turned *Intrepid* over to her eighteenth seagoing skipper, Capt. Robert J. Morgan.

Intrepid spent an easy summer in 1962 exercising her new air group and embarking a load of NROTC midshipmen. That autumn she went back to the Portsmouth shipyard for another major overhaul, receiving new paint, a new teak surface on her flight deck, an overhaul of her arresting gear and catapults, upgrades to her electronic equipment, and a general modernization of her crew amenities.

For the next year she operated along the East Coast, from Nova Scotia south to the Caribbean. In the spring of 1963, Captain Morgan was relieved by an old *Intrepid* hand, Capt. John Lawrence. As skipper of Torpedo Squadron 10, Lawrence had led his squadron of TBM Avengers during the epic battles for Okinawa and the sinking of the *Yamato*. He had been aboard during the deadly kamikaze attacks of March and April 1945, and then returned to the Pacific to enforce the peace after the surrender of Japan.

In May 1963, *Intrepid* docked at New York's 42nd Street pier for the annual Armed Forces Day celebration. She opened her decks to the public, and New Yorkers streamed aboard in droves. In a two-hour period on May 18, 17,751 visitors came aboard. The next day more than 21,000 boarded the ship. New Yorkers, it seemed, loved USS *Intrepid*.

In June 1964 *Intrepid* departed on her first Mediterranean deployment with an anti-submarine warfare air wing ("air wing" had replaced the anachronistic "air group"). Even though she no longer carried fighters and attack bombers, *Intrepid* and her sub-hunting air wing were still instruments of the Cold War. In between operating periods at sea, *Intrepid* showed the flag in a succession of Mediterranean ports. When a Soviet Navy task group sailed into the Mediterranean, *Intrepid* joined the U.S. forces assigned to shadow it.

That July *Intrepid*'s old skipper, Paul Masterton, now a rear admiral, came aboard to present the carrier with an award—the Admiral Flatley Memorial Safety Award for the best CVS operating safety record. In the autumn of 1963, while *Intrepid* was headed back to Norfolk, came news of an even more prestigious award. *Intrepid* had won another Battle Efficiency "E"—her first as an antisubmarine warrior—breaking the five-year winning streak of her sister ship *Randolph*.

Intrepid was, again, the best in the fleet.

In the fall of 1964 she was at Yorktown, Virginia, commemorating the surrender of Lord Cornwallis to American forces, when she received the news of a new—and familiar—assignment. Another U.S. spacecraft was leaving the earth.

Intrepid would be there when it returned.

22

Gemini

There was to be no misunderstanding about what the term "space race" meant. The operative word was race. America's mission in space was not a program, not an initiative, not even a scientific quest. The United States was engaged in a no-holds-barred, nose-to-jowl race with the Soviet Union. At stake was preeminence not just on earth but in the heavens.

The mission had been laid down by John F. Kennedy in 1961: the United States would land a man on the moon before the end of the decade. The stated objective seemed clear enough, but the *unstated* objective was so clear it might have been cast in concrete on the White House steps: the United States would get there before the Soviets.

Nearly three years had elapsed since *Intrepid*'s long-distance re-covery of Scott Carpenter after the flight of *Aurora 7.* In that time, two more Mercury astronauts had rocketed into orbit, each building on Carpenter's three-orbit flight. Wally Schirra flew a flawless six-orbit mission, returning to earth with such precision that sailors on the recovery ship USS *Kearsarge* watched from the flight deck as *Sigma*, Schirra's Mercury capsule, descended to the water four and a half miles away.

Gordon Cooper's twenty-two-orbit, thirty-four-hour flight in May 1963 put a satisfying finish to the Mercury program. Despite system shutdowns during the final orbits, much like those that plagued Carpenter's flight, Cooper put on a dazzling performance of the right stuff by manually positioning his capsule in the correct attitude for reentry, firing the retrorockets himself—and splashing down even closer to *Kearsarge* than Schirra had done. It was a textbook mission, and it opened the way for the next stage of orbital testing, the Gemini program.

Meanwhile, Soviet cosmonauts had been heating up the competition. A month after Cooper's flight, Valery Bykovsky flew a 119-hour flight during which he rendezvoused with another spacecraft—this one flown by a woman cosmonaut. In 1964 the Soviets staged a twenty-four-hour mission with a crew of three, and the next year flew an even longer two-man mission in which cosmonaut Alexei Leonov performed the first spacewalk.

The United States had fallen behind again. The Gemini program was intended to propel the United States back into the lead, and it would test the techniques and hardware that would take Americans to the moon. Gemini 1 and 2 were both unmanned launches to test the functionality of the rocket and capsule combination. The Gemini flights used the new Titan rocket, a mightier vehicle than the Atlas rockets used in the Mercury missions.

Gemini 3, flown by astronauts Gus Grissom and John Young, would be a shakedown flight preceding more ambitious missions that would practice orbital rendezvouses, docking, and EVAs— extravehicular activity, in street vernacular *spacewalking*—and hadn't yet been attempted by American astronauts.

The main objective of Gemini 3, beyond simply validating the new rocket and its manned capsule, was to prove that the astronauts could modify their orbit using Gemini's Orbital Attitude and Maneuvering System (OAMS). The OAMS thrusters were the tool that made it possible to join separated vehicles in space—an essential requirement for the future Apollo flights to the moon.

On the morning of March 23, 1965, the eyes of the world were again on Cape Canaveral, watching the launch of Gemini 3. And in the Caribbean some 10,185 personnel, 126 aircraft, and 27 ships were waiting to recover the spaceship and its crew. The principal recovery ship was, again, USS *Intrepid*.

———

When she left Norfolk in mid-March, 1965, a huge banner adorned her starboard flight deck edge: INTREPID HAS A DATE WITH GUS AND JOHN.

On board again were the representatives from all the services, NASA observers, tech reps from the manufacturers of the rocket and capsule, a horde of media people, and the commander of the recovery operation, Rear Adm. D. M. White.

En route to the recovery area, the helicopter crews practiced picking up the dummy capsule that NASA had supplied, and then they simulated retrieving astronauts from the capsule itself. They wanted to get it right. No one at NASA or high up in the Navy had actually come out and said it, but there was an underlying imperative to this operation: *don't screw up.*

Not that anyone actually *had* screwed up, at least too badly, but it was a fact that not all the astronaut pickups had gone smoothly. There was the unfortunate dunking of Scott Carpenter as he was being hoisted to the hovering Sea King. The dunking lasted only a few seconds, but it was enough to fill his pressure suit with seawater and trash half the photos he'd flown 80,000 miles to shoot.

But the closest brush with calamity happened during the retrieval of Gus Grissom and *Liberty Bell.* Because of the inadvertent blowing of the capsule's hatch, the spacecraft had filled with water and was about to sink. Fixated on saving the capsule, the helo crew was oblivious to the fact that Grissom was floundering in the ocean beneath them as his pressure suit took on water and began to drag him down. In the nick of time someone picked up on the fact that the astronaut seemed to be drowning. They hoisted the gasping, gagging Grissom aboard the helo, but the capsule was filled with too much water. In dismay, they watched *Liberty Bell* disappear beneath the waves.

Now the message couldn't be clearer: *don't screw up.* Anyone who even came close to drowning Grissom again could consider himself dead meat. With this grim directive fixed in their minds, the crew of *Intrepid* took their station in the recovery area to await *Molly Brown.*

In his contoured seat aboard the capsule *Molly Brown* high atop the Titan rocket, Lt. Cdr. John Young listened to the countdown. They had stopped at T-minus thirty-five minutes to fix an oxidizer line leak. It took only a few minutes, then the count resumed.

With Young in the Gemini capsule was Gus Grissom, the mission commander. Despite NASA's objections, Grissom had insisted on naming the spaceship *Molly Brown*, after the Broadway musical *The Unsinkable Molly Brown*. Grissom had a good reason for the name. After the sinking of his previous capsule, *Liberty Bell*, in 16,000 feet of ocean, Grissom vowed that his next spacecraft would be unsinkable, at least in name.

Outside their spaceship, the overcast that earlier threatened to delay the launch of Gemini 3 had miraculously cleared. There were no further leaks or problems with the rocket. The countdown continued.

This would be Young's first flight into space. He was a slim, boyish-looking Navy pilot from Orlando, Florida. The day before the launch, his hometown had surprised him with a 60-foot-long telegram wishing "their boy" a good flight.

A graduate of Georgia Tech, Young had gone directly into the Navy, where he served a year aboard a destroyer before entering flight training. His first assignment was to a fighter squadron flying F9F Cougars and then F8U Crusaders aboard the first supercarrier, USS *Forrestal*. After being selected for test pilot school, Young was assigned to the Navy's flight test center in Patuxent River, Maryland, evaluating the new Crusader and Phantom fighter weapons systems. In 1962 Young set two successive time-to-climb records in the new F-4 Phantom II. It was the same year he received news that he had been chosen for astronaut training.

Young's partner on *Molly Brown* was a hardscrabble little guy from the Midwest who had never wanted anything except to be a test pilot in the Air Force. Gus Grissom had been a World War II Army Air Force cadet, missed out on flight training when the war ended, married his high school sweetheart, worked his way through college, and then reentered the Air Force. He'd flown a hundred missions in F-86s in Korea, earned a reputation as a hot-rock fighter pilot, and was a well-regarded Air Force test pilot when he was chosen as one of the original seven Mercury astronauts—a certified possessor of Tom Wolfe's "right stuff."

Grissom had already achieved celebrity status when he became the second American, after Alan Shepard, to rocket into space. Now, as commander of Gemini 3, he would become the first human being to set off for space twice.

Young listened to the controller's voice counting down. At exactly 0924, he heard the ignition command. He felt the rumble of the Titan's mighty twin-chambered engine swelling like an erupting volcano.

The acceleration, Young thought, was hardly noticeable. And despite the thunderous roar of the engine beneath them, providing 430,000 pounds of thrust, the cabin was surprisingly quiet. He felt the rocket roll as it aligned its inertial guidance units, then a slight shift as the engine gimballed to maintain the rocket's upward alignment.

"You're on your way, *Molly Brown*," called astronaut Gordon Cooper, the CAPCOM—capsule communicator—for the first leg of the journey.

After two and a half minutes, the first stage shut down. The spent stage was blown away and the second-stage rocket kicked in. The trajectory was good. They were headed into orbit.

"*Molly Brown*, you're go from here," Cooper called from Gemini Control.

Young glanced outside his tiny half-moon window. The view was spectacular. He could see all the way down the Eastern Test Range. Waiting for them somewhere in that blue expanse of water was an aircraft carrier.

In their second orbit, Grissom and Young made history. Igniting the forward-firing thrusters of the spacecraft for a timed burn of seventy-four seconds, they slowed the capsule enough to change the shape of their orbit and thus adjust their altitude by several miles. It was the first time astronauts had actually "flown" a ship in space, and it had shown that Gemini could rendezvous with another spacecraft in orbit.

They had more mundane tasks to perform. The astronauts were supposed to eat the specially prepared "space food." Young, however, had smuggled aboard a contraband corned beef sandwich, which had the unintended effect of filling the capsule with crumbs and delicatessen smells.

Crossing the Pacific in their final orbit, the astronauts stowed their gear and prepared for reentry. Because several Mercury capsules had come down considerable distances from their targets, NASA had designed the Gemini capsule for a "controlled reentry." The shape of the capsule was intended to provide a certain amount of lift as it penetrated the atmosphere, allowing it to slightly change trajectory as it descended to splashdown. By monitoring the trajectory, the onboard computer—a new item of technology in 1965—could predict the splashdown point and display it to the crew, who could then adjust the capsule's lift by slightly changing its attitude.

But the actual lifting properties of the Gemini capsule hadn't been proven in flight yet. "The needles show us about twenty-five miles short," Grissom radioed. The capsule's blunt shape wasn't developing as much lift as the engineers had expected. *Molly Brown*'s splashdown point would be some 52 miles short of its target over USS *Intrepid*.

The main chute deployed on schedule. The capsule hit the water and submerged for a moment, just long enough to cause Grissom to have an unpleasant flashback to *Liberty Bell*. The capsule righted itself, and the astronauts learned by radio that recovery aircraft were on the way.

The original plan was for the astronauts to remain aboard their capsule while it was hauled by helicopter back to the ship. But the ship was too far away, so Grissom made a command decision: they'd ride the helo back, and the capsule could be retrieved separately.

Grissom hadn't forgotten his near-death experience with *Liberty Bell*. He refused to open the hatch of *Molly Brown*, unsinkable or not, until the swimmers had attached the flotation collar. But this took some time, and while the astronauts waited, the capsule rocked like a hunk of flotsam in the rough seas.

Grissom became seasick. Up came the space food. And up came the contraband corned beef sandwich. Navy man Young watched, doing his best to keep his own lunch down. "Gemini may be a good spacecraft," he reported, "but she's no boat."

Finally the collar was in place and a swimmer opened the hatch. Watching Grissom scramble out of the claustrophobic, unseaworthy ship, Young had to laugh. It was the first time in his Navy career, he reported, that he'd seen a commander be first to abandon ship.

Aboard the Sea King helicopter, Grissom had to think about public relations. It wouldn't do to meet the media on *Intrepid* wearing his barf-stained flight suit. He and Young stripped down to their long johns and put on the robes supplied by the helo crew.

Seventy-four minutes after splashdown, the crew of *Molly Brown* stepped onto the deck of USS *Intrepid*. Waiting for them was Rear Admiral White and *Intrepid* skipper Capt. Joe Smith. They were hurried straight down to sick bay for medical exams. While still there, they received a phone call. In his folksy Texas twang, President Lyndon Johnson congratulated the two on a successful mission. Johnson was followed by exuberant Vice President Hubert Humphrey, who wanted to throw in his own attaboy.

The astronauts were given a tour of *Intrepid* by Captain Smith. Cheerfully they posed for photographs, cut a giant cake baked in their honor, and signed autographs for happy sailors. With the Sea King helicopter that rescued them and the spacecraft *Molly Brown* in the background, they sat through a ceremony on the hangar deck in which Admiral White introduced "Gus and John" to the ship's crew.

It was a heady time for the men of *Intrepid*. For a brief moment in history, their aging warship had joined the glittering new age of space exploration. They were now a part of it.

The flight of *Molly Brown* was declared a huge success. The launch and recovery had been nearly flawless. The ship's instruments, computer, and hand control had worked as advertised.

The two astronauts would continue their careers at NASA. Gus Grissom's would end abruptly, however. He was named the commander of AS-204, intended to be the first manned Apollo flight. On January 27, 1967, Grissom was killed along with fellow astronauts Ed White and Roger B. Chaffee in a spacecraft fire while training for Apollo 1.

Young went on to have what was probably the most distinguished career of any astronaut of his time. He returned to space on another Gemini mission, then circled the moon on Apollo 10, the last dress rehearsal before landing on the surface. In 1972, as commander of Apollo 16, he became the ninth human being to walk on the moon. Nearly a decade later Young was picked to command the historic first flight of the space shuttle *Columbia,* then flew into orbit once more as commander of STS9. John Young remained with NASA as chief of the Astronaut Office, retiring at the age of seventy-four with the most impressive record in the history of space exploration.

After the Gemini operation, *Intrepid* went into the New York Naval Shipyard for a six-month, $10 million overhaul called FRAM— Fleet Rehabilitation and Modernization Overhaul. The overhaul included new flight deck planking, rebricking and retubing of her boilers, hull reinforcement, improvements to the steam catapults and arresting gear, renovation of the Combat Information Center, and renovation of the gun mounts. She was fitted with new electronic gear, a dry-cleaning plant, new radio equipment, antennas, and a new refueling-at-sea rig.

Intrepid received the equipment that was standard on the supercarriers—a new bow-mounted SQS-23 sonar, a PLAT (Pilot Landing Aid, Television) system that televised every carrier landing and flashed it live down to all the squadron ready rooms, and a Fresnel Lens Landing System in place of the old mirror optical landing system.

The Fresnel lens took the mirror system a step further. Instead of a real mirror, the lens was a vertical row of five glass boxes. The green datum lights were extended outward from the middle, or third, box. Each box projected a beam of light at a different angle, so that the pilot, seeing the light—the "ball"—from one of the boxes, could know his relative position, high or low, on the glide slope.

While *Intrepid* was still in the shipyard, she again changed skippers. Capt. Giuseppe "Gus" Macri was a muscular, tough-looking officer with a quick smile. A 1941 graduate of the Naval Academy, Macri was a decorated torpedo bomber pilot in World War II, an attack squadron skipper, and onetime air boss aboard USS *Oriskany.*

Her overhaul complete, *Intrepid* headed home to Norfolk, pulling into her berth on October 16, 1965. Three days later, in another ceremony on her deck, she received two awards—the Battle Efficiency "E" and the "A" award for excellence in anti-submarine warfare. It was *Intrepid*'s second straight "E" as the best CVS-type carrier in the Atlantic.

In accepting the award, Captain Macri paid homage to the crew and air wing. But in his speech, he planted a clue about the future. "After the completion of several months of training, *Intrepid* will again be ready to give full, flexible response in anti-submarine warfare, attack, or whatever missions carriers are called upon to perform." Macri was being circumspect, but anyone who was following events in the Far East had no trouble deciphering his meaning. *Intrepid* may have been the best anti-submarine ship in the business, but that was then. This was now.

Intrepid was returning to the Pacific.

23

Dixie Station

I doubt that Mister McNamara and his crew have a morale setting on their computers.

—Rear Adm. Dan Gallery, 1965

Another war had been heating up in increments for over ten years. Since the French defeat at Dien Bien Phu in 1954, the United States had gradually raised the stakes of its commitment in Vietnam. Ships of the U.S. Seventh Fleet now maintained a presence off the coast of Vietnam, gathering intelligence, supporting the small American ground presence in South Vietnam, and flying regular photo reconnaissance missions.

One afternoon in the Tonkin Gulf, 28 miles from the shoreline of North Vietnam, the 2,200-ton destroyer *Maddox*'s radar picked up three torpedo boats approaching at high speed. Undeterred by a warning shot fired from *Maddox,* the boats launched two torpedoes at the destroyer. *Maddox* took evasive action, dodging the torpedoes and returning fire. A flight of F-8E Crusaders from USS *Ticonderoga* was vectored to the scene to strafe the boats, sinking one of them. That seemed to be the end of the confrontation.

Two nights later, on August 4, 1964, *Maddox,* in company with the destroyer *Turner Joy,* detected what appeared to be five high-

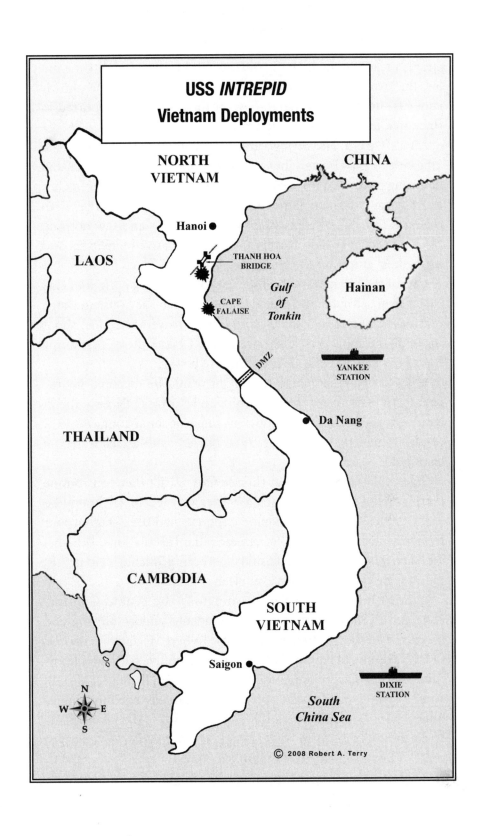

speed surface contacts. In a confused and frenzied nighttime melee, the two destroyers wheeled and evaded, firing at the ghostly contacts on sonar and radar. Several torpedoes were reported in the water, but none hit the destroyers.

Aircraft from *Ticonderoga* and *Constellation* were launched to attack the enemy boats. The weather was ugly, with low clouds and lightning pulsing in the overcast like a neon sign. The Tonkin Gulf, as *Maddox* radarman James Stankevitz put it, "was darker than the hubs of hell." The jets swept over the area—and saw nothing. Nothing except two destroyers swirling in evasive maneuvers and firing their guns into the blackness.

One of the pilots was Cdr. Jim Stockdale, leading a flight of Crusaders from *Ticonderoga*. "I had the best seat in the house to watch that event," wrote Stockdale, "and our destroyers were just shooting at phantom targets. There were no PT boats there . . . nothing there but black water and American fire power."

What actually happened that night would be disputed for the next forty years. Were the destroyers under attack? Or were the incoming torpedo boats only spurious radar or sonar contacts? Why would the North Vietnamese be so brazen as to attack a fleet of armored U.S. warships?

One explanation was that the *Maddox* wasn't there on routine patrol, as the secretary of defense later insisted in testimony before Congress. South Vietnamese gunboats had been staging commando attacks on North Vietnamese radar installations. Whether *Maddox* was supporting the raids, gathering intelligence, or just monitoring the events was never clear.

It didn't matter, at least in Washington. The Tonkin Gulf incident was all the provocation that President Lyndon Johnson and his closest advisor, Secretary of Defense Robert McNamara, needed. On the evening of August 4, Johnson went on live television to say, "Our response for the present will be limited and fitting . . . we will seek no wider war." As he spoke, it was already the morning of August 5 in Vietnam. Operation Pierce Arrow—a sixty-four-plane strike by aircraft from *Ticonderoga* and *Constellation*—was en route to targets in North Vietnam.

"That reply is given as I speak to you tonight," Johnson went on.

"Air action is now in execution against gunboats and certain supporting facilities in North Vietnam which have been used in these hostile operations."

Crusaders, Skyhawks, and Skyraiders bombed and rocketed the North Vietnamese bases at Hon Gai and near the Lach Chao estuary. Sixteen aircraft from *Ticonderoga,* led by Jim Stockdale, struck the petroleum storage complex at Vinh, setting it ablaze. Two pilots—Lt. (jg) Richard Sather and Lt. (jg) Everett Alvarez Jr.—were shot down. Sather was not seen again, and Alvarez earned the distinction of becoming the longest-held POW of the Vietnam War.

On August 7, 1964, after testimony by McNamara, Congress passed by nearly unanimous vote the Tonkin Gulf Resolution. The resolution authorized the president to use military force in Southeast Asia without a formal declaration of war by Congress. In the months ahead, the Johnson administration would use the resolution as its legal authority for the rapid escalation of military involvement in Vietnam.

From then on, the buildup was steady. In early 1965 U.S. Marines landed on the beach at Da Nang, becoming the first units of American combat troops into South Vietnam. By year's end, nearly 200,000 more troops were in the country. In the air, more retaliatory strikes were launched against North Vietnam. Then came a sustained bombing campaign called Rolling Thunder.

The idea of Rolling Thunder was to break the will of North Vietnam to invade the South. The list of targets kept expanding to include almost all of North Vietnam—airfields, supply depots, military barracks, power plants, and explosives factories, as well as dams and waterways in the Red River delta. Every road and bridge used to move supplies to the south became a target.

By the end of 1965, Navy pilots alone had flown 31,000 combat sorties, expending 64,000 bombs and 129,000 rockets. The Navy kept three to five carriers in the South China Sea, all under the command of the Seventh Fleet and, specifically, Task Force 77 (CTF-77). Carriers launching strikes into North Vietnam were deployed to Yankee Station, a point in the South China Sea roughly between the two Vietnams. Operations in South Vietnam were flown from Dixie Station, a hundred miles southeast of Cam Ranh Bay. Each "line period"—a session in combat mode—lasted from twenty-five to thirty-five days, followed by a break in the Philippines or Hong Kong or Japan. A carrier typically put in at least four line periods before rotating back to the United States.

In 1965, the commander of all U.S. ground forces in South Vietnam, Gen. William Westmoreland, informed the secretary of defense that he needed a Navy carrier specifically assigned to support combat operations in the South. He wanted carrier planes available on call from Dixie Station.

The problem was, every attack carrier was already committed. After a brief analysis, Secretary McNamara's "whiz kids" came up with a solution. It was simple. They would redesignate one of the anti-submarine carriers as a "special" attack carrier. In fact, they already had one in mind.

McNamara himself delivered the announcement. "In order to maintain the attack carrier force off Vietnam," said the secretary, "we are deploying one of the Atlantic-based carriers, the *Intrepid*, to Southeast Asia. Very minor modifications were required on this vessel to permit it to operate light attack aircraft and it can be quickly reassigned to its antisubmarine role."

The announcement filled no one with joy. *Intrepid* had excelled in her role as an anti-submarine carrier, repeatedly winning the "E" as best ship in the business, and her air group winning the "A" as the best anti-submarine air wing. Now all that was history. *Intrepid*'s crew, most of whom weren't around during *Intrepid*'s previous life as an attack carrier, had to learn an entirely new craft.

The first to go was the anti-submarine air wing with their S-2 Trackers and SH-3A Sea Kings. In their place came Air Wing 10, a hodgepodge of squadrons cobbled together to fit *Intrepid*'s unique mission. It would be an all-attack wing, with two A-4 Skyhawk squadrons (VA-95 and VA-15 from NAS Lemoore and NAS Cecil) and two A-1 Skyraider outfits (VA-165 from NAS Alameda and VA-176 from NAS Jacksonville). The Skyhawks were old A-4B models, mostly retrieved from shore-based reserve squadrons. Though they could carry the same basic bomb load as the more modern A-4Cs and A-4Es, they had no radar or missile warning equipment.

But what about fighters? asked the attack squadron skippers. Where were the fighters to protect the strike aircraft?

Not necessary, replied the whiz kids. *Intrepid*'s mission was to provide close air support in the South. Her aircraft wouldn't be operating in the North, where SAMs and MiG fighters were a threat. Never mind the fact that every other attack carrier air wing had either F-8 Crusaders or F-4 Phantoms embarked. *Intrepid* didn't need fighters.

Air Wing 10's commander, Cdr. Thomas B. Hayward, looked as though he'd been chosen by central casting to play the part of air wing commander. He was a tall, slender man with the unlined face of a movie star. To go with the looks, Hayward had the confident manner of someone who never doubted for an instant that he was destined to reach the very top of the Navy's pyramid. A former F-8 Crusader squadron skipper, Hayward was something of an elitist. It was no secret that he wasn't thrilled about running a mixed bag of attack birds with no fighters, deployed on an old ship whose *real* mission had been hunting submarines.

The job of CAG—air wing commander—was the ultimate flying assignment in naval aviation. By long tradition, the CAG was a former squadron skipper and a highly experienced carrier pilot. Also by tradition, he flew two or more of the different types of airplanes in his wing. It was a military maxim that good leaders led from the front, and in the case of CAG—the good ones, anyway—it meant leading the toughest strikes.

In *Intrepid*'s long history, she'd had almost as many CAGs as she'd had captains. But CAGs were not all the same. Some were commanders in name only, preferring to assign the tough missions to their squadron skippers and experienced strike leaders. For them, the job of CAG was a ticket punch on their route to higher command. Some, such as Johnny Hyland, who commanded Air Group 10 at Okinawa and participated in the sinking of *Yamato*, were brilliant leaders. Hyland, in fact, now wore three stars and commanded the Seventh Fleet, and would ultimately become commander in chief, Pacific.

Other CAGs were brave but unlucky warriors: John Phillips, who led Air Group 6 during *Intrepid*'s initial combat cruise in 1944, was lost in action on the first day at Truk. Some, such as Air Group 18's "El Gropo" Ellis, distinguished themselves as tough combat leaders, then went into obscurity in the shrinking peacetime Navy.

Intrepid's new mission was a culture shock for both the ship's company and the air wing. Most of the ship's crew and officers were still attuned to the sedate rhythm of ASW operations. The howl of jets and the specialized skills of loading bombs, rockets, and 20-mm ammunition were foreign to them.

For their part, the air wing sailors weren't thrilled about deploying on an aging *Essex*-class ship rather than one of the modern supercarriers. *Intrepid* lacked many of the amenities of the new carriers, including air-conditioning. Her cramped quarters were notoriously hot, making deployment to tropical climates a living misery for the crew. Besides having less deck space, she had only two catapults, which put her at an operational disadvantage compared to the supercarriers. To the airedales, deploying on *Intrepid* felt like going to school in a rusty truck while their privileged classmates were riding air-conditioned buses.

In November 1965, Captain Macri took his new ship and air wing to Gitmo for five weeks of intensive training. After returning to Norfolk for the holidays, they resumed the heavy workup schedule off the coast of Florida. By spring 1966, *Intrepid* was ready to go to war.

Gus Macri had seen a lot of departures, but this one was different. From his bridge, he had a view of the crowd on the pier. They were mostly women and children, families of his crew. Most of the wives were crying. They were weeping in the ancient, intuitive way women have always had when seeing their men off to war.

The U.S. role in the Vietnam War was in its second year. Newspapers and nightly television were reporting the casualty numbers, which were mounting. Polls showed that most Americans clung to the belief that Vietnam was nothing more than a police action, in the style of Korea. There were war protesters, but their voices were drowned out by patriotic Americans who saw Vietnam as a virtuous struggle in the long battle with Communism.

Against this backdrop, *Intrepid* left the United States on her 12,000-mile voyage to Vietnam. She crossed the Atlantic, passed Gibraltar, and cruised through the waters of the Mediterranean, stopping for two days of liberty in a familiar port, Naples. She transited the Suez Canal on April 22, then cruised eastward across the Indian Ocean to Subic Bay in the Philippines, which had become the staging base for carriers operating in the Tonkin Gulf.

Then came the first surprise. To the fury of Gus Macri, CAG Hayward, and particularly the ordnance crews, an order from the Seventh Fleet awaited them. *Intrepid*'s supply of modern Mark 80 bombs that had been carefully loaded back in Norfolk now had to be transferred to the carriers operating on Yankee Station. Since *Intrepid* would only be operating in the South, she would take on a load of old World War II "fat" bombs from an ammunition ship. Worse, the crews would have to assemble the weapons on the hangar deck. It was a backbreaking chore for the ordnance men—and the first clue that *Intrepid* had been relegated to second-cousin status in the hierarchy of carriers.

Grudgingly, *Intrepid* exchanged her modern bombs for the old ones. *Intrepid* proceeded to Dixie Station, where on May 15 the A-1 Spads and A-4 Skyhawks flew ninety-seven close air support missions, all within 50 miles of Saigon. It was *Intrepid*'s first day of combat in twenty-one years.

In the ship's cramped air intelligence office, Lt. Cdr. Scott Allen was trying to put together a strike operations intelligence facility. It was a frustrating task. *Intrepid*'s intel office—and its staff—still reflected her old ASW mission. Allen's background was as a patrol squadron air intelligence officer, not a strike ops officer. The thirty-three-year-old officer had reported aboard *Intrepid* while she was still in the New York shipyard from his previous job in the Fleet Intelligence Center, Europe.

Like most of his staff, Allen was learning strike warfare on the job. Unlike most of the big-deck carriers in 1966, *Intrepid* didn't have a computerized intelligence center from which it could pipe live briefings to the squadron ready rooms. Strike leaders, squadron skippers, and the CAG came personally to the intel office to receive one-on-one briefings from Allen and his staff. When pilots returned from missions, they were debriefed and their fifty-minute-old information about SAM sites and enemy gun emplacements was used to update the plotting charts.

It was old-fashioned, not any different from the way intelligence data had been processed in World War II, but it worked. In some ways, thought Allen, it worked better than the new systems. He later reflected, "The big decks had invested millions in automated intelligence centers, with new mainframes that could process tapes received every few days from the Defense Intelligence Agency. There was a myth that if it came from a computer, it must be golden. Bullshit at the speed of light was still bullshit."

Like everyone from Captain Macri down to the enlisted intel staff, Allen assumed that *Intrepid* would only be operating in South Vietnam. Accordingly, he had ordered several pallets from the Army Map Service of 1:25,000-scale sectional maps of South Vietnam.

But then something had nagged at him, and he also ordered a supply of maps of North Vietnam. Just in case.

General Westmoreland was getting what he asked for—close air support in South Vietnam from a dedicated attack carrier. For six weeks *Intrepid* launched strikes into South Vietnam from Dixie Station. Even the fat bombs were turning out to be effective against fixed targets in the South. The A-1 Spads could lumber off the ship carrying as many as four of the big 2,000-pounders. Ingenious FACs—forward air controllers—on the ground had come up with new uses for the big bombs. Armed with a "daisy-cutter" warhead, one fat bomb could clear a patch in the jungle large enough to land a helicopter.

But the real reason for replacing *Intrepid*'s modern weapons with the fat bombs was becoming apparent: the Navy and Air Force were running out of bombs. American warplanes were dropping ordnance in Vietnam in immense quantities—soon to exceed the total of all bombs dropped in World War II. Ordnance was being rationed, and to the frustration of pilots and air crews, they were often risking their lives only to dump a token load of bombs. The war, they began to suspect, was a numbers game. What mattered was the number of missions flown, not the number of bombs on-target.

Still, for the *Intrepid* pilots, providing close air support for the troops was a satisfying mission. They flew mostly in daytime, with the A-1s on three-hour missions and the A-4s on ninety-minute cycles. The Skyraider was perfectly suited for the job, with the ability to loiter on station with a big load of ordnance, then swoop in when called. The only serious threat was from small-arms fire, and on most strikes the aircraft stayed above the range of enemy guns.

Intrepid completed her first line period on Dixie Station, then returned for a second. During a total of fifty-nine days, *Intrepid*'s airplanes hit Viet Cong supply, storage, and training areas. They flew 4,738 sorties, dropping 5,500 tons of ordnance. The most significant statistic, however, was that they had accomplished their assigned mission without losing a single airplane.

In June the two senior commanders aboard *Intrepid* said farewell. CAG Hayward, towering by a head over his successor, Cdr. Ken Burrows, turned over command of Air Wing 10. The officers who regularly saw Hayward were still amazed. He had never looked old enough to hold the rank of commander, let alone command an air wing, and that hadn't changed. His face bore none of the signs of stress that combat leaders were supposed to show. He could still flash the quick, movie-star grin and come up with the right line for every occasion.

Hayward, the elitist fighter pilot, had earned the respect of the attack pilots the hard way. He put in full days, often flying two or more sorties, briefing and leading strikes. Before the Vietnam War ended, he would return to the South China Sea as the captain of the supercarrier USS *America*. In the years to come, Hayward would ascend to the top of the Navy's command structure, becoming chief of naval operations.

His successor, Ken Burrows, was less charismatic than Hayward.

He was short and stocky, with a gap-toothed grin and a round, tough guy's face. His manner tended to be blunt, lacking Hayward's easy charm. But there was more to Ken Burrows, as the air wing pilots learned. For one thing, he was a consummate attack pilot, with an instinctive grasp of how to run a strike without losing precious airplanes and pilots. He was like Hayward in one critical respect: he believed in leading from the front. Burrows regularly assigned himself to lead the toughest missions.

The next month, on July 15, 1966, Gus Macri turned over his ship to his relief, Capt. John W. Fair. Unlike his predecessors, Fair wasn't a Naval Academy grad. He came up the hard way, enlisting as a Marine in 1940, finagling his way into flight training, and receiving his wings and commission as a Navy ensign. A much-decorated fighter pilot in World War II, he'd held all the classic jobs—fighter squadron skipper, carrier air boss, air group commander.

Like many carrier skippers, Fair had a fetish. His was a railroad engineer's cap, scrambled eggs on the bill, which he wore as part of his working uniform on the ship. Soon after taking command, he had his photograph snapped wearing the cap while inscribing a thousand-pound bomb loaded on a Skyhawk. In large, legible script was the message "Warm regards, J. W. Fair."

John Fair was known as a man who didn't suffer fools gladly, being prone to bursts of anger that could vibrate bulkheads and rattle hatches. But he had also acquired a reputation as being a fierce protector of his men and airplanes.

Soon after taking command of *Intrepid*, Fair had a good reason to raise his voice in anger.

★ 24 ★

Up North

They couldn't believe it.

Even before leaving Norfolk, they'd been told that *Intrepid*'s mission was to provide close air support in the South. That was the reason for the hodgepodge, all-attack air wing—no fighters, no recon aircraft, no radar, no radar detection gear. They didn't need such luxuries. They were flying from Dixie Station. *South* Vietnam, right?

Wrong. The order came in when *Intrepid* had nearly finished her second line period. They were heading to Yankee Station. *Intrepid*'s planes were going up north.

Captain Fair's howl of protest was heard all the way to the flagship of the commander of Task Force 77. The next day a four-striper from the admiral's staff arrived aboard. Behind closed doors, the admiral's staffer and the carrier skipper had a nose-to-nose discussion. The result, though never made public, was to the effect that Captain Fair had made his point, thank you, and now he could shut up and comply with his orders.

Which he did, though not without more glowering and door slamming. The reason for the change in plan was that the scale of the bombing campaign in North Vietnam was ratcheting up. The task force commander wanted three carriers instead of two on Yankee Station, and *Intrepid* was the only one available. Never mind that her attack airplanes were not equipped with anti-missile warning gear or that she carried no fighters to protect the strike planes. It was a classic "needs of the service" argument—the military Catch-22 that trumped every form of logic.

The A-4Bs were ill-equipped for night or all-weather missions. With no radar, no radio altimeter, and a single TACAN navigation radio, the little Skyhawks were out of their element. Worse, they had none of the ECM—electronic countermeasures—gear to detect and thwart enemy surface-to-air missile radars. It hadn't been considered necessary, of course, since they weren't going up north.

For the A-1 Spad pilots, the ante had just gone higher. In the hostile environment of North Vietnam, the slow-moving propeller-driven attack planes were easy prey for anti-aircraft guns, surface-to-air missiles (SAMs), and MiG-17 fighters. Most of the missions were called "armed reconnaissance," which meant no specific targets were assigned. The pilots looked for targets of opportunity— trucks, trains, troops moving along the inland roads. The target areas for the Spads were mostly in the southern portion of North Vietnam, which was less heavily defended by SAMs and MiG fighters than the northern sector, around Hanoi and Haiphong.

Despite the lack of sophisticated equipment, the A-4 pilots of VA-95 and VA-15 flew the missions, dodged the SAMs and anti-aircraft artillery, and all managed to get back to the ship. Their first and only loss was on August 7, 1966, and it had nothing to do with combat. VA-15's Lt. Cdr. Richard "Moose" Moran was returning from a tanker mission. He flew over the ship at pattern altitude, broke to turn downwind for landing, and then, inexplicably, descended into the water and exploded. Moran didn't eject from the Skyhawk, and the cause of the accident was never determined.

The next month was a bad one for the A-1 Skyraiders. On September 2, 1966, VA-165 Executive Officer Cdr. Bill Jett was leading a flight of Spads on a road reconnaissance mission near Vinh Son when they came under heavy anti-aircraft fire. Jett felt the telltale thunk of a flak hit on his starboard wing. With flames streaming from his wing, Jett nursed the Skyraider toward the shoreline.

Knowing he had to bail out—the Navy A-1s had no ejection seat—Jett stretched it as far as he dared, torn between parachuting into enemy country and trying to make it to the open sea before the Skyraider blew apart.

Five miles past the beach, Jett clambered over the side and parachuted to the water. It was still too close to the enemy shore to suit Jett, but within minutes he heard the sound of rotor blades. A Navy helicopter swept in from the sea and hauled him to safety.

Nine days later, a flight of VA-165 Spads were bombing the heavily defended air defense site at Cape Falaise, 25 miles north of Vinh. Anti-aircraft bursts were already appearing like ugly mushrooms as Lt. (jg) Terry Dwyer rolled into his dive on the target.

The guns caught Dwyer's Spad while he was still in his dive. With his port wing shattered and streaming flames, he headed out to sea. Ten miles offshore, he went over the side and, like his executive officer the week before, was plucked from enemy waters by a Navy rescue helo.

The next week, like a recurring bad dream, it happened again. VA-176 pilot Lt. Charles Knochel and his flight were exiting the country after their armed reconnaissance mission when an unseen anti-aircraft battery opened up on them. Knochel took a hit in his starboard wing, which caught fire. Like Jett and Dwyer, he wanted to stay with his airplane, afire or not, long enough to put some ocean between him and the enemy.

He had made it out over the water when the 20-mm ammunition in his right wing detonated. His wingmen saw Knochel bail out, but the parachute appeared to be damaged. He hit the water hard and didn't wave or respond to his squadronmates as they swept overhead. When an Air Force SA-16 Albatross amphibian splashed down on the site twelve minutes later, Knochel was gone.

It was a grim evening in the VA-95 and VA-176 ready rooms. Everyone knew that sending Spads on strikes into North Vietnam was a lousy idea. The events of the past weeks had proved it.

And then the next month, something happened to change the mood in the Spad ready rooms. Something spectacular.

Lt. Cdr. Leo Cook heard the excited chatter on the strike frequency. Strike planes from *Intrepid, Oriskany,* and *Coral Sea* were hitting targets in the southern part of Route Package 3, near Vinh. Cook heard them talking about taking anti-aircraft fire. Someone was yelling about MiGs in the area.

Cook, the executive officer of VA-176, was leading a four-plane flight of Spads on a rescue patrol mission, or RESCAP. If one of the strike airplanes went down in Indian country—the pilots' term for enemy territory—it was the RESCAP's job to make contact with the guy on the ground, provide air cover, and to escort the rescue helo in and out of the site. Each A-1 had the standard RESCAP load—two 150-gallon drop-tanks on the stub racks, four pods with nineteen 2.75-inch rockets apiece, and 800 rounds of 20-mm ammunition for the four wing cannons.

RESCAP missions could be the most dangerous of them all, but most of the Spad drivers welcomed the assignment. Risking your life to bomb a mud bridge or blow a hole in the jungle didn't always make sense. Saving a fellow pilot's life was a worthwhile mission.

Then Cook heard the strike leader's voice cut like a knife through the jabber on the radio. Someone had just been shot down. Another voice reported that he thought he heard signals from the pilot and the flight officer on the ground. A rescue by helicopter might be feasible.

Cook ordered his second section, Lt. Pete Russell and Lt. (jg) Tom Patton, to escort the slower-moving SH-3A helicopter inland while he and his wingman, Lt. (jg) Jim Wiley, headed in to try to locate the downed crew. As Cook and Wiley headed toward the mountainous terrain where the jet had gone down, they came under heavy anti-aircraft fire. Dodging flak, they hugged the ridges and used the lowering cloud cover to hide from enemy gunners.

For fifteen minutes they searched the designated area without finding a trace of the downed pilots. They were still searching, flying at nearly treetop level, when Wiley called Cook's attention to something peculiar on the ground: orange flashes. It looked very much like tracers. What was peculiar was that the tracers appeared to be coming from *above* them.

"Break right!" yelled Wiley on the radio.

As Cook's Spad wheeled into a hard right turn, Wiley glimpsed over his shoulder a dark silhouette. It was a swept-wing fighter. He recognized the large circular jet intake of a Russian-built MiG-17. He could also see the flashing muzzles of the MiG's guns—two 23-mm guns and one 37-mm cannon.

Behind the MiG was another. Both were flying a pursuit curve toward the two Spads, guns blazing. Wiley saw Cook's Spad skim over a mountain ridge and disappear on the other side. More tracers tore into the ground beneath Wiley's airplane.

Now there were *three* MiGs after him.

He was on his own. At treetop altitude, and with the mountain ridge separating them, he'd lost radio contact with Cook. He yelled for the other Spad section—Russell and Patton—to come join the fight.

The other two Spads were still escorting the slower-flying search-and-rescue SH-3A helicopter. When they arrived, Russell in the lead, they saw Wiley's Spad being chased by two MiG-17s. In the turning, twisting duel, Wiley had traded shots with the MiGs and managed to score some hits.

Converting their altitude to extra airspeed, Russell and Patton dove in behind the North Vietnamese fighters. It was a one-sided fight, the slow, propeller-driven Spads versus high-performance MiG fighters.

But the MiG pilots were making a classic mistake. Instead of using the jets' superior speed and performance to pounce like hawks, then zoom up and out of the fight, they locked themselves into a low-altitude, turning duel with the Spads.

Russell found himself in a head-on pass with one of the MiGs. He put several rounds into the jet as it whooshed past. Then Patton rolled in behind one of the MiGs that was pursuing Wiley. Suddenly aware of the danger, the North Vietnamese pilot rolled his wings level and pulled up in a climb.

Which was another mistake. Patton pulled up behind him. With the MiG centered in his gun sight, he blazed away with all four 20-mm cannon. Pieces were flying off the jet, but somehow the MiG kept flying. He was still pointed upward, climbing for the safety of the overcast.

Patton's guns ran out of ammunition. Frustrated, he fired all his rockets at the escaping MiG. Before he could see the results, the MiG vanished in the murk of the cloud layer.

The Spad pilot was a man obsessed with one burning desire: to kill MiGs. He punched into the clouds behind the MiG, not sure what to expect.

Seconds later, he popped through the top of the overcast, and there was the MiG-17. Directly above the MiG was another object. It was the North Vietnamese pilot, descending in his parachute. The shattered MiG-17, smoking and trailing fire, was plummeting back toward the earth.

With one MiG down, the emboldened Patton dove back through the clouds to find more. Beneath the cloud deck, he saw that he and his fellow Spad pilots were alone. The MiGs had cut their losses and run for home.

Back aboard *Intrepid*, still in their damp and sweat-stained flight gear, the Spad pilots were summoned to the captain's bridge. Captain Fair, wearing his engineer's cap, wanted to hear every tantalizing detail about the dogfight.

That evening the story was retold over the ship's PA. Word of *Intrepid*'s MiG killers spread to the other carriers and ready rooms on Yankee Station. Downing a MiG was a spectacular feat—but not unique. A year ago, Spads from *Midway* had a similar engagement and flamed a MiG-17. Still, it was a terrific morale-boosting event for the entire attack community.

Tom Patton received credit for a MiG kill, and a Silver Star to go with it. Pete Russell got credit for a probable, and Jim Wiley was given a possible. It was a rare moment of glory for the Spad and the men who flew it. Someone pointed out that the first flight of the A-1 Skyraider had been on March 18, 1945, when most of *Intrepid*'s Spad pilots were preschoolers. Some hadn't even been born.

The Skyraider's long career as a U.S. Navy attack plane was nearly finished. That day's action, everyone agreed, made a hell of a good last chapter.

The pilots of VA-176 made the most of it. For the rest of the deployment, their ready room door was emblazoned with a big, audacious symbol—of a MiG kill.

Another thing everyone agreed on: if the A-4s and A-1s *were* going to go up north and survive, they had to have better equipment. During *Intrepid*'s next break in Subic Bay in the Philippines, a piece of classified equipment called a radar warning receiver was installed in the noses of the A-4Bs. It provided a rudimentary SAM warning—the capability the pilots had previously been told they wouldn't need because they weren't flying into a missile environment. Likewise, the A-1s were fitted with SAM alert devices, but they had to be installed in the cockpits on the glare shields.

An even more useful item of equipment still wasn't available to *Intrepid*'s pilots. A new air-to-ground weapon, the AGM-45 Shrike, was an anti-radiation missile with a tracking head that could lock onto a radar-emitting SAM site and home in as if it were a beacon. Shrikes were in short supply in 1966, and so was the onboard equipment the A-4s needed to launch them. Not until later in the war were Shrikes in regular use.

The A-4 pilots had already devised their own anti-SAM tactics, lofting 5-inch HVARs—high-velocity aerial rockets—from low altitude at a SAM site. It was primitive and imprecise. The rockets rarely destroyed the sites, but the rain of unguided explosives usually motivated the North Vietnamese to shut down their acquisition radars long enough for the strike aircraft to deliver their bombs and make a hasty exit.

Intrepid's assignment to Yankee Station, along with *Oriskany* and *Ranger*, was one of the first times three attack carriers had been deployed in the North. One of the targets most struck—and most heavily defended—was the Thanh Hoa Bridge, a massive structure spanning the Song Ma River in Thanh Hoa province. The Vietnamese nicknamed the bridge "Ham Rong"—Dragon's Jaw—and it lived up to its name. Between 1965 and 1972, 873 strikes were flown against the Dragon's Jaw. In the 75-square-mile area around the bridge, an estimated 104 U.S. Navy and Air Force airmen were shot down. Although the bridge took hundreds of hits, rockets and bombs seemed to ricochet off the massive steel structure. Not until 1972 was the Dragon's Jaw finally destroyed by Air Force F-4s and Navy A-4s dropping 2,000-pound laser-guided bombs.

Another target, the anti-aircraft site on the peak of Cape Falaise, on the coast of North Vietnam, was a source of ongoing pain. *Intrepid*'s three Skyraider losses were attributed to the guns at Cape Falaise. But the Spads kept returning, and persistence finally paid off. The Spads' precise delivery of lethal 2,000-pound "fat" bombs finally put most of the Cape Falaise air defense site into the South China Sea.

When air intel officer Scott Allen debriefed *Intrepid*'s pilots after strikes, he liked to record the sessions on tape. While their memories were fresh and adrenaline still surged in their veins, pilots gave real-time intel data about SAM sites, gun emplacements, and targets of interest they'd just observed. Allen knew how to stimulate the airmen's memories. With the collaboration of *Intrepid*'s flight surgeon, they dispensed rations of "medicinal" alcohol. Allen's debriefing tapes often had in the background the telltale squeak of caps twisting off bottles, followed by the soft tinkle of ice plopping into glasses. Some pilots, he found, tended to stretch the debriefings out as long as possible.

Intrepid remained on Yankee Station. The days of close air support missions, dodging nothing heavier than small-arms fire and dropping fat bombs on undefended targets, were over. For the rest of her deployment *Intrepid* alternated line periods on Yankee Station with port calls in Yokosuka, Japan; Hong Kong; and the now-familiar Subic Bay.

While the aircraft carriers of the Seventh Fleet were delivering tons of conventional bombs and rockets on Vietnam, they were prepared for war on a wider scale. The war in Southeast Asia was viewed by the Pentagon as a manifestation of America's larger engagement in the Cold War.

Each attack carrier carried a store of nuclear weapons. USS *Intrepid* was no exception. *Intrepid*'s nukes resided in a heavily guarded compartment directly beneath the officers' wardroom. Lt. Cdr. Scott Allen was the custodian of the nuclear authentication codes, and at regular intervals the ship's senior officers would have to conduct tedious authentication drills, just in case.

Finally came the day—October 18, 1966—when *Intrepid* turned her bow southward and left Yankee Station. After nearly eight months away, she was going home. In forty-one days of operations in North Vietnam, *Intrepid*'s attack planes had flown 2,595 combat missions, dropping 3,704 tons of ordnance.

The Seventh Fleet's oldest attack carrier, embarking a wing of ancient Douglas attack planes, had posted one of the most impressive records of the war. On one exceptional day, her catapult crews launched an entire strike from her two catapults with an average of twenty-six seconds between launches, better than the big-deck ships with their four catapults. Unlike her sister ships on Yankee Station, neither of *Intrepid*'s catapults had delivered a "cold" catapult shot—shooting an airplane with insufficient flying speed off her bow and into the sea. For *Intrepid*'s extraordinary performance in combat operations, Capt. John Fair, who had railed against sending his ship up north, was awarded the Legion of Merit.

Homeward she sailed, retracing her route across the Indian Ocean and through the Suez Canal. En route through the canal, *Intrepid* received a visiting delegation of senior officers from the Egyptian Ministry of Defense. The guests were treated to a drill by the ship's Marine detachment and a tour of the ship. One of the visitors, resplendent in riding uniform and carrying a whip, was the commander of the MiG-21 wing from Helwan Air Base. He wanted to see the airplanes that he heard had engaged the MiGs in Vietnam.

The Egyptian officer was taken to the flight deck and shown the Spads. The four that had fought the MiGs had kill symbols painted on their fuselages. The Egyptian was incredulous that these old airplanes had shot down a MiG-17, and wanted to know what sort of devices had been installed in the A-1s to allow them such an incredible victory.

None, he was told. None except four skilled pilots and sixteen 20-mm guns. The Egyptian refused to believe it.

Intrepid left the Suez and entered the Mediterranean, passed Gibraltar, and on November 21, 1966, put into Mayport, Florida, for five hours—long enough to debark the men and planes of Air Wing 10. A storm slowed her progress northward, but at 1400 on November 23 the great gray shape of *Intrepid* appeared in the entrance to the Norfolk Naval Station.

A crowd of nearly 3,000 was waiting at her old berth at Pier 12, including Adm. Tom Moorer, commander, Atlantic Fleet, and Vice Adm. C. T. Booth, Naval Air Forces, Atlantic.

The presence of the heavy brass was nice, thought the men of *Intrepid*, but it didn't matter. What mattered were the wives, kids, and girlfriends waving and cheering. It was a joyous homecoming, almost as joyous as those of a generation before when *Intrepid*'s men returned from war in the Pacific. Christmas was a month away, and they were home. They could forget about Vietnam and sea duty and Yankee Station.

But not for long. Five months, to be exact.

★ 25 ★

Rolling Thunder

This time was different. The Egyptians weren't friendly. In fact, they were howling mad.

The men aboard *Intrepid* could see them lined up on the banks of the Suez, waving shoes over their heads, spitting on the ground, hurling insults at the gray warship gliding past them. Egyptian torpedo boats were zigzagging across *Intrepid*'s bow like terriers chasing a car.

It was June 1967, and another war was about to ignite, this one in the Middle East. The Egyptian army, along with the armies of Syria and Jordan and troops from most of the Arab countries, was massing in the Sinai for what appeared to be an invasion of Israel. The United States, in the view of the Arab countries, had allied itself with Israel. Now Egyptians were venting their anger at the highly visible symbol of the United States passing their shore.

Intrepid had left Norfolk on May 11, 1967, on her long voyage back to Vietnam. It was a now-familiar route—eastward across the Atlantic, past the hulking rock of Gibraltar, and on through the Suez Canal. But instead of entering the canal, she stopped in the eastern Mediterranean, with orders to remain clear of the canal. There she stayed for the first days of June 1967 while the U.S. Sixth Fleet and the commander, Naval Forces Europe, evaluated their options. War was likely. What were U.S. forces supposed to do?

"We've got *Intrepid,* a combat ready carrier in the Med," the commander flashed to Washington. "Can we keep her?"

They could. No one knew what would happen, or what the United States' role ought to be. *Intrepid*'s attack planes were loaded with bombs and pilots were put on standby, all poised for a strike on an unspecified target for an undetermined purpose.

The uncertainty lasted two more days, and then *Intrepid* received orders to transit the Suez Canal—and do it quickly. Relations with Egypt were deteriorating. War in the Sinai was imminent.

With epithet-yelling, shoe-waving Arabs lining the shore, *Intrepid* and her destroyer escort slid through the canal, then into the Red Sea, harassed all the way by Egyptian warships and aircraft.

She just made it. On June 5, as *Intrepid* was exiting the Red Sea and entering the Indian Ocean, the Six-Day War between Israel and the Arab nations exploded. *Intrepid* and her escort would be the last American ships to pass through the Suez Canal for eight years.

Since *Intrepid*'s last combat deployment, America's commitment in Vietnam had grown more costly and more controversial. Protesters were taking to the streets. The bombing campaign in North Vietnam, called Operation Rolling Thunder, was exacting a toll on both sides. Lyndon Johnson and his "best and brightest" team were determined to bring North Vietnam to its knees, and every attack carrier was being rotated back to the Tonkin Gulf on short turnarounds.

During *Intrepid*'s brief respite between deployments, she had gone through another overhaul in the Norfolk Naval Shipyard at Portsmouth. Then came a quick series of four-day exercises to get ready for her operational readiness inspection. The same month, April 1967, *Intrepid* received word that the ship had again won the Battle Efficiency "E." By now this was no big deal—it was the third year in a row. To the men of *Intrepid,* it was just a replay of the old days when she beat her sister *Essex*-class carriers at the ASW game. Now she was beating the big-deck carriers at the attack game.

Some hard lessons had been learned during the previous combat deployment. Small deck or not, she needed fighters of her own. Relying on other carriers' fighters to escort her attack aircraft was awkward and, as in the case of the Skyraiders at Cape Falaise, potentially catastrophic. The hodgepodge composition of her air wing (CVG-10) now included a detachment of supersonic F-8 Crusaders from VF-111. Experience had also shown that she needed her own photo reconnaissance capability, so she now carried a detachment of RF-8 photo-Crusaders.

Except for VA-15, none of the air wing's squadrons from the first deployment were still aboard. An A-4B squadron, VSF-3, which had originally been formed to deploy in detachments aboard antisubmarine carriers, was now assigned as a pure attack unit aboard *Intrepid*. Two additional A-4 Skyhawk squadrons, VA-34 and VA-66 from Cecil Field, were assigned to the air wing. To make room for the extra Skyhawk squadron, only one A-1 squadron, VA-145, was embarked. The days of the Spad aboard Navy attack carriers were almost over.

This time the air wing included the traditional "cats and dogs"— detachments of E-1B Tracer early-warning aircraft, electronic warfare EA1-F Guppies, and UH-2A Seasprite helicopters.

Nothing on Yankee Station had gotten easier. The sky over North Vietnam contained the same perils as before, except that it had become deadlier. By 1967 North Vietnam had more than 300 SA-2 surface-to-air missile sites concentrated around vital targets. The sites were linked by a network of communications, air alert stations, early-warning ground control interceptors, and fire control radars.

The list of killed and captured American pilots was steadily growing.

Intrepid's A-1 Spads were being assigned to more and more search-and-rescue missions, which were often more dangerous than actual strike missions over North Vietnam. Rescue attempts turned into vicious traps in which the downed airman *and* his would-be rescuers were all lost.

Morale of the aircrews had become a factor in operations from

Yankee Station. Pilots flying almost daily strikes into North Vietnam were acutely aware that their targets were being selected by officials back in Washington who had only the vaguest sense of value versus risk. Targets that *should* have been hit—ammunition supply ships, MiG fighter bases in Hanoi, the docks of Haiphong—were off-limits.

Adding to airman discontent was the ongoing bomb shortage. It had become so bad that the United States had to buy back from Germany large stocks of conventional ordnance sold under NATO contract. Soon after *Intrepid*'s arrival on Dixie Station in 1966, they had run out of napalm, a highly effective close air support weapon. Even "dumb" bombs—500 pounds, 1,000 pounds, 2,000 pounds—were in such short supply that they were rationed among strike aircraft. A-4s capable of carrying 8,000 pounds of ordnance were launching with a single Mark 82 500-pounder on each wing.

The belief was growing stronger among the pilots that their mission was not so much to inflict damage on the enemy but to rack up an impressive number of sorties flown. Just as the generals in Saigon were equating success with enemy body count, the officers running the air war were impressing the Pentagon with numbers of missions.

On a steamy afternoon in June 1967, *Intrepid* took a short break in the action. John Fair removed his engineer's cap, donned his summer white uniform, and turned over *Intrepid* to her new skipper, Capt. William J. McVey.

The name "Rolling Thunder" had a sonorous, Wagnerian ring to it, and deliberately so. It was the bombing campaign against North Vietnam that lasted from March 2, 1965, four weeks after Lyndon Johnson's election as president, until November 1, 1968, when Johnson ordered a halt to the operation. Its stated threefold purpose was to persuade the North Vietnamese to cease their support for the Communist insurgency in the South; to destroy North Vietnam's transportation, industrial, and air defense systems; and to interdict the flow of troops and supplies to the South.

Rolling Thunder was the most difficult aerial campaign flown by

U.S. military aircraft in the Cold War. The operation was plagued by seasonal foul weather, an erratic on-again, off-again course by Washington, and the most deadly air defense network ever faced by American airmen. Nearly 400 Navy airplanes were shot down in Rolling Thunder, and 450 Navy airmen killed or captured.

Flying from Yankee Station, *Intrepid*'s pilots hit targets from the demilitarized zone near the border between North and South Vietnam all the way to the border of China. The A-4s struck bridges, military warehouses, industrial complexes, railroad lines, highways, and military bases.

Two key targets were the Hon Gai and Ben Thuy thermal power plants. Others were army barracks and SAM storage areas around Hanoi, the Port Wallut naval base near the Chinese border, and Haiphong's Kien An MiG base. *Intrepid* pilots picked up a name for themselves: "bridge busters." They dropped four major bridges fanning out from Haiphong, along with a bypass bridge built to replace one that had been previously destroyed.

Ken Burrows was now the "old man" of the air wing. With 135 combat missions to his credit, he was one of the few Vietnam-era CAGs to put in two successive combat deployments. He had led his air wing continuously since taking command in June 1966, before *Intrepid* was ordered for the first time north to Yankee Station, and would still be in command when she returned to the United States.

By now Burrows had earned the respect of his pilots. "He was a no-bullshit, organized, disciplined senior commander," recalled Lt. (jg) Bernie Fipp, a VA-34 Skyhawk pilot. One of the things Burrows insisted on was "zip-lip," or radio-silent operation. "No gab whatsoever on the air around the boat and over the beach," remembered Fipp, "unless it was an emergency or critical information." Zip-lip was tough discipline for adrenaline-charged young pilots in combat. Sometimes it was just as tough when they returned to the ship.

Standing on the LSO platform, Lt. (jg) R. R. "Boom" Powell squinted into the hazy sunlight. *Intrepid* was heading into the wind to recover aircraft returning from strikes. Powell was an LSO trainee, which meant he assisted the qualified LSOs, checking for them whether the deck was clear for the next landing and dutifully recording their comments in a notebook that they used later to debrief the pilots.

Boom Powell was a twenty-three-year-old nugget on his first combat deployment. He'd gotten his wings, gone to the Replacement Air Group at NAS Lemoore to learn to fly the A-4 Skyhawk, then been assigned to VSF-3, whose original mission was to fly fighter cover aboard ASW carriers such as *Intrepid*. Now VSF-3's mission was the same as the other A-4 squadrons—flying strikes against targets in Vietnam.

Powell liked it out here on the platform. This was where the action was. You saw everything out here—combat-damaged planes streaming fuel, gear or flaps or tailhook inoperative, pieces missing from the airplanes. Sometimes the LSO had to sugar-talk a stressed-out pilot to get him back aboard.

Powell was watching an A-4 in the groove, a quarter mile behind the ship. There was something wrong with this jet. The guy had shown up all by himself, landing gear and tailhook extended. They were operating zip-lip, but it wasn't an unbreakable rule. If the pilot was in trouble, he could break radio silence.

This pilot in the groove hadn't radioed any indication that he was in trouble, but now Powell could see why. The A-4's nose was missing—which explained why he wasn't talking on the radio, since the radios were in the nose compartment.

As the jet flew closer to the ramp, Powell wondered how the thing stayed in the air. The entire front section of the jet was gone, shot away. There was just the blunt, flat bulkhead ahead of the cockpit.

It was Powell's job to inform the LSO whether the landing deck was clear or not. It wasn't. Powell saw that the jet that landed previously was still trying to get clear of the arresting cables. "Foul deck!" he warned the LSO.

The LSO nodded, keeping his eye on the incoming jet. He'd keep it coming, hoping the deck would clear in time.

It didn't. The damaged A-4 was almost at the ramp. The deck was still fouled.

Damn. The LSO flashed the red wave-off lights and transmitted, "Wave off! Wave off!" even though he knew the A-4 pilot couldn't hear him.

As the noseless, radioless jet staggered back into the sky, Powell saw just how badly shot up it really was. Not only was the nose shot away, but the rest of the jet was full of holes. He was wondering again how the A-4 managed to keep flying when, abruptly, it didn't, suddenly pitching over like a shotgunned pigeon. Powell saw the dark shape of the pilot eject from the cockpit. The white canopy of the parachute blossomed for two seconds before the pilot splashed into the sea off *Intrepid*'s port quarter. Seconds later, the plane guard helicopter was over the pilot, snatching him back out of the water.

Powell shrugged and turned his attention to the next jet in the groove. He was too busy to reflect on what happened. The guy was okay, and that was all that mattered. Just another day on Yankee Station.

In 104 such days on Yankee Station, Air Wing 10 expended more than 10 million pounds of ordnance on North Vietnamese targets, flying more than 9,000 missions and logging 17,400 hours of flight time.

But not without a bitter price. Whereas the previous combat deployment had produced very few losses, this time was different. Three A-4Bs of VSF-3 were shot down, as were nine A-4Cs from the other two squadrons. Three of the pilots were lucky. Lt. (jg) A. D. Perkins, Lt. (jg) R. W. Gerard, and Lt. Cdr. S. H. Hawkins all were snatched to safety by heroic search-and-rescue teams. Three other Skyhawk pilots—Lt. (jg) Fred Kasch, Lt. Phil Craig, and Lt. LeGrande Cole Jr.—were killed in action. Three more—Lt. Cdr. Pete Schoeffel, Lt. Cdr. Ed Martin, and Lt. Denny Key—spent the rest of the war as POWs.

In December 1967, a sober and war-weary *Intrepid* turned south and headed for home. As before, she cruised across the Indian Ocean, but this time she turned south, toward the Cape of Good Hope at the tip of Africa. The Israeli-Arab war of June that year had ended in only six days, but the Suez Canal was now closed to U.S. warships. The added distance meant that *Intrepid* would spend Christmas at sea.

On December 30, after eight months at war, the familiar gray silhouette of USS *Intrepid* glided toward her pier at the Norfolk Naval Station. The joy of the men on her deck and the 3,000 family members waiting to greet them was unbounded.

While the snows of winter descended on Virginia, *Intrepid* went into the shipyard at nearby Portsmouth for another refurbishment of her machinery, upgrades to her electronics array, and modernization of her quarter-century-old spaces. The crew had five precious months to become reacquainted with their families before returning to the business of war in Southeast Asia.

In January 1968, they threw a welcome-home bash at the Virginia Beach Civic Center complete with dancing girls, music, and lots to drink. Everyone loved it, including the officers and especially Captain McVey, who came with his wife and grinned his way through the evening.

It was a great way for everyone to unwind. It also helped take their minds off what was happening half a world away.

What was happening was a holiday called Tet. In observance of the Vietnamese lunar new year, each side had agreed to a temporary cease-fire. Then in the predawn darkness of January 31, 1968, South Vietnam exploded like a powder keg. Every city and every major U.S. and South Vietnamese base was under siege. Over a thousand Viet Cong troops infiltrated the city of Saigon and seized part of the U.S. embassy. To the north, Viet Cong captured the Citadel in the ancient city of Hue.

Stunned Americans watched the fragmented news reports from Vietnam. Polls were already showing that half the population opposed the war. Americans had become disaffected by the mounting loss of young lives, the huge monetary cost, and the seemingly endless nature of the conflict. Protesters had taken to the streets, marching on Washington and picketing military bases.

Now this. On television they were watching their own embassy in Saigon being occupied by the enemy. The war seemed to be spiraling out of control.

The fighting raged on for two weeks. In the end, Tet amounted to a colossal military defeat for the Communist forces, but it no longer mattered. It marked a turning point in the war. It was the beginning of America's disenchantment not just with the war but with the administration that had taken them into Vietnam.

On March 31, 1969, President Johnson, who had been campaigning for reelection, went on television to declare that he would not seek another term as president. In the same speech, he announced that he was suspending all bombing attacks above the 12th parallel, which meant bombing would continue in the lower portion of North Vietnam but not in Hanoi and Haiphong. And then Johnson announced that he'd authorized the opening of peace negotiations with North Vietnam.

For the men of *Intrepid,* nothing had changed. Like a relentless ticking clock, the days before they deployed were slipping away. Peace negotiations or not, *Intrepid* would return to Yankee Station.

When the ship emerged from her overhaul in Portsmouth, the crew had to undergo an annual ordeal called the admin inspection, wherein each department's records received a going-over by a team of inspectors from AIRLANT—Naval Air Forces, Atlantic—and were then given a grade. In war or peace, some things in the Navy never changed.

Intrepid headed for her traditional training site in the warm seas around Guantánamo Bay. Embarked again was Air Wing 10, still a mixed bag of attack and fighter planes. CAG Burrows had been relieved in January by Cdr. J. A. Chalbeck, who had been an attack pilot and a Skyhawk squadron skipper.

Finally gone were the slow, lumbering Spads. From now on, *Intrepid*'s attack planes would all be A-4 Skyhawks. Three new squadrons were embarked—VA-36 and VA-66, both flying A-4C Skyhawks, and VA-106 with new A-4Es. The A-4E was an upgraded Skyhawk with a more powerful J-52 engine, two extra ordnance stations beneath its wings, and a "humpback" upper fuselage compartment for added avionics.

Back were the fighters—a detachment of F-8C Crusaders and

photo reconaissance RF-8Gs. Also aboard were early-warning E-1B Tracers—called "Willie Fudds" because of their previous designation, WF—and a detachment of elderly EA-1E electronic warfare Guppies.

Intrepid spent two weeks drilling in Gitmo, rehearsing the wartime basics—fire drills, abandon-ship drills, man-overboard drills—as well as giving her airedales a refresher course in carrier operations. Then she returned to the waters off Mayport and drilled some more.

On June 4, 1968, the drills were over. *Intrepid* was headed south on her third voyage to Vietnam.

Alpha Strike

If you had to go to war, *Intrepid*'s crew agreed, you might as well take the scenic route. And it didn't get any more scenic than this. Corcovado Mountain and Rio's famous Sugar Loaf pinnacle jutted in the background. Around them spread the strikingly lovely Guanabara Bay of Rio de Janeiro, Brazil.

Intrepid's destination was the same, but the route had changed. The Suez Canal was closed and would stay closed to U.S. warships for several more years. Instead of crossing the North Atlantic to enter the Mediterranean, *Intrepid* had headed south, stopping in Rio.

It was an exotic change of venue for the men of *Intrepid*—and a suitable place for a change of command. Almost exactly a year ago Capt. Bill McVey had stood in this same spot beneath *Intrepid*'s island when he relieved John Fair. They were under way then—in formation with *Intrepid*'s carrier group on Yankee Station—and the ceremony was necessarily brief. McVey's relief, Capt. Vincent F. Kelley, had a personal knowledge of the situation in Vietnam. He'd been the deputy chief of staff for plans at the Military Assistance Command in Saigon.

With her new captain at the helm, *Intrepid* set off for the Far East, rounding the tip of Africa, making her usual provisioning and arming stop in Subic Bay. She arrived on Yankee Station at 2300 on July 23, 1968.

At dawn the next morning, it was business as usual. The voice of the air boss boomed over the darkened flight deck. "Good morning, gentlemen. In fifteen seconds the time will be zero-five-forty-five. Stand by . . . *mark*. Flight deck temperature eighty-three degrees. Helmets on, goggles on, sleeves rolled down. Stand by to start jets. . . ."

Thus began *Intrepid*'s third time around. The mission was the same: cut enemy supply lines to the South—bridges, roads, ferries, railroads. Throughout the day, every hour and a half, the launch and recovery cycle was repeated. It was grueling and dangerous work. Flight deck crews labored in deadly proximity to howling jets, afterburners, catapults, arresting gear cables, and high explosives.

So far *Intrepid* had been spared the horrific accidents that befell other carriers on Yankee Station. A fire ignited on *Oriskany* as two seamen were returning unused parachute flares to a storage locker. The blaze leaped into the nearby hangar bay, touched off other ordnance, and burned through three levels, reaching the officers' staterooms. Many of the pilots who'd just returned from the strike were caught, unable to escape. Forty-four men aboard *Oriskany* were killed, including the Air Wing 16 commander.

Several months later *Forrestal* was readying jets for a strike when a Zuni rocket accidentally fired from an F-4 Phantom. The rocket hit the external fuel tank of a Skyhawk occupied by a former *Intrepid* pilot, Lt. Cdr. John McCain. The tank exploded in flames, spilling over the flight deck, igniting bombs and rockets and engulfing the entire aft end of the ship. McCain managed to jump from his cockpit, roll through the sheet of flames, and escape the inferno.

It took an hour to extinguish the fires on *Forrestal*'s flight deck, but secondary fires below took twelve more hours to contain. When the dead and wounded were finally counted, 134 men had lost their lives. Twenty-one aircraft were destroyed and forty-three damaged. *Forrestal* was out of the war, rotated back to Norfolk, where the cost to repair her was placed at $72 million.

One of the squadrons aboard *Forrestal* then was VA-106, now embarked on *Intrepid*. The squadron lost eight men in the fire. By now every crewman on *Intrepid*'s deck knew what happened to *Oriskany* and *Forrestal*. Could it happen to their ship? Yes, if they were careless. Or unlucky.

So far *Intrepid* had been lucky.

Her luck held. In the daily grind of launching and recovering aircraft on Yankee Station, handling deadly high-explosive ordnance on the flight and hangar decks, there were no serious accidents.

There were combat losses, but not in the number other ships and squadrons were enduring. On August 1, 1968, Lt. (jg) Edward J. Broms of VA-66 was shot down by anti-aircraft fire over the North. For nearly three more months the A-4 squadrons flew missions over the North without another combat loss. The string was broken on October 21 when Lt. Ken Knabb flew his Skyhawk into the ground on a strafing run. He was VA-106's first combat loss since World War II. Knabb and Broms were listed as missing in action, but neither was ever seen again.

In the next few weeks, more airplanes were lost, but in each case the pilot was rescued. One of the losses happened in late August, and it wasn't in combat.

Shortly after midnight on August 20, 1968, Cdr. Hawley Brooks and his wingman, Lt. (jg) Rich Holden, catapulted off *Intrepid* on a night mission over the North. Brooks was the skipper of the VA-36 Roadrunners, a veteran A-4 squadron that had already made one combat deployment aboard *Enterprise*. So far the Roadrunners had had good fortune, taking no losses on their *Intrepid* deployment.

Brooks and Holden threaded their way inland, jinking the whole time, only to find the target area obscured in thunderstorms and low clouds. With indications of SAMs firing at them they were forced to jettison their bombs and take evasive action.

On the way back to *Intrepid*, they were getting a time hack from the ship's controller when Brooks felt a thump on his port side. Startled, he looked out to see the round yellow tailpipe of his wingman as the plane dove past him out of control. Seconds later, Brooks heard Holden radio that he had regained control, but his

Skyhawk was barely flyable. The young pilot, distracted for a moment in the inky blackness over the Tonkin Gulf, had collided with Brooks's jet.

Brooks was having troubles of his own. His left wing was badly damaged, spewing fuel, and he needed full right aileron trim to keep the Skyhawk from rolling out of control. He heard the voice of Vince Kelley, Intrepid's captain, come over the radio. The two crippled A-4s were cleared for an immediate landing.

Holden, whose aircraft seemed to be the most badly damaged, made the first pass at the ship. It didn't work. Forced to eject from the damaged jet, Holden floated down in his parachute so low over the ship he could shout to the crewmen on the deck. He splashed into the black water directly behind the carrier.

While the helo was searching for Holden, Brooks brought his own damaged jet aboard, 20 knots too fast, plunking it down to snatch the first arresting wire. He was still in the cockpit, pleased to be alive, when he heard that Captain Kelley wanted to see him.

"Where do you think we are?" Kelley asked when Brooks reported to the bridge.

Brooks shrugged. "Somewhere in the Tonkin Gulf."

"How about fifteen miles from North Vietnam?"

Brooks's eyes widened. To get the damaged Skyhawks back aboard, the captain had kept Intrepid into the wind, on a westerly course toward the shoreline. They had come almost within stone-throwing range of North Vietnam.

Brooks thanked the skipper. A few minutes later he thanked the helo crew that had just hauled his shaken wingman out of the Tonkin Gulf. Brooks's own jet would never fly again. For the rest of the cruise it would be used for spare parts, then scrapped.

The next day Brooks and Holden resumed flying combat missions. The experience had brought Rich Holden to a career decision. To hell with the war. He was going to become a doctor.

The two Vietnams were visited by regular monsoon seasons, and they were on almost opposite schedules. In the winter the northeast monsoon descended from China to engulf North Vietnam in low ceilings and drizzle. Combat flight operations became problematic, and only all-weather bombers such as the A-6 Intruder could reach their targets with any kind of accuracy. Weather in the South during North Vietnam's monsoon season was more benign, and commanders on both sides used the alternating weather patterns to their advantage. North Vietnam was able to shuttle supplies and troop reinforcements down the trails to the South without heavy interdiction from American planes. American commanders used the good weather in the South to hammer Viet Cong positions from the air and consolidate their gains on the ground.

While the summer weather in the Tonkin Gulf was usually clear, the downside was the heat and humidity. Unlike the big-deck carriers, *Intrepid* didn't have central air-conditioning. Work spaces, particularly those just beneath the flight deck, were oppressively hot. Some of the spaces were jury-rigged with window-unit air conditioners, which exhausted hot air into the passageways. Living quarters could be miserably hot, and crewmen sought out spaces near vents and open bay doors where they might catch the slightest breeze.

Boom Powell shared a junior officer bunk room with seven others in the forward area they called "Boys Town." "We had a Sears and Roebuck air conditioner stuck right into the bulkhead," said Powell. "It worked okay, lowering the temperature a few degrees. The problem was, it exhausted directly into the next compartment next door—the officers' head—and turned it into a permanent sauna."

Lt. Cdr. Linn Felt, *Intrepid*'s strike operations officer, had been an A-4 pilot in VA-34 before reporting aboard the carrier. He had a room under the flight deck. Working eighteen-hour days, he'd try to grab a nap between launch cycles. He didn't have to worry about oversleeping. Directly over his head was one of the steam catapults. Each time the catapult fired, he got another wake-up call.

Most of the missions over the north were Alpha strikes. These were large-scale operations focusing most of the carrier's strike force on a single target complex, usually in coordination with other carriers. *Intrepid* would launch as many as three Alpha strikes a day from Yankee Station. Each strike involved twenty or more Skyhawk bombers with Crusader fighter escorts taking position on either side of the strike force. In advance of the main force would go the "Iron Hands"—designated anti-SAM aircraft and flak suppressors. Orbiting offshore were the A-4 tankers carrying "buddy stores"— refueling packs from which they could extend a hose and pass fuel to the returning strike birds.

SAMs and heavy anti-aircraft fire went with the territory. Going in first, the flak suppressors would try to spot the muzzle flashes of the big guns and hit them with Zuni missiles or Rockeye cluster bombs. Meanwhile, the main force would divide, attacking the target from at least three directions. The Skyhawks would plunge down in a 45-to-65-degree dive, releasing their bombs at about 4,500 feet, pulling up hard so as not to go lower than about 2,800 feet above the ground. Then they ran like hell. They tried to rejoin in pairs, climbing and jinking, resisting the urge to fly straight toward the beach and the safety of the open sea. A straight course made them predictable, easy to track and shoot down. Speed and altitude were their friends. Speed gave them the kinetic energy to keep jinking—flying an erratic, flak-dodging path. Altitude gave them time to glide if, God forbid, they took a hit and lost their engine.

When things went well, it took only a few minutes to exit North Vietnam. When things didn't go well, it might take years. When things went very badly, as it did for some, it took forever.

After what seemed like several eternities came the radio call: "Feet wet." It meant they were over water, away from the guns and SAMs. Time to resume breathing and check for battle damage: hung bombs, telltale streams of hydraulic fluid or fuel, then refocus on the mundane but demanding task of plugging into the tanker's refueling drogue before landing back aboard a tiny flight deck in the middle of the Tonkin Gulf.

It was already known that carrier landings, particularly at night, induced more stress than combat missions. Physiologists had gone so far as to wire up pilots flying missions over North Vietnam, and the result came as no surprise, at least to the pilots. Their pulse rates spiked the highest during the last thirty seconds of landing aboard the carrier.

All the more reason, pilots concluded, for the time-honored debriefing enhancer—the flight surgeon's ration of medicinal alcohol.

"MiG-21 high!"

The voice of Lt. Tony Nargi crackled on the radio. A second later, he heard his wingman, Lt. (jg) Alex Rucker, acknowledge the call. The two Crusader pilots had just left their CAP station, where they had been covering an A-4 strike force from *Intrepid*. The airborne controller had warned them about an incoming MiG threat.

Tony Nargi was a tall, good-looking young man of Italian lineage. Like two other VF-111 pilots on *Intrepid*, Nargi was on his second consecutive combat deployment. This was Alex Rucker's first combat cruise. Most Crusader pilots, given a choice, preferred flying off the big-deck carriers, but not Rucker. He'd actually volunteered for the *Intrepid* deployment. His brother, Lt. (jg) Bill Rucker, was also on *Intrepid* as a communications officer.

The noses of the VF-111 Crusaders were painted with ferocious shark's-mouth grins and glowering eyeballs, a takeoff on the Flying Tigers nose art of World War II. The squadron name, Sundowners, dated back to World War II, when they were renowned for shooting down "suns"—the red balls on Japanese wings.

So far the war had been frustrating for the fighter pilots. It was an all-attack war, which meant long hours of escorting the A-4 to their targets and flying tiresome CAP orbits to protect them from the MiGs, which almost never came out to fight. The only MiGs any of *Intrepid*'s pilots had encountered were on her first cruise, and the attack airplanes—clunky propeller-driven Spads—had dispatched the MiGs with no assistance from real fighters.

Now it was September 19, 1968, three months into *Intrepid*'s third combat cruise, and the MiGs had finally shown up.

Nargi shoved the throttle up on the Crusader and climbed toward the incoming enemy fighters. The MiG-21—code-named "Fishbed"—was the most formidable of the North Vietnamese fighters. Most kills had been against the aging MiG-17, a subsonic late-1950s fighter. The sleek MiG-21 was a next-generation fighter capable of speeds in excess of Mach 2 and was at least a match for the F-8 Crusader. But the MiG-21 had been designed as an interceptor, not a dogfighter. Unlike the tight-turning MiG-17, the MiG-21 depended on high energy to attack, then get out fast.

By 1968 North Vietnam had established a network of 200 air defense radar sites that gave them complete radar coverage of the country. North Vietnamese pilots took their tactics from the Eastern Bloc air forces, maneuvering in four-plane divisions strung out in a line-astern column. U.S. Navy fighter pilots learned to capitalize on this tactic, going after the number one MiG, then the others in succession.

Nargi and Rucker were flying a "loose-deuce" formation, spread laterally about a mile apart, with the wingman crossing from side to side to keep the cone behind them clear. Loose-deuce was a refinement of the World War II Thach weave—the fighters continually clearing each other's aft sector—that succeeded brilliantly against Japanese Zeroes.

Nargi and the lead MiG pilot spotted each other at the same time. The MiG went into a hard evasive turn, with Nargi closing on him, trying to maneuver into a position behind him to fire an AIM-9 Sidewinder heat-seeking missile. After half a circle of turn, the MiG pilot sensed that he was losing ground and pulled the MiG-21 into a high-G loop.

That was a bad move, as Nargi followed the MiG into the loop. Using the Crusader's tighter turning ability, he pulled up into the firing cone behind the MiG. He heard the growling tone in his headset that told him the missile's infrared sensor was locked on, and squeezed the trigger.

In the next instant the Sidewinder leaped from the rail on the Crusader's fuselage, leaving a zigzag smoke trail. Nargi watched his heat-seeking missile streak toward the fleeing MiG-21. The Sidewinder had only an 8-pound warhead. To cause lethal damage, it had to score a direct hit or be detonated by its proximity fuse close to the target.

Nargi's Sidewinder scored a direct hit. He saw the tail separate, and the burning hulk of the MiG plummeted toward the earth. Seconds later, a figure ejected from the flaming wreckage and an orange-and-white parachute canopy blossomed.

But the fight wasn't over. A second MiG-21 swept toward the pair of Crusaders. Again the F-8 pilots pulled inside the MiG's wide, overshooting turn, and each fired a Sidewinder. They saw both missiles explode just behind the MiG's tail. The MiG kept flying. The Sidewinders had detonated too far behind the MiG to mortally wound it. Frustrated, Nargi and Rucker watched the MiG escape to the north, accelerating in full afterburner, joining his two surviving wingmen, who had already exited the fight.

The Crusader pilots landed back aboard *Intrepid* to a tumultuous welcome. Nargi had scored the Navy's twenty-ninth MiG kill of the war, for which he was decorated with the Silver Star. It also happened to be the eighteenth confirmed aerial victory for the F-8 Crusader—and, as it turned out, the last. The sleek Crusader, last of the classic Navy gunfighters, was on its way out. Every aerial victory for the rest of the war would be won by the new McDonnell F-4 Phantom.

Twelve days later, Rolling Thunder ended.

In a televised address on the evening of October 31, 1968, five days before the U.S. presidential election, Lyndon Johnson announced the unconditional cessation of "all air, naval, and artillery bombardment of North Vietnam." For several weeks U.S. negotiators had been meeting with North Vietnamese representatives in Paris. Finally Hanoi had agreed to allow the South Vietnamese to participate in the talks. Johnson, in turn, had consented to allow a role for the National Liberation Front—the Viet Cong—in the talks.

Cynics argued that Johnson was playing politics with the war, trying to tilt the coming election in favor of Hubert Humphrey, the Democratic candidate, who was lagging in the polls. Other cynics insisted that the Republican candidate, Richard Nixon, had tried to sabotage the negotiations by persuading South Vietnamese president Nguyen Van Thieu to disavow the bombing halt.

For *Intrepid,* which had already put in three line periods on Yankee Station, it meant she'd spend her last combat line period on Dixie Station, where she'd begun two years earlier. The schedule was just as heavy, flying air support missions for ground operations in South Vietnam. The threat of MiGs and SAMs and intense antiaircraft fire was replaced by the more subtle dangers of small-arms fire from the concealed enemy.

On November 24, after six months of war, *Intrepid* departed Dixie Station. After the usual stop at Subic Bay for unloading war provisions and reprovisioning for the voyage home, she headed for home.

Again, it was the scenic route, but instead of returning the way she came, she continued eastward, via Australia and New Zealand, taking Magellan's route around Cape Horn at the tip of South America, and stopping again at a now-favorite port, Rio de Janeiro. On a frigid winter day, February 8, 1969, *Intrepid* nudged against her berth at the Norfolk Naval Station, ending her 17,000-mile journey. In her voyage to and from Vietnam, *Intrepid* had circumnavigated the planet.

Though no one had yet said it, they all knew what was coming. *Intrepid*'s days as an attack carrier were over.

★ 27 ★

Hunter-Killer

Back to the Cold War hunt-and-kill anti-submarine games.

But first *Intrepid* needed some serious renovation. The strain of three combat deployments was showing. Her catapults, arresting gear, and main engines needed overhauling. Her teak flight deck was a mess and would have to be resurfaced. In her absence, the technology of anti-submarine warfare had evolved to a new level, and *Intrepid* required updating.

In February 1969, she entered the Philadelphia Naval Shipyard, which for the next five months became her home port. For most of the crew it was an idle summer. Many took apartments in Philadelphia. They stood watches aboard the ship and did little else except watch the shipfitters overhauling their carrier. Moored next to *Intrepid* was the World War II battleship *New Jersey*, which was being restored for duty in Vietnam. Several *Intrepid* crewmen were so fascinated by the famous warship they volunteered to return to Vietnam aboard her.

Refurbished and gleaming in new paint and teak flight deck, *Intrepid* was ready to leave Philadelphia. She had a new captain, Horus N. "Whitey" Moore Jr., who had relieved Vince Kelley on August 1. And she had a new home port—Quonset Point, Rhode Island, where she'd relieve *Yorktown* as the flagship of Carrier Division 16.

A patchy coastal fog hung over the northeast coast on the morning of September 9, 1969, the day *Intrepid* began her short voyage to Quonset Point. It was the ship's—and the captain's—first trip into Rhode Island's Narragansett Bay. As it turned out, it was a day Whitey Moore wished he could forget.

From *Intrepid*'s bridge, Moore could see the silhouette of Jamestown Island on the port side, and on the starboard side the towers and rooftops of Newport, but not much more. The morning fog still hadn't lifted. They moved from patches of fog into bright sunshine and back into fog. A harbor pilot had come aboard to guide the ship along the channel to the naval air station carrier pier.

Intrepid's arrival at Quonset Point had received a huge splash in the press. The media had turned out in full strength, and a crowd of nearly 10,000 waited on the pier. An assemblage of Navy brass and Rhode Island dignitaries including a congressman and a local mayor were there, as well as the throng of Navy families. A band was entertaining the crowd with a medley of perky marches and show tunes.

With sailors in dress whites lining the rails, *Intrepid* made her stately procession into the foggy bay, beneath the span of the Newport Bridge, along the shore of Jamestown Island. Because of the spotty visibility, the harbor pilot was "buoy hopping"—following the navigation markers that identified the channel to Quonset. *Intrepid* rounded the northern tip of Jamestown Island, then turned toward the pier at Quonset, where the reception waited.

On the ship's fantail, Fireman Apprentice Joe Richardson was looking straight down at the water behind *Intrepid*'s stern. What he saw didn't look right. A dense cloud of mud and silt was churning in the thin wake behind the carrier.

Richardson was a welder in the "R" division shipfitter shop. He was good at his job. In his words, he could "weld anything from a broken heart to the crack of dawn." Indeed, he'd just received a commendation from Captain Moore for his expert welding of steam pipes while *Intrepid* had been in the Philadelphia shipyard.

Now Richardson was staring at the ominous brown cloud beneath the fantail, wondering what it meant. In the next moment he knew. He felt a grinding, shuddering sensation. The ship stopped moving.

They had run aground.

From several hundred yards away, the guests and dignitaries on the pier could see the gray silhouette out there in the water. It wasn't getting any closer. Minutes passed. Then hours. It still didn't move. They could see boats swarming around the carrier, but the ship seemed fixed in position.

For the rest of the afternoon *Intrepid* remained stuck. The single little tugboat attending her couldn't pull her off. A seagoing tug from Boston was summoned.

Machinist's Mate Second Class Charlie Wladyka was one of the sailors standing on the number two elevator. "We amused ourselves flirting with the girls in the small craft that surrounded us," he remembered. "Some sailors lowered buckets and were rewarded with cold beer and blown kisses for their efforts, while others speculated about their first liberty in Quonset."

This went on for most of the afternoon. Joe Richardson went down to the hangar deck, where several hundred white-uniformed crewmen had gathered. Sailors being sailors, they were making the most of the occasion, wisecracking and making up ditties. Then someone passed the scuttlebutt that it was Captain Moore's birthday. Charlie Wladyka remembered the result. "Either out of frustration or dislike, the approximately six hundred men in the hangar bay broke into a spontaneous verse of 'Happy Birthday.' The Mormon Tabernacle Choir couldn't have done it better."

It took a combination of the high tide, a partial defueling of *Intrepid* to lessen her displacement, and strenuous hauling by the powerful tug from Boston to break the ship free. By the time she reached the pier at Quonset, it was nearly dark.

The music was finished. The guests and the dignitaries had gone home. "It looked like the day after a Super Bowl party," recalled Wladyka, "nothing but litter and a lone staff car flying a two-star flag." The boarding ladder was barely in place before a tight-lipped admiral in summer white uniform stormed aboard.

Whether the harbor pilot, the captain, the navigator, or all of them were at fault was not made public. The cause and effect were obvious: *Intrepid* had passed to the wrong side of a channel marker buoy. Other than the ingestion of muck and sand in the engine cooling intakes, there was no significant damage—except to egos and careers.

"To err is human," went an old Navy saying. "To forgive is not Navy policy." Captain Moore's tenure as skipper of *Intrepid* lasted only eight months. For years after the incident, bars and honky-tonks around Quonset Point advertised a special drink called "Intrepid on the Rocks."

Intrepid's crew loved the new base. The sprawling air station had been constructed at the beginning of World War II and served as a home port for ships and squadrons of the Navy's carrier anti-submarine force. At one time it had been the off-season headquarters of VX-6, the Navy's Antarctic Development Squadron, and in nearby Davisville was a Seabee—Construction Battalion—base. The base had given its name to the Quonset hut, the ubiquitous temporary structure put up around the world by the U.S. military.

Just as *Intrepid*'s crew had to relearn the attack business before going to Vietnam, now they had to relearn ASW. Operating in hunter-killer groups, anti-submarine carriers spent their time at sea tracking subs and running simulated kills. ASW was a tedious and often frustrating exercise. Sometimes you scored, and sometimes you were shut out.

In April 1971, *Intrepid* deployed to northern Europe with her new air wing, CVSG-56. Embarked again were the Grumman S-2E Trackers, which tradition-loving Navy men still called "Stoofs" after their old designation, S2F. Also aboard were the SH-3A Sea King helicopters and Grumman E-1B Tracers; the E-1B was called "Willie Fudd" or "Stoof-with-a-roof." *Intrepid* would also carry a "jet-det"—a detachment of five A-4 Skyhawks—to provide air cover.

The jets were an idea implemented in the early 1960s. Anti-submarine task groups had become easy targets for Soviet bombers such as the four-engine turboprop TU-95 Bears and jet-powered

M-4 Bisons and TU-16 Badgers, which liked to make passes over the ASW groups mainly to demonstrate that they could. The Skyhawks were configured to carry heat-seeking AIM-9 Sidewinders. With controllers aboard the E-1B Fudds vectoring the Skyhawks, *Intrepid* had its own onboard air defense system.

One of the A-4 pilots on *Intrepid* was Lt. Cdr. Larry "Worm" Elmore. He'd already made a Vietnam cruise, left the Navy to join the airlines, then found himself furloughed in the 1970s recession and airline cutbacks. Elmore was flying Skyhawks in the reserves when his old ops officer, Cdr. John "Pygmy" Paganelli, who now commanded the VA-45 Blackbirds, called with a job offer. Paganelli needed a seasoned A-4 pilot who was also an LSO to take a detachment of A-4s aboard USS *Intrepid*. Would Elmore consider coming back to active duty?

He did, and he never looked back. "It was the best deal I had in twenty years in the Navy," Elmore remembered.

For Navy men used to the steamy humidity of the Tonkin Gulf or the tossing seas of the North Atlantic, it was a cruise made in heaven. The first stops were Lisbon; Plymouth, England; and Kiel, Germany. Then in early summer they went into the Mediterranean for port calls in Naples, Cannes, and Barcelona. After that *Intrepid* sailed back to northern Europe, pulling into the legendary Scandinavian port of Copenhagen, back to Britain for several port calls, and across the North Sea to Bergen, Norway, before a visit to Scotland.

Much of *Intrepid*'s at-sea time was in the GIUK gap—the chokepoint in the ocean created by the landmasses of Greenland, Iceland, and the United Kingdom, through which Soviet ships and subs had to pass on the Atlantic route to the United States. *Intrepid*'s sub hunters hunted and tagged Soviet and NATO submarines, making numerous "blue nose" forays above the Arctic Circle.

If pursuing Soviet subs was exciting work, *being* pursued—not just by Soviet submarines—could be even more exciting. Almost daily came the announcement over the bullhorn: "A-4s to condition one!" The men of VA-45's Det One would scramble to get their

Skyhawks airborne within three minutes of the alert. Vectored by radar controllers, the little delta-wing fighters intercepted incoming Soviet aircraft. When the big bombers made their pass over the carrier, they were invariably in close formation with *Intrepid*'s fighters.

It became a favorite photo op. Hearing the scramble alert, *Intrepid* sailors would run to the gallery decks to snap photos of the low-flying swept-wing Soviet aircraft escorted by the tiny, Sidewinder-armed Skyhawks. During *Intrepid*'s North Atlantic deployment, they made more than 125 intercepts.

Some were repeat visitors. One day Worm Elmore intercepted a TU-95 Bear bomber over the North Sea. Elmore slid in so close he could see the face of the tail gunner, a friendly type who waved back at him and showed Elmore the box lunch he was eating. Then he held up a sign in English that said, HOW DO YOU DO?

Elmore laughed and waved back.

A few days later came another alert. Again Elmore catapulted off the deck and raced to intercept the Russian TU-95 Bear. When he came alongside the intruder, he saw that it was the same airplane. In the back was the friendly tail gunner. Elmore held up his own sign, this one in Russian: COME ON BACK WITH ME.

The tail gunner cracked up laughing. For a tiny moment over the North Sea, the Cold War had thawed by a few degrees.

Peering out the cockpit window of his S-2E Tracker, Cdr. M. R. "By" Byington kept his eyes fixed on the object 200 feet below. He was watching the long, gray shape of a Soviet-built Whiskey-class submarine. The Whiskey-class boats had been around since the early 1950s. They were diesel-powered subs, mostly relegated to coastal patrol duty, though some had been fitted with tubes for launching cruise missiles. ASW pilots from *Intrepid* often caught them trailing the ship. This one was motoring along on the surface, and Byington could see Soviet seamen clustered in the sail peering up at him.

Intrepid had just spent a blissful week in the picturesque port of Copenhagen, where the sailors had fallen in love with Danish beer,

Intrepid Sea, Air & Space Museum at its home at Pier 86, located at West Forty-sixth Street and Twelfth Avenue, on Manhattan's West Side.

Children show their pride for *Intrepid*. More than 150,000 school-aged children visit *Intrepid* each year.

Hector Giannasca, an *Intrepid* World War II veteran, shares his stories of heroism with visiting children.

Visitors on the flight deck of *Intrepid* during Fleet Week. More than 100,000 people visit *Intrepid* and the U.S. and foreign ships berthed around *Intrepid* over Memorial Day weekend each year.

A huge American flag displayed on *Intrepid*'s flight deck during its annual Memorial Day ceremony. Veterans are asked to take hold of the flag during the three-volley rifle salute to the fallen.

Barrington Irving, the first African American to fly solo around the world, speaks with students as part of the *Intrepid*'s unique Power of One educational program.

The Center for the Intrepid, a 65,000-square-foot advanced physical rehabilitation center at Brooke Army Medical Center in Texas, serving severely injured military personnel who have suffered amputations and serious burns during war—a project of the Intrepid Fallen Heroes Fund.

One of the twenty-one-suite Fisher Houses built as part of the Center for the Intrepid complex in San Antonio, Texas. There are thirty-nine Fisher Houses around the globe serving as a home away from home for families of injured service members.

White asks His Holiness Pope Benedict XVI to bless the zucchetto of His Eminence John Cardinal O'Connor, who had presented it to the *Intrepid* at Zach Fisher's funeral. Archbishop Celestino Migliore, the Papal Nuncio to the UN, looks on in celebration.

Bill White pointing toward Marine One with President Clinton during his visit to *Intrepid* in 2000. This was the first time the presidential helicopter landed on *Intrepid*'s flight deck and the only visit of a sitting U.S. president to the museum to date.

McAllister Towing tugboats attempting to move *Intrepid* on November 6, 2006. Their valiant attempt ultimately failed due to the mud built up around *Intrepid* over two decades. After emergency salvage operations led by the Army Corps of Engineers and the U.S. Navy, McAllister was subsequently successful in moving the ship on December 5.

Intrepid entering dry dock for the first time in thirty-eight years. She underwent a $15 million renovation in Bayonne, New Jersey.

Intrepid in dry dock showing the enormous rudder and the four massive, bronze propellers, together weighing 50 tons.

Intrepid, in dry dock, receives a new coat of paint: 5,500 gallons of battleship gray. Thirty million gallons of water are drained from the dry dock to allow for this work.

Photo of the 2005 Board of Trustees of the Intrepid Museum Foundation

the amusement parks, and the blond Scandinavian women. Leaving port, the carrier had rounded the tip of Sweden and entered the Baltic Sea.

The presence of a U.S. warship in the Baltic was a rare sight. The body of water was enclosed by Sweden and Finland on the north and the Eastern Bloc satellite countries on the south, and the Soviets had come to regard the Baltic as their private lake. So many Eastern Bloc ships were maneuvering and crisscrossing the Baltic at any given time, the sea appeared to be in gridlock.

To Byington, anti-submarine warfare was more than a job. He loved the hunt, matching wits with Soviet sub skippers, puzzling out the hiding places of enemy subs. The thirty-nine-year-old officer, a 1954 Naval Academy grad, had been one of the few in his flight training class whose first choice of assignments was the sub-hunting Grumman S-2 Stoof. He'd never been sorry. He stayed with ASW, making two squadron tours in Stoofs, then a shipboard job aboard *Yorktown*, getting his prize in early 1971. Now he was skipper of VS-24, deployed aboard USS *Intrepid*.

Still studying the Soviet submarine, Byington decided to drop a sonobuoy. A sonobuoy was a 36-inch-long, 4-inch-diameter "listening stick" that floated on the sea. Its hydrophone picked up the noises of a sub and transmitted the data to the circling S-2, where they could be data-linked back to *Intrepid*'s ASW command center. When the Soviet submarine submerged, the S-2 could continue to track it.

Byington dropped the sonobuoy about 10 miles astern of the sub—far enough away, he figured, that they wouldn't see what he was doing. Nearly invisible in the water, the presence of the sonobuoy could only be detected by homing in on its radio transmissions, which was how Byington's two detection equipment operators in the back of the S-2 kept track of the device.

That, in fact, was how the Soviet submariners also kept track. Byington saw the sub changing course, swinging its bow like a bloodhound sniffing the air as it homed in on Byington's sonobuoy. Byington saw an officer in the sub's sail pointing to where the sonobuoy was bobbing in the waves. A sailor went out on the bow and fished the sonobuoy out of the water with a boat hook.

Oh, well, thought Byington. It was no big deal, the Russians capturing a sonobuoy. It was an SSQ-53 passive listening sonobuoy, one of the older models that everyone knew about. The only thing that annoyed Byington was that the other guys had just scored a few points, however small, in the ASW game.

He saw the Russian seamen carry their prize belowdecks. The sonobuoy's hydrophone was still working. The transmitter was relaying the sounds back to Byington's airplane. He knew the next thing they'd do would be to snip off the hydrophone.

But they didn't. To Byington's amazement, he was now listening to the internal sounds of a Russian submarine. They were coming loud and clear over the sonobuoy's transmitter. Russian voices were chattering away, oblivious to the fact that every word was being sent to the circling airplane overhead.

Byington couldn't believe it. Either the Soviets were playing dumb, pretending to be unaware that their sub was bugged, or else they really *were* dumb. Byington couldn't wait to get back to *Intrepid.* If they were lucky, they'd just scored a huge intelligence coup. For the first time, someone had planted a listening device *inside* a Soviet submarine.

Back aboard ship, the taped transmissions were translated. The voices belonged to Russian sailors. On the tape, the sailors could be heard bitching about the things sailors have always bitched about— food, weather, women, vodka, their officers, their shipmates.

And that was all. Nothing of intelligence value. A few hours later the submarine dove beneath the surface, and the transmissions faded. By Byington was disappointed, but he could be philosophical about it. It was all part of the game.

New England was in the thrall of Indian summer when they came home in October 1971. Everywhere the foliage was transitioning to a brilliant gold. Best of all, their wives and children and sweethearts were waiting there on the pier to greet them.

Coming home to Quonset had a different feel from the old Norfolk days. When a ship pulled into a sprawling naval base like Norfolk, there was no mistaking where you were. Everywhere you looked, you saw gray—gray slab-sided Navy buildings, rows of look-alike Navy office buildings and shops, neat blocks of base housing with identical fixtures and paint jobs. Even the off-base businesses up and down the access roads had a drab sameness to them, all oriented toward the military trade.

Quonset Point was different. Just outside the gate were the quaint towns and seaside villages that looked as if they belonged in a Norman Rockwell painting. Quonset, the men of *Intrepid* agreed unanimously, was a glorious place to come home to.

After a month-and-a-half yard period in the Boston Naval Shipyard, *Intrepid* was back at sea, working up for her next deployment. In March and April 1972, she exercised with ships of the Spanish and Portuguese navies. In July *Intrepid* and her sub-hunting air wing were headed back to Europe. As before, they joined in a series of NATO exercises in northern Europe, returning to the crew's favorite, Copenhagen. After another blue-nose foray above the Arctic Circle, they pulled into Bergen, Norway, then down to the port of Rotterdam in the Netherlands, and on to the British Isles, where they made stops in Portsmouth, England, and Greenock, Scotland.

It was another European idyll, but this one was short, only three months. In October 1972, *Intrepid* was back in Quonset Point to be reconfigured for a new mission. The world was changing again, and once again the Navy was short of carriers.

The air war in Vietnam was building to a final, thunderous climax. The Nixon administration had resumed the bombing of North Vietnam. The renewed air offensive, called Linebacker II, was in full fury. To support the campaign, two Atlantic Fleet carriers, *Saratoga* and *America,* were sent on emergency deployments to the Tonkin Gulf.

Now the Sixth Fleet was lacking a carrier in the Mediterranean that had both anti-submarine and strike capability. There were no big-deck carriers available. Thus would the Atlantic fleet's oldest active carrier—and only remaining anti-submarine carrier—be again configured for an attack mission.

And she had exactly one month to do it.

Watching his men working their tails off to get ready for the deployment, Cdr. Raoul "Al" Alvarez could only marvel at how they did it. He was the new officer in charge of VA-45's fighter detachment. What had begun as a little five-jet A-4E Skyhawk detachment had just grown to sixteen airplanes. His men's workload had more than tripled.

There was a subtle but important distinction between officer in charge and commanding officer. Regular squadrons had commanding officers. The COs got to wear the command-at-sea insignia—a star over a circular wreath—on their right breast pocket, and with the insignia went all the perks of being skipper of a seagoing unit.

Detachments were offshoots of a mother squadron whose real skipper was back ashore. Each detachment had an officer in charge, and the job didn't merit an insignia or carry the pedigree of a real command.

Which was okay with Al Alvarez. He had been more than pleased at the prospect of a nice European deployment as officer in charge of a little Skyhawk detachment. While many of the VA-45 pilots were grousing about missing the war in Vietnam, Alvarez had no such sentiments. He'd seen plenty of the war as a Spad pilot on *Intrepid*'s first Vietnam deployment.

But Alvarez's little fighter detachment was no longer little. Instead of a single-mission, seven-officer, sixty-five-man detachment, he had sixteen officers, 210 men, and three distinctly different missions. In addition to intercepting Soviet Bear and Bison bombers, the A-4s were tasked with all the attack squadron missions, including conventional and nuclear strike capability. They had thirty days to configure the additional airplanes and find space on the ship for living quarters, squadron offices, weapons, and the reams of manuals and records. They also had to learn a myriad of new jobs to go with the new missions.

And then in November, in the midst of the frenzy to get ready for deployment, Alvarez received a message from the chief of naval personnel. He was no longer a detachment officer in charge. Because of the unit's enhanced size and mission, it was now considered a squadron. Al Alvarez was a real commanding officer. Which was nice, thought Alvarez, but it didn't really change anything. He pinned on his new command-at-sea insignia and went back to work.

After two more weeks of intense work, his squadron was ready. It was an impressive accomplishment. When someone asked how they got the job done, Alvarez had an answer. "The American Bluejacket," as he put it, "with his bitching and swearing about eighteen-hour days and seven-day work weeks. That's what got the job done."

Intrepid put to sea for ten days to exercise the newly configured air wing, then came home long enough to say goodbye. The day after Thanksgiving, 1972, she threaded her way out of Narragansett Bay, cleared Point Judith, and pointed her bow eastward.

On the bridge was the ship's navigator, Cdr. By Byington. He'd completed his squadron command tour with VS-24 and then been reassigned as *Intrepid's* navigation officer. Being an aircraft carrier navigator was considered a plum job, normally the number three slot in the chain of command beneath the executive officer. *Intrepid's* current executive officer, Cdr. Lee Levenson, had been her navigator before moving up the ladder.

Navigation had been one of Byington's favorite subjects since Naval Academy days. Already he'd won a $10 bet with the ship's damage control officer over exactly how many feet of draft *Intrepid* would have when she entered the harbor at Copenhagen. The DCO had made precise calculations, factoring in every pound of flesh and machinery, every gallon of fuel, and each airplane, predicting the ship's exact displacement in the water on the day she entered the harbor. Byington had bet him that his draft estimate was off by 6 inches.

As soon as they'd dropped anchor in Copenhagen, the DCO ran to the dock to study the draft measuring marks on *Intrepid's* hull. He was off by 6 inches. Gleefully, Byington told him where he'd gone wrong. He'd overlooked one tiny physical property of the environment. The salinity in Copenhagen's harbor was infinitesimally less than that of normal seawater, a fact that caused the ship to float just the tiniest amount deeper in the water—6 inches, to be precise, which was enough for Byington to win ten bucks.

In early December *Intrepid* steamed past Gibraltar and chopped into the Mediterranean, relieving USS *Franklin D. Roosevelt* on station. It was like old times, almost. Officially, she bore her old designation, CVS-11, but the new multi-mission put her in the same league as her big-deck sisters. She was armed and ready for aerial combat, undersea warfare, or all-out nuclear war. *Intrepid's* crew was feeling some of the old pride they used to sense when *their* ship was out there on the front line, the point of the spear.

But they also had the sense that it wouldn't last. Nothing official had come down, but a rumor was circulating through the crew spaces. This could be *Intrepid's* last hurrah.

End of the Line

It was a wistful, uncertain holiday season.

Four days before Christmas, 1972, *Intrepid* dropped her anchor in the harbor of Palma de Mallorca in the Balearic Islands, south of Barcelona. Her skipper, Capt. C. S. "Chuck" Williams Jr., turned over the helm to Capt. Ray Barker, an old anti-submarine warrior and decorated Korean War veteran. On Christmas Eve, many of *Intrepid*'s crew went ashore to celebrate midnight mass at the ancient cathedral of Palma.

While the faithful were praying in Palma, B-52s were raining tons of bombs on Hanoi and Haiphong. It was the Nixon administration's final push to drive the North Vietnamese to the negotiating table, the so-called Christmas bombing. The world was becoming increasingly incensed with the United States. American servicemen, including sailors from *Intrepid*, were feeling the resentment of their European hosts.

And then on January 27, 1973, while the carrier was in Lisbon, came an announcement that everyone aboard *Intrepid* sensed would change their lives. The war in Vietnam was over. Negotiators from North Vietnam and the United States had signed a peace accord in Paris. It meant that attack carriers would no longer be deploying to Yankee Station. No more American airmen would be killed or imprisoned. POWs who had languished for years in North

Vietnamese prisons were coming home. The Navy was no longer short of carriers.

Almost immediately speculation was flying through the crew compartments. *Intrepid* was now the oldest capital ship still in U.S. Navy service. If she were no longer needed, what would happen to the crew? Would there be a cutback in military manning? In the number of ships? Would they get transfers to new ships and bases?

The uncertainty continued while *Intrepid* kept up her Sixth Fleet commitments. She alternated at-sea periods with port calls in Cannes, Lisbon, Malaga, Barcelona, and Athens. In the eastern Mediterranean, the weapons division conducted a nuclear weapons exercise, loading and unloading the bombs that *Intrepid*'s A-4 squadron would deliver on a Soviet enemy if the order came down. The Mediterranean winter mellowed, and the sea temperature finally topped the magic 65-degree cutoff that allowed the pilots to shed the hated poopy suits.

On March 1, 1973, came the message that ended all the speculation about *Intrepid*'s future.

It was official: *Intrepid* was being retired. When she returned to Quonset Point in May, she would begin the process of what the Navy called "inactivation." Only half her crew would stay with the ship while she was being prepared for mothballing.

Thus began the scramble for orders. Part of the earlier speculation was turning out to be true. With the war ended, the military *was* downsizing. The names of dozens of ships and bases were on a closure list.

Intrepid's crewmen were urged to fill out "dream sheets"—lists of where they would like to be reassigned. Many wouldn't be reassigned at all. Enlisted men with less than a year remaining in their obligated service would be offered "early outs," as would junior officers who were ready to return to civilian life.

Just as *Intrepid*'s career had begun with a series of firsts—first arrested landing, first launch, first combat sortie—she was now in a final succession of lasts. On April 25, 1973, she left Rota, Spain, and chopped out of the Mediterranean for the last time. After completing her last Atlantic crossing, she rendezvoused off the U.S. East Coast with the ammunition ship USS *Santa Barbara* and off-loaded her nuclear weapons for the last time.

Her last homecoming would have to be special. Neither the Navy nor the state of Rhode Island was going to let *Intrepid*'s final voyage end without pomp and ceremony. A helicopter flew out carrying Rhode Island governor Philip W. Noel, Rear Adm. George Cassell, and a party of dignitaries to ride along on the final portion of *Intrepid*'s voyage.

It was a brilliant spring day, May 4, 1973, just past 0900, when *Intrepid* rounded Castle Rock and slid beneath the bridge that connected Jamestown Island to Newport. The yachts and mansions along the shore glistened in the early light. A swarm of private boats joined the carrier on her trip up the bay. Fireboats from Newport came out to salute her with horn blasts and geysers of water.

Intrepid eased up to the Quonset Point carrier pier. The white-uniformed sailors lining the rails were stunned at what they saw. A crowd of thousands stretched from one end of the pier to the other. The base commanding officer had opened Quonset Point's gates, and Rhode Islanders had come out in droves to greet the carrier. A uniformed fifty-member high school marching band from North Kingston was on hand to entertain the crowd.

It was an emotional moment. The sailors swarmed off the ship to embrace their loved ones. The adoring crowd applauded, snapped pictures, and gazed admiringly at the mighty warship at the pier. The warm glow of *Intrepid*'s triumphant return lasted until the next day.

That's when reality sank in. Even those who were anxious to leave couldn't help feeling a certain sadness. It was impossible to look at the great warship without realizing that she would never again charge through the high seas at over 30 knots. The old teak deck would never again reverberate with the thunder of engines. Her mighty catapults wouldn't be hurling 20-ton warplanes like toys into the sky. It was over. *Intrepid* was like a beloved old aunt at the end of her life.

Somehow it didn't seem right.

———

Half the ship's men and officers were leaving. One of those *not* leaving was By Byington, whose job as navigator had ended when *Intrepid*'s lines were fastened to the pier. Now Byington was pondering his new assignment: inactivation coordinator.

He was staying until the bitter end. In fact, he was the officer responsible for making the bitter end happen. It wasn't a job at the top of a squadron skipper and anti-submarine warrior's wish list.

The process of inactivating a large ship was normally accomplished in a shipyard by professional shipfitters. Someone had decided that *Intrepid* would be inactivated here in her home port by her own crew. Then, pickled and preserved like a floating mummy, she would be towed to the Philadelphia Shipyard to join another Mothball Fleet.

Byington's problem was that there were no clear directions as to what he was supposed to do. The objective, as stated in his orders, was classic military gobbledygook: "To conduct inactivation at Quonset Point to specified standards within given time and manpower constraints."

Which meant that he was on his own. The job was a tangle of organizational and engineering problems, which nothing in his naval career had prepared him for. Nothing, that is, except a background in the intricate, puzzle-solving craft of hunting Soviet subs. The truth was, they'd just handed Byington a job he was supremely suited to perform.

At the same time that *Intrepid* was being inactivated, so was her home port. Quonset Point Naval Air Station was another victim of the post-Vietnam drawdown and was being closed. So were the adjoining aircraft overhaul facility and the nearby Boston Naval Shipyard. The entire military presence in New England was shrinking, and the local economies were already feeling it. For Byington's crew, the base closures were good news. They could grab up all the surplus tools and equipment they needed for their inactivation work.

All *Intrepid*'s interior spaces had to be sprayed with preservative. All fuels and fluids had to be drained, including the oil from her massive engines and drive units. The ship's interior voids and tanks would have to be pumped dry and sealed and all the vents closed. The steam catapults had to be deactivated and the shuttle assemblies and pistons removed. The flight deck arresting cables would be removed and stored. All the ship's radio and radar antennas, sonar dome, and electronic equipment would be sheathed in a preservative envelope. Every item of reusable equipment—desks, bunks, workbenches, shelves, tables—had to be off-loaded.

Amid the drudgery they had fun. Before they deactivated the catapults, someone came up with the idea of having one last ceremonial launch. With Captain Barker presiding and the V-2 catapult division crew in position, *Intrepid*'s "shooter," catapult officer Lt. Cdr. Art Kilpatrick, removed his work shoes and fastened them to the catapult shuttle. With great showmanship, he went through the traditional shooter's choreography—hand twirling overhead, an overhead sweep with the right arm as the signal to fire the catapult.

Watching the brown objects fly off the bow and splash into the water of Narragansett Bay, the shooter had to smile. The record would show that after thirty years of service the last objects catapulted from the deck of *Intrepid* were his shoes.

On August 10, 1973, they took a break for a change of command. Ray Barker turned *Intrepid* over to his executive officer, Cdr. Lee Levenson. When he disembarked after the ceremony, Barker took with him the distinction of having been her last at-sea commander.

Levenson and *Intrepid* already had a shared history. He'd reported aboard as her new navigator back in September 1971 while the ship was in northern Europe. After ten months, he'd moved up to the number two slot, serving as executive officer for a northern European cruise and then a Mediterranean deployment. Now he was her last skipper.

Like By Byington and most of *Intrepid*'s officers, Levenson came from the anti-submarine warfare community. He'd won his wings through the Naval Aviation Cadet Program in 1953, then spent his career in a succession of sub-hunting units, including command of Anti-submarine Squadron 29.

Levenson had no illusions about his new command. He was a caretaker skipper of an inert warship. The job was neither glamorous nor gratifying, but he didn't care. After these many years, he'd acquired his own personal involvement with *Intrepid*. He would preside over the nine-month-long grind of sealing and draining and preserving, and when it was finished he and the old ship would have a lifelong bond.

The mournful sound of the boatswain's whistle echoed through the ship. It was March 15, 1974, one of those biting cold days that come at the end of a New England winter. A crowd of 1,500 was gathered on the hangar deck, including *Intrepid*'s crew, now down to 670. They were in dress blues, lined up by divisions, department heads and division officers standing in front.

This was the day they would say goodbye to *Intrepid*.

In four more days *Intrepid* would leave Quonset Point. Her engines were already secured and preserved. From now on she would move only with the external power of a tugboat. Her next—and probably last—destination was the Philadelphia Shipyard.

A Navy band from the New London Submarine Base played the national anthem. *Intrepid*'s chaplain, Lieutenant Commander Gill, delivered a properly somber invocation. Vice Adm. Frederick H. Michaelis, commander, Naval Air Forces Atlantic, was there to deliver his remarks. A small, compactly built man, Michaelis took the podium and recounted *Intrepid*'s history—her battle ribbons and awards of excellence, her record in World War II and Vietnam.

Intrepid's current and final commanding officer, Lee Levenson, took the podium. Levenson was wearing four stripes now, having recently been promoted to captain. He praised *Intrepid*'s crew past and present, delivering special praise to the men standing before him.

Kenneth J. Shea, representing Governor Noel, presented Levenson with a proclamation declaring USS *Intrepid* Day in Rhode Island. The people of the state were greatly honored to have the *Intrepid* based there, said the proclamation, and she "will long be remembered as part of our naval heritage."

The speakers tried to be upbeat. *Intrepid* was just being preserved until the day came that she would be recalled to active duty. After all, this was her third decommissioning, and each time she'd made a comeback. What no one felt like pointing out was that her previous decommissionings—the post–World War II mothballing in 1947 and the decommissioning prior to recommissioning in 1954—were transitory events. In those days *Intrepid* was young. This time was different. Thirty-year-old aircraft carriers didn't make comebacks.

The ceremony came to its most emotional part. *Intrepid*'s commissioning pennant, the long, whip-shaped flag that had first been hoisted on an August afternoon in 1943, was slowly lowered. A silence as heavy as the grave descended over the hangar deck. With great solemnity, Master Chief Quartermaster B. E. Franklin presented the pennant to Captain Levenson.

There was more tradition to be observed. With the ship officially decommissioned, Captain Levenson turned her over to Cdr. W. D. O'Toole, the commanding officer of a unit called the Naval Inactive Ships Maintenance Facility, which was current Navy-speak for the Mothball Fleet. O'Toole was, in effect, the caretaker of embalmed ships.

Levenson ordered *Intrepid*'s watch secured. The ship's log was closed. The captain issued his final order: "Debark the crew."

The band played a melancholy version of "Auld Lang Syne." Then came a prolonged drumroll. In column, *Intrepid*'s crew marched across the deck and disembarked for the last time.

After the decommissioning ceremony, some of the guests came to shake Lee Levenson's hand. Some were former *Intrepid* crewmembers who felt an emotional attachment to their old ship. Some were dignitaries—mayors of local cities, the commander of the Rhode Island National Guard, local businessmen. Some were military history enthusiasts who wanted to tell Levenson about a great idea they had. They wanted to acquire a ship such as *Intrepid,* take it to a public pier somewhere, and convert it to a museum. Wasn't that a great idea?

The Navy captain listened politely. Were these guys serious? Make a carrier into a museum? It sounded like a pipe dream.

★ 29 ★

Deliverance

Gray. It was all that drivers on the expressway saw when they slowed to peer at the mummies on the river below. The same drab monotone ran from the Schuylkill inlet for a mile up the Delaware. Ships were moored side by side in long rows, each wearing the same gray death pallor.

One of the ships was *Intrepid*.

From the day she entered the Philadelphia Navy Shipyard, *Intrepid*'s days were numbered. Despite the upbeat speeches at her decommissioning and the painstaking work of the inactivation crew, the truth was there for everyone to see. *Intrepid* wasn't waiting to be recalled. She was waiting to die.

On October 13, 1975, by act of Congress, she was given a reprieve. *Intrepid* was declared the official vessel of the 1976 U.S. Navy and Marine Corps Bicentennial Exposition. It happened also to be the 200th anniversary of the Declaration of Independence, which meant Philadelphia—and *Intrepid*—would be at the center of the nation's gala celebration.

For *Intrepid* it was a new—but temporary—lease on life. She moved downtown to Penn's Landing, at the heart of Philadelphia's waterfront. Her decks were cleaned, her spaces opened and freshened, and she was spruced up to host thousands of bicentennial visitors and veterans. For most of the next year, *Intrepid* presided over the celebration like an aging hostess throwing her last grand party.

Then came winter. The party was over. Down came the bunting and the bicentennial displays and the entertainment stages. *Intrepid* made the lonely trip back down the river to the shipyard to rejoin the fleet of embalmed gray warships. There would be no more reprieves. She was on the block to be sold for scrap.

One day in late November 1978 a *Vogue* magazine ad director and publisher named Dick Shortway set up a business breakfast on behalf of a group called Odysseys in Flight. The group had been formed in the mid-1970s for the purpose of acquiring a retired aircraft carrier and converting it into a museum. The founders of the group—Michael Piccola, Bruce Shearer, and several others—were joined by a naval historian named Larry Sowinski and Jim Ean, a World War II Navy pilot and airline public relations officer. They had made contacts inside the Navy Department, enlisted a number of celebrities and military leaders as advisors, and zeroed in on a carrier—USS *Intrepid*.

One of the corporate leaders at the breakfast was a New York developer named Zachary Fisher. He was intrigued by the idea. He wanted to know more.

When he saw it, Zach Fisher didn't know whether to laugh or cry. This old ship, a *museum*?

The carrier was closed to the public, and the only access was up a steep, narrow ramp. Fisher's bad leg couldn't make the climb, so Sowinski hauled him up piggyback. Now he was standing on the flight deck, out of breath, his knee aching like hell.

Old ships, Fisher could attest, were a lot like old men. When they reached a certain point of decrepitude, no amount of makeover could restore them to fighting shape. Zach Fisher was sixty-eight, with a bum leg, several years beyond his prime. So was this ship he was looking at. *Intrepid* had spent the last four years here in the Philadelphia yard waiting her turn to be recycled into slabs of processable steel. The notion of saving her from the blowtorch, turning her into a floating museum in Manhattan, now seemed as far-fetched as launching pigs into space.

Fisher saw acres of peeling paint, bulkheads festooned with splotches of orange rust, compartments that smelled of ancient sweat, smoke, and machine oil. *Intrepid* appeared to be in an advanced state of decay. The immensity of such a restoration was overwhelming.

For a long while he stood there on the flight deck, looking around, thinking about what to do. A part of him was daunted by all the peeling paint and rust. Heading up such an effort would be a Herculean task. He didn't need any more Herculean tasks.

But there was another part to Zachary Fisher. Inside the shrewd businessman and visionary builder beat the heart of an old-fashioned patriot. Fisher was a man who had lived the American dream, and now he wanted to give something back.

He was born in Brooklyn in 1910. The son of Russian Jewish immigrants, he learned about discrimination at an early age. He dropped out of school at age sixteen to join his brothers, Martin and Larry, in the construction business. He became a bricklayer, earned his union card, and was soon supervising construction crews. When he was seventeen he was badly injured in a construction accident. In that pre-penicillin era, the doctors wanted to amputate his leg, but his brother Larry refused to let them. Fisher kept his leg, but for the rest of his life he walked with a limp.

The construction business prospered. Over the next several years Zach Fisher evolved into a hugely successful New York developer and businessman. When Pearl Harbor was attacked in 1941, the old leg injury made him ineligible for military service. Looking for a way to join the war effort, he helped the Army Corps of Engineers build coastal fortifications.

The family construction firm continued to flourish after the war. Along the way Fisher married a gorgeous former Ziegfeld showgirl named Elizabeth Kenowsky. Elizabeth had performed for the USO in 1943 in Sicily with Bob Hope, and it was she who led Zach Fisher into the work of supporting wounded veterans. The Fishers helped finance the Veterans Bedside Network, which afforded hospitalized veterans the chance to write, direct, and act in their own shows and broadcast them from one veterans' facility to another. Zachary Fisher was transforming from builder to patriot to philanthropist. He was also acquiring a reputation as the kind of man who made things happen.

But this—a neglected and condemned warship? It was too much. It was too far gone. The problems were too overwhelming. The cost was too outrageous. Fisher was too old to take on such a project. The list of reasons not to do it was endless.

But Fisher was, above all else, a builder. Never mind the peeling paint and rust and smell of mold. Those could be fixed. He knew about such things because had spent a lifetime constructing edifices that now filled the New York skyline.

Fisher did what he had always done when confronted with a daunting project: he closed his eyes and tried to imagine the job already completed. He imagined the *Intrepid,* refurbished and gleaming in fresh gray paint, silhouetted against the Manhattan skyline. He imagined crowds of people—*young* people—walking her decks, studying the displays, feeling the glow of pride that Americans take in their rich history. He imagined *Intrepid* as a place where America's heroes would be honored.

He could see it clearly. It wouldn't be easy, but it could be done. Standing there on the deck of the deserted warship, Fisher arrived at a decision: "I will save the *Intrepid.*"

And then he went to work.

He was right about one thing. It wasn't easy. It turned out to be one of the most difficult—and expensive—undertakings of Fisher's life.

The first challenge was in getting the carrier transferred from the Navy rolls to the not-for-profit Intrepid Museum Foundation, which Fisher formed in February 1979. The president of the new foundation was Jim Ean, one of the original Odysseys in Flight members. Fisher's official title was executive vice president of the foundation, and he also served as chairman.

One of the requirements in getting the carrier transferred to the foundation was that he had to prove his own financial capability. It was the least of the problems. For years Fisher had held a place on the *Forbes* magazine list of the top 400 wealthiest Americans. Another problem was bureaucratic: the transfer of the ship required, literally, an act of Congress. It was an agonizing process that ground along for another twenty-six months, through the tenures of three secretaries of the navy, two presidents, and two mayors of New York.

The Intrepid Museum Foundation needed funding for the proposed renovation of the ship. In addition to Fisher's contributions, more private donations flowed in. A tax-exempt bond sale and a loan from the city of New York were planned.

A cast of celebrities came aboard to add the weight of their fame to the fund-raising effort. Among them was Tex McCrary, a radio talk show pioneer who had a knack for compressing the foundation's goals into catchy taglines. Other prominent supporters were Maureen O'Hara, Arthur Godfrey, and Helen Hayes. Sportscaster Howard Cosell joined the group, and so did Senator Barry Goldwater.

Another important question had to be answered: Where to locate the new museum? Zach Fisher had a spot in mind—a pier on the West Side of midtown Manhattan, which no one, including Mayor Ed Koch, thought made sense. The West Side waterfront in the early 1980s was a run-down and neglected area, considered by New Yorkers to be the dark side of the moon. Fisher insisted that *Intrepid*'s presence would revitalize the area. Because Koch believed in Zach Fisher, he gave in and agreed to make it happen.

Then they encountered another stumbling block, this one in the form of New York's building codes. No bond sale or loan could go through until the city's plethora of codes had been satisfied. When applied to a 40,000-ton floating edifice, the codes were a bewildering mountain of red tape. "The codes treated the *Intrepid* like a building laid on its side," recalled a frustrated Zach Fisher.

To the rescue again came New York's mayor. With Ed Koch running interference, New York adapted its byzantine building codes to the new floating museum, applying safety modifications so thorough that they would serve as guidelines for future ships used as moored structures. Through Koch and his commissioner of ports and terminals, Linda Seale, the city donated $2.4 million toward the renovation of Pier 86.

Finally, in February 1982, enough red tape had been sliced that the Intrepid Museum Foundation was cleared to sell $14.2 million in tax-exempt bonds. Thereafter came another $4.5 million in the form of a federal Urban Development Action Grant loan, obtained through the city of New York.

That same month, *Intrepid* left her berth at the ship graveyard in Philadelphia. Under tow, she moved up to Hoboken's Bethlehem Shipyard in New Jersey for the restorations she would need in order to make her grand debut in Manhattan that coming summer. The idea was to time the museum opening with the Fourth of July holiday and attract the huge crowds in the city.

Then more complications ensued. The extent of the renovations to *Intrepid* had been underestimated. She had become the embodiment of one of her old World War II nicknames, "Decrepit *Intrepid*." The old ship would take more renovating—and money—than Zach Fisher or anyone else had guessed.

By the time of the museum's opening, the bills had run to nearly $22 million. Through it all, Fisher kept writing checks. The renovation was well behind schedule, but the glorious day was nearing when *Intrepid* would cruise up New York Bay to her new home port. Zach Fisher could only hope it would be worth it.

It wasn't the kind of day he had hoped for. From where Fisher stood on *Intrepid*'s flight deck, he could see the wisps of cloud dangling like ragged curtains over the bay. It was Sunday morning, June 13, 1982, and between Manhattan and the Bayonne, New Jersey, shipyard, where *Intrepid* now resided after her restoration, lay a solid wall of gray murk. Rain was coming, and Fisher guessed they'd have to scrub the military aerial display that was scheduled.

It didn't matter. Nothing was going to dampen his spirit, not even the monsoon-like weather. Gathered on the deck were the 1,300 invited guests—museum supporters, donors, former crew members, and Navy personnel. Most had come from Manhattan early that morning on chartered Circle Line ferries. Now they were going to ride *Intrepid* on her triumphal voyage to Manhattan. The media was out in full force to record the event. Despite the gloomy weather, everyone was in a celebratory mood, wearing *Intrepid* baseball hats with the scrambled-egg visors.

By the time the tugs nudged the carrier away from the pier and into the bay, the light drizzle had become a steady downpour. It still didn't dampen the party atmosphere. The guests looked for shelter in passageways, or hunkered down beneath overhangs, or went down to the hangar deck. A flotilla of small boats gathered around the ship, including Malcolm Forbes's yacht *Highlander*.

It was less than 6 miles to the West Side pier, but at the tortoise-like pace of the carrier and tugboats, the voyage dragged on for over six hours. As *Intrepid* neared the newly prepared berth at Pier 86, New York City fireboats showed up to spray red, white, and blue streams of water, which were nearly invisible in the rain. It took another two hours to secure *Intrepid*'s lines to the pier and position the disembarking brows.

It had been a long day. They held a brief dedication ceremony on the hangar deck. Foundation president Jim Ean took the podium to give a short speech, then Zach Fisher gave an even shorter one. Elizabeth Fisher, who had been a trouper throughout the four-year ordeal, presented *Intrepid* with a bronze plaque honoring her new status. The wet and fatigued guests applauded, then disembarked.

Intrepid was safe in her new home—for the moment.

Her troubles weren't over. The hoped-for Fourth of July debut had to be scrubbed because of the renovation delays. The new gala opening—the *real* opening—was scheduled for August 4, 1982, only seven weeks away. Now even that goal was looking doubtful.

The problems kept mounting. Most of the displays and aircraft exhibits still had to be hoisted aboard and made ready. There was no electric power to Pier 86 yet. This was New York, and no amount of arm-twisting by Fisher or the foundation or even an *Intrepid* booster such as Ed Koch could expedite the process of hooking up electric service. Portable generators had to be brought aboard and kept running full-time while the exhibit company workers scrambled over the ship getting her ready.

And then the exhibit company workers went on strike. It looked for a while as if the museum opening would again be scrubbed. Through all the turmoil, Fisher remained calm. He had spent his working life in this city, and better than anyone he understood the New York labor culture. Railing against a strike was like shaking your fist at a snowstorm. You had to wait until the storm passed.

So he did. In a short while, the labor dispute was resolved. The work on *Intrepid* went ahead.

On August 4, 1982, the Intrepid Sea, Air & Space Museum opened to the public. There to add glitter to the occasion were Mayor Ed Koch, astronaut and Navy captain Wally Schirra, actress Helen Hayes, and a cast of military and civilian dignitaries. They were the first of a long procession of celebrities whose names would grace *Intrepid*'s decks.

That October, Vice President George H. W. Bush flew to New York to attend the dedication of Intrepid Hall, on the ship's capacious hangar deck, honoring the veterans of the Pacific war. Bush was one of those veterans, having been a Navy pilot in the Pacific. Impressed with the new museum, Bush told everyone how he, as a twelve-year-old boy, had visited a Navy destroyer in the Hudson. It was that experience, he said, that inspired him to join the Navy.

Intrepid took her place against the Manhattan skyline and joined the list of tourist attractions. But the late opening in August caused the new museum to miss most of the summer crowds. Attendance was good, but not good enough. Consequently, the museum operated in the red. Jim Ean, the foundation president, told the *New York Times* that "a drop in foreign visitors, combined with an unusually rainy spring and a hotter than normal summer this year, also cut attendance." In its first fiscal year, the Intrepid Museum ran a deficit of $3.5 million.

Things didn't improve the next year. Or the next. Attendance wasn't picking up, and museum officials were blaming it on the slower-than-expected development of the area west of midtown

Manhattan. But they expected a surge in attendance with the opening of a new Marriott hotel in Times Square and the new convention center the next year. Best of all, the 1986 rededication of the Statue of Liberty would bring in hundreds of thousands of tourists. It would be *Intrepid*'s big turnaround.

The problem was, *Intrepid* might not last that long. The museum was hemorrhaging money, mostly in the 16 percent interest payments on the $14.2 million bond issue. Still outstanding was the federal loan obtained through the city of New York. In the fiscal year ending in 1985, *Intrepid* racked up a deficit of $4.3 million. As news about *Intrepid*'s financial plight became public, Zach Fisher tried to put a brave face on it. "This museum will never close," he told the *New York Times*. "No two ways about it."

Things didn't get any better. That year attendance was below its first-year number of 708,000, which itself was woefully short of the predicted number of 1.4 million visitors per annum. Adding to *Intrepid*'s woes was the discovery that a Manhattan crime gang called the Westies had infiltrated the unions working at the Intrepid Museum and had been systematically siphoning off hundreds of thousands of dollars in box-office receipts.

In July 1985, just before bondholders were to receive a $1.2 million interest payout that would have emptied the foundation's bank account, the Intrepid Museum filed for bankruptcy.

The Fighting I—the ship that had battled kamikazes and escaped the scrap yard—was fighting for her life again.

★ 30 ★

The Patriot

It's a privilege to live in this great country of ours. They don't owe me a thing. I owe them.

—Zachary Fisher

It took two years, and Zach Fisher, as always, continued to write checks. He forgave debts owed him by the foundation and renegotiated *Intrepid*'s loans. It was a laborious, painful process. *Intrepid* emerged from the storm with a reorganized management and a solid new financial footing.

As everyone had hoped, 1986 was a better year. The Statue of Liberty centennial drew thousands of tourists to New York for the spectacular Fourth of July celebration. It was also the year the National Park Service declared the *Intrepid* a National Historic Landmark. The Intrepid Museum now had a prominent place among New York's must-see destinations.

The list of exhibits and displays continued to grow. In 1988, through the efforts of Dick Torykian, a trustee of *Intrepid* and a prominent New York businessman, the museum acquired the historic submarine *Growler*. *Growler* was the fourth nuclear missile constructed in the United States and was the predecessor of the more advanced Polaris submarines. Via White House chief of staff

John Sununu, Torykian persuaded President George H. W. Bush to negotiate with the Soviets an exception to the Strategic Arms Reduction Treaty, which required destruction of nuclear missile submarines once they were decommissioned. *Growler* won a reprieve. After making the 6,000-mile journey from Washington's Puget Sound to New York, she joined *Intrepid* as a featured attraction at Pier 86.

The city of New York had hosted an event each spring called Fleet Week—during which Navy and Coast Guard ships visited the city and their crews enjoyed a week of liberty—but by the mid-1980s it was floundering. At the request of the Navy League, Zach Fisher stepped in, injecting nearly $1 million of his own to revitalize the Fleet Week celebration. The event expanded to include a parade of ships, a stem-to-stern relay race, tug-of-war crew competitions, live demonstrations of military skills, and the Best Chow competition. Fisher hosted parties for thousands of service personnel on *Intrepid* with hot dogs and beer and live music, making their week in New York one they'd never forget.

Fisher wanted Fleet Week to include not just Americans. The world was changing. The acquisition of the Cold War submarine *Growler* coincided with the dismantling of the Iron Curtain and the Soviet Union. On his own initiative, Zach Fisher extended an invitation to the Russian Navy to visit New York for Fleet Week 1993.

Which sparked a protocol controversy. Zach Fisher's one-man invitation lacked any official U.S. government sanction. Private citizens, even those as well intentioned as Zachary Fisher, weren't authorized to invite foreign navies to visit U.S. ports. Before the initiative was lost in a storm of diplomatic red tape, Fisher's friend Colin Powell, Chairman of the Joint Chiefs of Staff, stepped in to coordinate with the Navy and the State Department. The protocol issues were resolved, and Fisher's invitation to the Russians stood.

In May 1993 New Yorkers beheld a spectacle unseen in their city for 130 years—warships of the Russian Navy sailing in New York Harbor. The destroyer *Bezuderzhny* and her accompanying refueling ship received a twenty-one-gun salute from U.S. Navy warships. Four hundred Russian Navy men swarmed ashore to join 7,300 U.S. sailors and Marines on the streets of New York.

To Zach Fisher, the son of Russian immigrants, it was a glorious sight—and irrefutable proof that the forty-year-long Cold War had ended.

Forty-nine years.

That's how long Alonzo Swann Jr. waited after the day—October 29, 1944—he battled a kamikaze pilot in the Philippine Sea. Nine of his fellow African American sailors—all steward's mates in the still-segregated Navy—were killed when the flaming fuel from the destroyed Japanese Zero engulfed Gun Tub 10. When Swann recovered from his wounds, he returned to duty as an anti-aircraft gunner. He survived the next kamikaze strikes in November 1944 and the final fury of the "divine wind" off Okinawa in March and April 1945.

For their actions, Swann and five of his surviving crewmates from Gun Tub 10 were awarded in 1944 the Bronze Star, the military's fourth highest award for valor in combat. Swann accepted the medal, but he quietly insisted that he had been promised the Navy Cross, the Navy's highest award, one order of magnitude beneath the Medal of Honor.

Swann left the Navy at the end of the war, a tougher and more determined young man. Using the GI Bill, he graduated from Pennsylvania State University with a degree in political science. He married and became the father of ten children. For twenty-two years he worked as a city planner in Gary, Indiana.

Through it all, Swann never forgot what he considered to be the great injustice of his life. He'd been denied the Navy Cross for his actions aboard *Intrepid* in 1944, in his view, for one simple reason: he was black. In Swann's unyielding opinion, the whole affair was an extension of the Navy's discriminatory attitude toward African Americans. Of the 3,376 Navy Crosses awarded in World War II, only three had gone to black Navy men.

Swann kept up his one-man crusade for most of the next four decades. He badgered the Navy Department. He wrote to congressmen. He talked to veterans' organizations. When he finally grew tired of being stonewalled, he hired a lawyer named Ron Layer, and in 1991 they filed a suit in federal court in Hammond, Indiana. The suit dragged on for another two years before federal judge

Rudy Lozano ruled in Swann's favor. Swann's attorney charged him $1 for his services.

The ruling landed on the desk of Secretary of the Navy Sean O'Keefe, who gave the Swann case a thorough review. What he saw convinced him that Swann's case was legitimate. The decoration would receive the endorsement of the White House. The only remaining question was, where should they have the ceremony?

To Zachary Fisher, there was only one conceivable answer. Alonzo Swann Jr. was one of *Intrepid*'s own. There could be no place more appropriate to honor one of *Intrepid*'s heroes than the ship on which he served. In classic Fisher fashion, he set about making it happen.

They held the event on a chilly autumn evening, November 3, 1993. Alonzo Swann Jr. looked distinguished in his tuxedo, in the company of his multitudinous family. He was sixty-eight, his hair gone mostly gray, but still recognizable as the nineteen-year-old gunner of 1944, a genial man with a lively sense of humor. He bore no rancor about the years of being denied his medal. All that was history. Now it was his night.

Zach Fisher remained out of the limelight, but he couldn't help hovering over the arrangements like a doting father. The Alonzo Swann Jr. story had touched the most patriotic spot in his heart. He made sure that the Navy, after years of ignoring Swann, gave the old veteran his due respect.

And they did. The Navy dispatched a contingent of flag officers led by the vice chief of naval operations, Adm. Stan Arthur. With him were the three senior African American Navy officers, all admirals, as well as a Marine Corps three-star and the commandant of the Coast Guard.

It was an emotional evening. Several of Swann's former shipmates from *Intrepid* were there. Each of the old sailors was asked to stand and receive applause. Then they dimmed the lights. On a screen appeared the grainy black-and-white footage of the events leading up to the kamikaze strike on Gun Tub 10 on October 29, 1944. The film showed the violence and cacophony of the kamikaze attack. Smoke gushed from the destroyed port side gun mount where Swann and his fellow stewards had manned their 20-mm anti-aircraft guns. The movie ended with the memorial service for the fallen gunners, each body bag draped with an American flag, awaiting burial at sea. A hushed silence fell over the crowd.

Vice Adm. Paul Reason, the Navy's senior-ranking African American officer, told about being "one generation behind" Alonzo Swann Jr. Men such as Swann, he said, had made it possible for his own generation to succeed. Reason was followed by Adm. Stan Arthur, who pinned the Navy Cross on Alonzo Swann Jr.

In his own remarks, Swann was humble. He thanked Zach Fisher and the Navy. Then he asked the crowd to join him in a moment of silent prayer for the men who were lost on *Intrepid*. In closing, he offered advice for the next generation: "If you think you're right, fight your heart out."

The evening ended, but Zach Fisher had more plans. Through the White House he had arranged for the president's U.S. Marine Band to come to Carnegie Hall, which he rented for the evening. Alonzo Swann Jr., his family, and 2,000 public guests were entertained in a concert by the Marine Band.

Swann was impressed and grateful. "What a difference this would have made in my life fifty years ago," he told a reporter. "Not only in spirit but in opening the doors of opportunity for me in America."

A few months later came another black-tie gala, another honor. *Intrepid* hosted its annual Salute to Freedom gala. The recipient of the 1993 Intrepid Freedom Award was former president Ronald Reagan. It would be one of Reagan's last appearances before illness forced him out of the public arena.

Seated at the president's table, hosted by noted philanthropist Paul Tudor Jones, was Alonzo Swann Jr. When Reagan addressed the guests, he singled out Swann. "Alonzo," said Reagan, "will you please stand and receive fifty years of admiration."

To the roar of applause, the old gunner rose. Zach Fisher, standing beside him, urged him to hoist his hands over his head in a victory gesture. For one memorable evening, half a century of injustice was erased.

Zachary Fisher was pleased with the honor given to one of America's heroes. He was so pleased, that he was already thinking about the next year's Fleet Week, which coincided with the fiftieth anniversary of the D-Day invasion.

For this Fisher had something special in mind.

The old Navy pilot was speechless.

He was staring at the airplane parked on *Intrepid*'s flight deck. It bore the same Navy blue paint scheme as the TBM Avenger he'd flown in the Pacific. On the starboard side of the warbird was painted the name Barbara. On the port side was *his* name: Lt. (jg) George H. W. Bush. Slowly, a huge smile spread across his face.

It had been Zachary Fisher's idea to invite former President Bush, a World War II hero, to be guest of honor at *Intrepid*'s observance of the D-Day fiftieth anniversary. In his second year of private life after the White House, Bush was busy traveling and speaking. His office replied that he'd already received dozens of similar invitations from around the world, including several from foreign governments. To Fisher's great delight, Bush declined them all and announced that he was coming to the *Intrepid*.

That was when Fisher began working on his surprise. He located the Avenger—the same type Bush had flown off the light carrier USS *San Jacinto* in 1944—and had it painted in the scheme of Bush's unit, Torpedo Squadron 51. Then he had the names painted on the sides.

George and Barbara Bush arrived on *Intrepid* by helicopter. The first thing they noticed was the crowd. The word had gotten out that the ex-president was coming, and over a thousand visitors were there on the flight deck. Now they were applauding and yelling, "We miss you, we miss you."

Then Bush saw Fisher's surprise. It was one of the few TBM Avenger torpedo planes still in existence. Bush was still staring at the artifact from his past, delighting in the names emblazoned on the sides, when he saw the rest of the surprise. Standing beside the Avenger were two grinning old men—crewmen Bush had flown with from the *San Jacinto* half a century ago. With them were their children and grandchildren.

For the next twenty minutes the old fliers hugged, laughed, and crawled around the Avenger, poking into wheel wells and ammo compartments. They huddled by themselves for a while, recalling events of half a century ago.

For Bush, it was a time of elation and nostalgia. Burned into his memory was the day in the Pacific—September 2, 1944—when his Avenger was hit by anti-aircraft fire over Chichi Jima, an island 600 miles southeast of Japan. He steered the smoking torpedo bomber over the water and managed to bail out at low altitude. Neither of the two crewmen with him in the Avenger survived. Bush was rescued by a submarine, the USS *Finback,* and eventually returned to his squadron. For his actions, the twenty-year-old pilot was awarded the Distinguished Flying Cross.

Standing now on the deck of the *Intrepid,* looking at the dark blue shape of the Avenger, Bush had to fight back the tears. He'd never stopped thinking about the crewmen he'd lost, he said. Now, seeing the beautiful blue Avenger and his two later crewmen was one of the greatest moments of his life.

Zachary Fisher's support for America's military families was on-going. In 1982 he had established the Zachary and Elizabeth M. Fisher Armed Services Foundation, through which he made significant contributions to the families of the Marines lost in the bombing of the Marine barracks in Beirut in 1983. When forty-seven sailors died in a gun turret explosion aboard the battleship *Iowa,* Fisher's foundation sent $25,000 to each of their families. He and his brother Larry also made donations to the families of New York City firefighters, policemen, and New York State troopers who lost their lives in the line of duty. The program continued to grow and, in 2000, Arnold Fisher, Tony Fisher, and Richard Fisher, Zachary's nephews, founded the Intrepid Fallen Heroes Fund.

In 1990 Fisher heard about a Navy man who, while his wife was being treated at Bethesda Naval Hospital, had to sleep in their car because he couldn't afford a hotel and there were no facilities for him on base. The story motivated Fisher to propose building a guesthouse next to the hospital where military families could stay at no charge. He cut through the government red tape, received approval, and the first Fisher House opened at Bethesda the next year.

Zach Fisher dedicated more than $20 million to the construction of Fisher Houses at military and VA hospitals throughout the world. "Zachary is a brilliant point of light," said President Bush in 1991 at the dedication of the first Fisher House at Bethesda. "He saw a problem, moved in and solved it."

By the mid-1990s, Zachary Fisher's health was deteriorating. As he neared the end of his life, a grateful nation bestowed honors on him. A longtime friend, Secretary of the Navy John Dalton, announced in 1995 that the second ship of the Navy's *Bob Hope*–class of sealift ships would be named after Fisher.

Fisher was honored and grateful—but he balked. Instead of naming a ship *Zachary Fisher,* he asked that the vessel bear only the name *Fisher.* It should honor not just him but his entire family.

Dalton conceded, and on October 18, 1997, the USNS *Fisher* was christened in New Orleans. The diesel-powered ship was one of the Military Sealift Command's large roll-on/roll-off cargo ships, displacing 62,000 tons fully loaded, and designed for transporting the military's heavy weaponry—tanks, trucks, and helicopters. *Fisher* entered service in 1999 and became a vital transport in Operation Iraqi Freedom and Operation Enduring Freedom. The *Fisher* and the *Bob Hope* were among the very few Navy vessels named after private citizens who never held public office or military rank.

But the nation wasn't finished honoring Zach Fisher. On the evening of September 18, in the last year of his life, he received an even greater honor.

"Zachary Fisher," said the president of the United States, "has with selfless compassion enhanced the lives of service members, veterans, and their families. His generosity towards our military families is unsurpassed in our Nation's history. Through his efforts, he has helped repay the debt all Americans owe to our Armed Forces and has honored the service that preserves our Nation's treasured freedoms."

They were gathered in a suite reserved for heads of state at the Waldorf-Astoria in New York. With the president was First Lady Hillary Rodham Clinton, whom Fisher personally admired. Looking on was an assemblage of four-star generals and admirals, the chiefs of all five services. Secretary of Defense Bill Cohen had come, as well as New York governor George Pataki, Mayor Rudy Giuliani, and Police Commissioner Howard Safir. The president was there to bestow on Zachary Fisher the nation's highest civilian honor, the Presidential Medal of Freedom.

"There is no single individual in the history of our country," said Clinton, "who has done more philanthropically for the men and women in our armed forces than Zachary Fisher." Borrowing from Adlai Stevenson, he went on to say, "Patriotism isn't the quick bursts of emotion from time to time but the steady dedication and love of one's country for a lifetime." He looked directly at the man seated before him. "Zachary Fisher, you are a great American patriot."

It was time for Fisher to deliver his own remarks, but he needed help. At age eighty-eight, he was in frail health, his fingers crippled with arthritis. He couldn't turn the pages of his typewritten speech. "Bill?" he said, peering around the room for Bill White, his chief of staff.

White was stuck in the back of the room behind a cordon of security agents. Bill Clinton, thinking *he'd* been summoned, bounded back to the podium. Somewhat embarrassed, Fisher read his speech while the president of the United States good-naturedly flipped the pages for him. It brought a warm glow to the room, the scene of the young president serving as the old patriot's page-turner. The crowd loved it.

Afterward, the two men clasped hands warmly. Fisher and the Clintons had become close over the past few years, and this evening bound them closer. It was the last time they would see one another. Zachary Fisher died nine months later, on Friday, June 4, 1999. President Clinton ordered the secretary of defense to ensure all DoD installations and the Pentagon flags to be lowered to half-mast.

The list of guests and speakers read like a who's who of government and military leaders. The service aboard *Intrepid* began with the en-

trance of the U.S. Marine Drum and Bugle Corps—"the Commandant's Own." CBS special correspondent Walter Cronkite served as
master of ceremonies. With Zachary Fisher's flag-draped casket in
the foreground, the speakers, one after another, took the podium—
the nephews of Zachary Fisher, Joint Chiefs chairman Gen. H. Hugh
Shelton, Gen. Colin Powell, Governor George Pataki, Mayor Rudy
Giuliani, Archbishop John Cardinal O'Connor, Secretary of the Navy
Richard Danzig, Senator Charles Schumer, Congressman Henry
Hyde, and others. Each delivered his own tribute to Zach Fisher.

The most moving tribute of them all came from Air Force Master Sergeant Glynn Davis. With his wife beside him, the sergeant
told the hushed crowd about the premature birth of their son. After
spending two nights in a chair beside his wife in a civilian hospital
far from home, he wondered where he could go. When he called
the nearby Fisher House, he was told, "You are welcome here. Our
doors are always open to you."

The sergeant choked back tears as he said, "Every day we thank
God for our son—and for sending this world people like Zachary
and Elizabeth Fisher."

The eulogies went on. It was a unique outpouring of praise for a
man who had never worn a uniform or held a government office.
"We are a better country," said General Shelton, "a richer people,
and a stronger military for his life."

A 6-inch replica of *Intrepid* carved from the old teak of her deck
was placed in Fisher's hand in his coffin. It was signed by two members of *Intrepid*'s World War II crew, Hector Giannasca and Joe
Liotta. "This ties us with him forever," said Giannasca.

U.S. Army chief of staff Gen. Dennis Reimer, Chief of Naval
Operations Admiral Jay Johnson, Marine Corps Commander Gen.
Chuck Krulak, Coast Guard Commandant Jim Loy, and Air Force
Vice Chief of Staff Ed Eberhart presented Elizabeth Fisher with the
American flag that flew over the Pentagon on the day Zachary died.
The U.S. Marine Drum and Bugle Corps played taps.

The ceremony ended. It was impossible not to feel sadness, because everyone present had lost a great friend. But inside the gray
steel interior of *Intrepid,* they could feel the spirit of Zachary Fisher.
He was there, a part of the ship he had saved.

★ 31 ★

Condition Zebra

A new century. A new war.

This one began at 8:46 in the morning. The Intrepid Museum hadn't opened yet. It was a late summer morning in New York, dry and clear, the visibility unrestricted. Only a small number of staff members had shown up yet. A few were on the flight deck basking in the morning sun. Across the river, they could see every detail of the New Jersey skyline. To the south, the towers of lower Manhattan jutted like monoliths against the azure sky.

And then something odd appeared: jetliners flying low *down* the Hudson. They seemed out of place. Usually they flew the other direction, upriver, approaching LaGuardia or Newark, and they weren't this low.

No one paid much attention. The morning was too pleasant, too filled with promise. Then . . . *a plume of smoke.*

Every head turned to the south. Flame and black smoke were gushing from the nearest tower of the World Trade Center. Stunned, they struggled to understand what they'd just seen. An airliner flew into the building? It didn't make sense.

Sixteen minutes later they saw another spurt of flame, a new gush of smoke. The smoke from both towers was forming a pall over lower Manhattan. New Yorkers poured into the streets and went to rooftops. All across the country people stared in disbelief at televised replays of the Boeing 767s, one after the other, skimming down the Hudson, each turning left to bore into the Twin Towers. The truth was coming to them in sharp, sudden increments, like punches to the gut.

New York was under attack.

Within an hour after the second impact, Tony Fisher, Intrepid Museum chairman, received a phone call from Museum president Lt. Gen. Marty Steele, who had just got off the phone with the FBI. The Bureau's New York headquarters, located at 7 World Trade Center, had been destroyed. The FBI-NYPD Joint Terrorism Task Force wanted to use the *Intrepid* as an emergency headquarters. As an all-steel structure within five miles of Ground Zero, with road, water, and helicopter access, *Intrepid* was the most secure fortress in a vulnerable city. Fisher agreed without hesitation.

The museum closed, and hundreds of agents streamed aboard the ship. A temporary command center was set up inside the ship, with many of the agents camped out on sleeping bags in *Intrepid*'s capacious hangar bays. For the next two weeks *Intrepid* served as the task force's nerve center. Using *Intrepid*'s information technology facilities, agents fielded thousands of phone calls. Military and Federal Emergency Management Agency helicopters alighted and took off from *Intrepid*'s flight deck.

By the time the task force moved out, *Intrepid* had added another entry to her service record—and a new mission. The ship was retrofitted with an onboard facility that could be quickly converted to a full-fledged, secure auxiliary emergency operations post. If the unthinkable happened—another crippling terrorist attack—the tough, steel-hulled *Intrepid* was a secure headquarters. "It will stand ready should we need her," the head of the FBI New York office told the *New York Times*.

For *Intrepid*, it was like old times. She was back in service.

By 2005, *Intrepid* was enjoying good numbers. The museum was about to receive its 10 millionth visitor since opening. More than 700,000 paying museum-goers would come aboard that year. It seemed almost too good to last . . . and it was.

In late 2005 New York City engineers informed Bill White, the museum's president, that *Intrepid*'s Pier 86 was in danger of "imminent catastrophic collapse." Time and entropy had caught up with the old pier, which was *Intrepid*'s footing in Manhattan. The pier provided access, utilities, and virtually all the services needed to operate the museum. After twenty-four years of being mated to a 40,000-ton aircraft carrier, the structure was literally being pulled apart.

It was estimated that rebuilding the pier would take from eighteen months to two years and cost upward of $35 million. The *Intrepid* would have to leave, as reconstructing the pier with the carrier attached would cost much more, an estimated $100 million. Which meant the museum would close. It was bad news in the short term, but rebuilding the pier was an essential investment in the museum's future. The nearly hundred-year-old pier would be transformed into a modern park-like setting with gracious shade structures, walkways, and a café. While the pier was being replaced, *Intrepid* would enter dry dock at Bayonne, New Jersey, where her hull would undergo an inspection and receive a sandblasting and new paint, and the ship's structure would get some long-overdue repairs.

While the museum was closed, *Intrepid*'s interior would also be revitalized. Through the leadership of the Intrepid Museum Foundation's board and generous donations from trustees and other friends, $8 million was raised. A world-class architectural firm, Perkins & Will, was hired to redo *Intrepid*'s interior display spaces. The latest in high-tech audiovisual devices would be installed.

The cost for rebuilding the pier and renovating *Intrepid* was staggering, but there was no alternative except to close *Intrepid* permanently. From the federal government came grants totaling $35.5 million. The state of New York contributed $5 million, and through the initiative of Mayor Michael Bloomberg and City Council Speaker Christine Quinn another $23 million came from the city of New York, which considered *Intrepid* to be the keystone of the revitalized West Side and the new Hudson River Park.

On October 1, 2006, the museum closed its doors. They had one month to prepare *Intrepid* for her first voyage in a quarter century.

———

Move the *Intrepid?*

The immensity of the task was daunting. No one knew how deeply the aircraft carrier's hull was embedded in the floor of mud and silt beneath her. Over the years she had become more of an edifice than a ship, resting in a bed of silt and attached to her land base by a network of umbilicals.

In charge of readying *Intrepid* for the move was a tall, sandy-haired young man named Matt Woods, who had the title of vice president of facilities, engineering, and security. Woods was a marine engineer who'd graduated from the Massachusetts Maritime Academy, traveled the world on oceanographic survey ships, put in two tours in Iraq surveying beaches and rivers in the country's reconstruction, and worked as a port engineer managing shipyard repairs and dry dockings.

But this job—moving a sixty-year-old, 40,000-ton aircraft carrier—exceeded anything Woods had ever tackled. The problems seemed endless, and each cost money and time. Wood's solution was to block off each of the phases.

Dredge a path behind the ship
Check for structural problems
Remove obstructions from the pier
Remove gangways, ramps, and utilities
Arrange generators, fire safety, and services
Lift aircraft elevators

The starboard aircraft elevator was a problem. The elevator behind the carrier's island superstructure was in the down position and had been since anyone could remember. With only a couple of weeks before moving time, Woods was informed by the tugboat company that the elevator would interfere with the tug pushing against the ship. No one had a clue how to get power to the ancient drive motor of the elevator. Even if they did, no one really expected that the thing would move.

Then came an unexpected break. In an old storage room they

found an oil-stained elevator operations manual. Woods was ecstatic. The manual spelled out the exact combination of switches and power supply required to activate the elevator. Holding their breath, Woods and his crew actuated the switches and, to their astonishment, motors whirred, cable spools turned, and the creaky old elevator made a stately ascent to the flight deck for the first time in a quarter century.

Woods crawled through every space in the old ship. Some hadn't been visited in decades. Paint was peeling in strips from old bulkheads. Hatches and doors were encrusted with rust. The boiler room hadn't made steam in over thirty years and had the eerie stillness of a tomb.

"Set Condition Zebra" was the objective. It was the Navy term for making the ship watertight and ready for action. It had a macho ring to it, but Woods was a realist. The best he could hope for was that *Intrepid* wouldn't come apart under the strain of towing or take on water while she was under way.

To balance the ship, the display aircraft had to be moved from the far extremes of the flight deck to the middle. It was an operation that had once been accomplished aboard *Intrepid* by a hundred Navy aircraft handlers. Now it was a tedious chore performed by a tiny staff of museum workers.

The biggest worry was the 17 feet of mud that encased *Intrepid's* hull. A dredging company went to work excavating a 200-foot-long cavity in the muddy bottom behind *Intrepid's* stern. The idea was that as the ship moved backward, the silt that piled up behind her would be pushed into the deeper trench. To excavate the trench, the barge-mounted dredging cranes hauled up 30,000 pounds of silt. While the dredging continued, other crews ran hydrographic surveys, using sound waves to measure the depth of the mud around the ship's hull. Time, money, and environmental restrictions prohibited excavating the mud from beneath the entire ship.

Would it be enough? No one knew for sure.

The dredgers kept working. And then, twenty-six days before the move, a calamity occurred. Matt Woods heard it from where he was working on the flight deck. It was the unmistakable sound of a large metallic object crashing into the ground. Woods ran to where he could see the dredging barge, and he groaned. The 120-foot-long crane had toppled onto the barge. The long boom lay across the barge, bent like a giant pretzel. By a miracle, none of the workers was hurt. But in New York's post-9/11 posture, the scene transformed within minutes into a maze of flashing police car lights, fire trucks, and public safety officials.

Woods was exasperated. With a little more than three weeks to go, dredging had come to an abrupt halt. There were still thousands of pounds of mud to be hauled out. The November 6 deadline was hard and fast. That was the day of the year's highest tide, and there was no way to change it except by moving the moon.

The crane was replaced, and two days later dredging resumed. Matt Woods was back on schedule, but he knew better than to relax. Something could still go seriously wrong.

On November 6, 2006, even the weather cooperated. It was one of those balmy Indian summer days before the first blast of winter walloped New York. The temperature hovered near 60 degrees, the sun was out, and everyone was in a good mood. There were bands and color guards and a crowd of over 2,000 standing on the pier. New York senators Chuck Schumer and Hillary Rodham Clinton were there along with former mayors David Dinkins and Ed Koch and City Council Speaker Christine Quinn. The politicians delivered speeches, cameras whirred, and helicopters clattered overhead.

Aboard the ship, Felix Novelli was standing in the starboard catwalk, a few feet below flight deck level. He was there with forty other FCMs—former crew members—who had been invited to ride the carrier during her 5-mile cruise. Waiting for the ship to get under way, Novelli felt the old excitement flowing through him. Being a nineteen-year-old sailor on the deck of a carrier under way had been the high point of his life. Now he was back. It didn't get any better than this.

The ship even had a ceremonial captain. On the deck with the FCMs, wearing his service dress blues, was Rear Adm. J. Lloyd "Doc" Abbot Jr., who had commanded *Intrepid* in 1961–62. Now the eighty-eight-year-old skipper was kibitzing with his crew, issuing orders, and thoroughly enjoying himself. "Okay, men," he barked to the old sailors, "no liberty until we get this ship to Bayonne."

It was time to leave. The tide was nearly at its peak, and the moment would never again be this right. On cue, Captain Abbot issued the order: "Cast off all lines." The hands on the dock—an unlikely crew of New York mayors and senators—obeyed by casting off the lines. *Intrepid* was free of all connections to dry land.

On the ship's fantail, Jeff McAllister, chief pilot of the towing company, gave the order to his tugboat captain: "Slow ahead." The growl of the tugboat's engine swelled over the water. The cable fastened to *Intrepid*'s fantail tautened. The tugboat's stern lowered in the water as her 6,000 horsepower began to churn the water.

Seconds passed. Pat "Popeye" Kinnier, the port captain, yelled, "She's comin' out! She's comin', baby!"

And she was. Inch by grudging inch *Intrepid* was moving sternward. No one dared speak another word. No one wanted to break the spell. *Intrepid* was moving.

And then she stopped.

Something was wrong. She had moved 15 feet, and no more. *Christine McAllister,* the big 6,000-horsepower tug, was hauling with all her might. A cloud of angry brown silt roiled as the boat's screws flailed at the water. McCallister reconfigured the tow lines and ordered two of the smaller tugs to join the effort. Now they had a collective 13,000 horsepower hauling on *Intrepid*'s tow cables.

From the fantail came an ominous clunk. Matt Woods knew what it was: the chock through which the tow cable passed had torn from its mount on the stern. Now Woods had more to worry about. Even if *Intrepid* wasn't moving, some of her parts were about to.

They were running out of time. Minute by minute, the tide was receding. The operation was turning into a B-grade suspense movie with a ticking clock, a ship coming apart, and a crowd of perplexed spectators waiting to see what happened next.

Pilot Jeff McAllister wasn't giving up. In a last-ditch effort, he summoned another tug, this one a 7,000-horsepower super-tug that belonged to a competitor and was out on the river to observe the festivities. With the added thrust, the fleet of tugs had a collective might of 20,000 horsepower. The roar of their engines washed over the shore. The water behind the tugs turned an earthy brown.

Intrepid didn't budge. She creaked and groaned and refused to move one more inch. The carrier had become an immovable object.

The tide was still going out. No one was smiling on the ship, the pier, or the tugboats. The bands had stopped playing. The guests on the pier were staring as if they had witnessed a massacre.

McCallister sighed. "Okay, that's a wrap," he said into his microphone. "All boats down to dead slow."

Gloom settled like a dank cloud over the flight deck. Felix Novelli nodded glumly and joined the other FCMs as they disembarked. Doc Abbot said a polite farewell and made his own quick departure. Bill White talked to the press. Trying to sound upbeat, he told them, "The old gray lady dug in her heels and didn't want to leave her home of twenty-four years here in New York."

That much was true. But the question was, now what?

Twenty-four hours later, a scuba diver confirmed what they had already surmised. Each of *Intrepid*'s four huge propellers and her massive rudder were buried in a solid mountain of mud. The silt and sludge had built up as she moved sternward until they created an impassable wall. It was the same effect as a car backing down a snow-covered driveway until the snow piled up behind it in a solid dam.

For White and his staff, it was both a public relations nightmare and a windfall. *Intrepid* was the subject of the nightly news. Most of the coverage was sympathetic, with reporters emphasizing *Intrepid*'s importance to New York. Not all the reporters were charitable, however. One paper ran a story with the headline "USS Stuck in the Mud," which infuriated some of the old crewmembers. Felix Novelli was one of those most enraged. The old sailor snapped at the reporter, "If the Empire of Japan couldn't stop us, what the hell makes you think a ton of mud can?"

Even before the tugboats had stopped straining at *Intrepid*'s tow cables, Bill White was working the phones. From Gordon England, deputy secretary of defense, and Don Winter, secretary of the Navy, he received an immediate commitment to salvage the ship. Senator

Hillary Rodham Clinton and Congressman Bill Young immediately weighed in with the Pentagon on *Intrepid*'s behalf.

As *Intrepid*'s predicament became known around the world, ideas for unsticking her came pouring in. The suggestions ranged from the weird to the wacky—lifting her with helicopters and balloons, rebalancing her with tractor trailers, blowing her free with explosives. Priests in the Vatican held a special mass for *Intrepid*. A seventy-three-year-old woman showed up at the museum office to donate $10, with which she wanted to start an *Intrepid* rescue fund.

The Defense Department made good on its promise. The Army Corps of Engineers (USACE) arrived, and right behind came a unit from the Naval Sea Systems Command, whose jobs included heavy salvage operations. The rules had changed since the previous attempt to free *Intrepid*. She had been declared a "salvage" project, which meant a more advanced dredging technique could be used.

The commander of the USACE team was Gen. Todd Semonite, a crew-cut army engineer with a can-do attitude. Under Semonite's direction, the dredgers, led by District Commander Col. Nello Tortora and Operations Chief Tom Creamer, filled up six New York City sanitation barges a day, scooping a total of 40,000 cubic yards of mud behind the ship, thanks to former Marine and sanitation commissioner John Doherty. They ran computer simulations of *Intrepid*'s hull buried in the sludge, from which they developed a strategy. They came up with a technique called "drag dredging"—lowering a heavy beam into the silt next to the ship's stern and screws, then dragging it out laterally with a load of silt.

The dredging went on for five weeks. The countdown clock was ticking. The next window for a sufficiently high tide was in early December. Again, the phase of the moon and its unalterable sway over the tides would decide *Intrepid*'s fate.

Showtime.

Gone was the balmy autumn weather. The morning of December 5 was cold and gray, much like the mood of the crew. The temperature dwelled in the low thirties. Everyone aboard *Intrepid* and the fleet of tugs was wearing parkas, gloves, and wool hats.

Gone too were the bands and honor guards and politicians. Instead of a party, this would be more like a stealth operation. "I don't know how moving an aircraft carrier around in New York could ever be low-key," Bill White told the press, "but we had the celebratory event the first time and we're not having that again." Though the guest list was small, twenty former crew members in heavy jackets and scarves were huddled on the flight deck, determined to stay with *Intrepid* regardless of what happened that day.

The Army engineers and Navy salvage crews had dredged as much mud as they could, but they couldn't completely clear the port side propellers, which were adjacent to the pier. Sonar images showed the big screws still partly embedded in the wall of mud.

Would *Intrepid* come out anyway? No one was willing to make a promise. "Once she starts to go," predicted Pat Kinnier, the port captain, "she's gonna go"—about as optimistic a statement as anyone wanted to make.

Intrepid's mooring lines were cast off. Jeff McAllister was on the fantail again, directing his tugboats by radio. When all his boats were in place, McAllister gave the order. The eight tugs churned the water, pulling with 30,000 horsepower.

After a couple of minutes, McAllister saw something. It was almost imperceptible at first, but . . . she was moving slowly, inch by inch.

And then she stopped. Again!

The tugs strained harder. The familiar brown clouds of silt roiled again in the Hudson. Minutes ticked by. Nothing happened. *Intrepid* wouldn't move another inch. It was a repeat of the previous month's debacle.

The mood on the fantail was one of grim, silent supplication. Pat Kinnier looked like a man waiting for his own execution. A look of dejection was spreading like a mask over Matt Woods's face.

McAllister changed tactics. He ordered one of the smaller tugs to push against the stern of the ship, to move it slightly and loosen the silt beneath. He directed the big tugs to pull straight back instead of at an angle, as they had been doing. Then he ordered the smaller tugs to pull in different directions to "wiggle" the hull free.

The agony continued for nearly half an hour. The tugs were hauling so hard, *Intrepid* creaked and groaned from the strain. Matt Woods tried not to think about the forces being applied to the sixty-three-year-old hull. Lips moved in silent prayer. Someone on deck yelled, "Move, baby, move!"

And then she did.

It took several seconds to be sure. The movement was tiny, halting—but they could see it. It was real. Slowly she was inching away from the pier. Still, they held their breath. They'd been here before, and they were braced for the inevitable stop.

But she kept moving. Faster now, gliding away from the pier. The cheering started, then swelled into an animal roar that echoed through the ship: "We did it, we did it!" They hugged one another and slapped hands, and some wept unabashedly. They'd ridden an emotional roller coaster. In the space of minutes they'd been transported from utter desolation to unbounded joy. *Intrepid* was free!

She slid into deep water, then turned south on her stern-first journey down the Hudson. Approaching the site of the World Trade Center, the former crew members manned the starboard rail at attention. While the ship paused abeam Ground Zero, all tugboat engines to neutral, they unfurled a 100-foot American flag— *Intrepid*'s salute to the Americans lost in the attack of September 11, 2001.

Not long after came another emotional moment. The crew members, many of them octogenarians, gazed in awe as the Statue of Liberty slid slowly past *Intrepid*'s port rail.

Intrepid nudged against the pier in Bayonne at 3:40 in the afternoon. By now most of the old sailors had fallen silent. One after the other they filed off the ship. Several stopped on the dock and turned back for a long last look at the ship. The same unspoken thought was in all their minds. It would be nearly two years before *Intrepid* returned to Manhattan. For some, this would be the last time they saw her.

As they headed off into the cold autumn evening, their thoughts kept returning to the ship. *Intrepid* was a repository of all their youthful hopes, their memories, their finest moments. They'd grown to manhood aboard her. Their lives would always be intertwined with this old ship. The story of *Intrepid* was *their* story.

★ ACCOLADES AND ACKNOWLEDGMENTS ★

The story of *Intrepid* would be incomplete without recognizing a cast of remarkable people. They are the quiet heroes whose service and generosity have kept *Intrepid* and its causes alive. With the passing of *Intrepid*'s beloved founder, Zachary Fisher, on June 4, 1999, members of the Fisher family stepped forward to continue Zach's mission. Zach's nephew, Tony Fisher, who had served as vice chairman of the Intrepid Museum Foundation since 1995, took his place as chairman. A visionary who was determined to bring a more business-oriented management to the museum, Tony recruited Maj. Gen. Don Gardner, USMC (ret.), to be the museum's president. General Gardner's mandate was to streamline the operation and steer *Intrepid* clear of the turmoil she suffered in the mid-1980s. In this mission he succeeded brilliantly and was followed two years later by a fellow Marine, Lt. Gen. Marty Steele, who magnificently completed the museum's business redevelopment. General Steele coined the mission statement: "Honor our heroes, educate the public, and inspire our youth." Steele was a true visionary.

In 2003 the Intrepid Museum Foundation lost Tony Fisher and his wife in a tragic airplane crash. Arnold Fisher, who had been Tony's partner in the family business and was the son of Zach's older brother Larry, assumed the job as chairman and backed up his commitment on day one by personally pledging half a million dollars to the museum. The Board of Trustees quickly embraced the new leader, and Arnold became one of *Intrepid*'s most passionate and devoted commanders. With board member Jim Kennedy and news anchor Marvin Scott, Arnold managed to acquire G-BOAD, the sleek British Airways Concorde, for the museum. It was Arnold who built the Michael Tyler Fisher Center for Education, an 18,000-square-foot, $10 million state-of-the-art facility, on *Intrepid*'s fantail. We are grateful to "the Growler."

Arnold Fisher continued as the foundation chairman until *Intrepid*'s refurbishment project was safely launched, then stepped aside to devote himself to the Intrepid Fallen Heroes Fund. He continues to serve actively on the Board of Trustees along with three other family members: his sons, Steven and Kenneth, and Richard Fisher's son, Winston. Richard, who was a founding trustee and passionately devoted to the Intrepid Fallen Heroes Fund, passed away in August 2006.

To succeed Arnold Fisher, the foundation board elected as co-chairmen two brilliant corporate leaders and dedicated patriots, the first outside the Fisher family to take the helm: Charles de Gunzburg, vice chairman of First Spring Corporation, and Richard Santulli, chairman and CEO of NetJets, Inc. Under their leadership, the board has steered *Intrepid* into a new chapter of its history that would make founder Zachary Fisher proud. We are truly grateful to them and to the entire board. A current list of our extraordinary and generous board as photographed in 2005 can be found on the last page of the second insert.

Another trustee and key figure in the *Intrepid* story is Martin Edelman, rainmaker, a part of the fabric of New York real estate, and the attorney who helped Zach Fisher bring the ship to New York. Marty is tirelessly devoted to *Intrepid*'s mission. Since the museum's inception he has provided wise counsel on every major project and initiative. With the help of Sara Marks of *Vanity Fair* and Craig Hatkoff of Tribeca Films, Marty organized a trip in June 2003 to entertain troops in Iraq, Kuwait, and Qatar. Robert DeNiro, entertainer Kid Rock, the Dallas Cowboys cheerleaders, Wayne Newton, and a group from *Intrepid* traveled through the region, helicoptering aboard the carrier *Nimitz* in the Arabian Sea and on to Khalil, Iraq, in 127-degree heat, entertaining some 67,000 U.S. soldiers, sailors, airmen, marines, and coast guardsmen. Deserving of special credit for their help and personal contributions to *Intrepid*'s mission are actors Denzel Washington and Cher, and artist/songwriters Big and Rich, John Mellencamp, and Jon Bon Jovi.

Intrepid has likewise been very fortunate to have the help and wise counsel of Mike Stern, famed World War II journalist, author, film producer, adviser, partner to titans of industry, and Zachary Fisher's closest friend, whom Zach referred to as "the billion-dollar brain." They were true partners in these efforts.

One of *Intrepid*'s trustees and most generous contributors is Howard Lutnick, chairman of Cantor Fitzgerald. Headquartered on the 105th floor of 1 World Trade Center, Cantor Fitzgerald lost 658 employees, including Howard's brother, Gary, on the morning of September 11, 2001, more than any other single company. In the dark days following the tragedy, dozens of *Intrepid* employees came forward to help run a support center for Cantor Fitzgerald families.

Intrepid has been fortunate to have staunch allies in the military. Joint Chiefs chairman Gen. Colin Powell regularly consulted with Zach Fisher and often volunteered to give inspirational talks to New York City schoolchildren aboard *Intrepid*. General Powell's successors as chairman, Gen. John Shalikashvili, Gen. H. Hugh Shelton, and Gen. Richard Myers, were all solid *Intrepid* supporters, as was chief of naval operations Adm. Jeremy "Mike" Boorda, who helped Fisher achieve many of *Intrepid*'s goals. Special thanks to Adm. William A. Owens, former vice chairman of the Joint Chiefs and well-respected Fortune 500 CEO, who was very close to Zach and one of *Intrepid*'s most active supporters. Other staunch supporters have included Gen. Ed Eberhart, USAF; Adm. Bud Flanagan, USN; Gen. Mike Carns, USAF; USCG commandant Adm. James Loy; Adm. William Fallon, USN; Gen. David Petraeus, USA; Gen. and Mrs. Jim Amos, USMC; Capt. Kevin Wensing, USN; and Col. Tom Tyrrell, USMC, who served with excellence as CEO of the Intrepid Museum from 2001 to 2004.

Secretary of the Navy John Dalton was one of Zach Fisher's greatest friends in the Pentagon. So was Deputy Secretary of Defense Gordon England, who committed the military to rescue *In-*

trepid from her grounding in the Hudson. Two others were Army vice chief of staff Gen. Dick Cody, who dispatched the Army Corps of Engineers to join the effort, and Secretary of the Navy Donald Winter, who ordered the salvage unit from the Naval Sea Systems Command to lend its expertise in freeing the ship.

Over the years *Intrepid* has received generous support from corporate and private sources. Through the donations of more than 600,000 individual Americans, the Intrepid Fallen Heroes Fund was able to raise over $80 million for the families of our nation's heroes killed in action and to construct the Center for the Intrepid, a privately funded $40 million advanced-technology physical rehabilitation facility for wounded warriors at Brooke Army Medical Center in San Antonio, Texas. In 2008 the fund launched a new project, the National Intrepid Center of Excellence, a research, diagnosis, and treatment facility for troops suffering from traumatic brain injury. The Intrepid Relief Fund, begun by Zachary Fisher, provided scholarship help to more than 800 children of military personnel and veterans. Led today by Fisher's grandnephew, Winston Fisher, the fund, among many other projects, now supports a program created by philanthropists and dear friends Ron and Maddie Katz with Dr. Tim Miller and the UCLA Medical Center to provide advanced plastic surgery to service members who have suffered severe facial burns from horrific explosions in Iraq and Afghanistan.

A devoted corps of volunteers donates more than 40,000 hours a year to the Fisher Houses—homes away from home for families of patients receiving medical care at major military and VA medical centers. Since Zachary Fisher established this unique program in 1991, the Fisher Houses have accommodated more than 70,000 families, saving them more than $100 million in transportation and lodging costs. Under the direction of Ken Fisher, Zachary's nephew, the network of Fisher Houses has grown to thirty-nine facilities around the world, with more planned and under construction. The foundation also sponsors a program called Hero Miles, which has received over 1 billion donated frequent flier miles, used to provide more than 13,000 airline tickets to Iraqi Freedom and Enduring Freedom veterans and their families, saving them more than $17 million.

Intrepid owes a huge debt of thanks to George Steinbrenner, Fred Wilpon, and Nelson Doubleday for the tens of thousands of baseball tickets contributed each year during Fleet Week.

Local and national media have been outstanding in their reporting about *Intrepid*. In particular, Pat Milton, Heidi Collins, Don Imus, Lou Dobbs, Anderson Cooper, Bill O'Reilly, Matt Lauer, Brian Williams, Jim Cramer, Joe Scarborough, Barbara Walters, Larry King, Pete Williams, and Jeremy Bitz have had great interest in the *Intrepid*. Rubenstein Associates, led by über PR master Howard Rubenstein and his son Steven, and all *Intrepid*'s friends throughout the media world deserve huge credit for getting the great *Intrepid* story out there. Special thanks to Suzie Halpin, Debbie Raskin, Kathy Lynn, and all at Rubenstein for their love of *Intrepid*'s mission.

Intrepid has been blessed with bipartisan support from elected and appointed officials, most notably from Senators Chuck Schumer and Hillary Rodham Clinton; Representatives John Murtha, Carolyn Maloney, and Jerry Nadler; New York governors George Pataki and Eliot Spitzer; State Assembly Speaker Sheldon Silver, State Senate Majority Leader Joe Bruno, comptrollers Alan Hevesi and Bill Thompson, Manhattan Borough President Scott Stringer, Staten Island Borough President James Molinaro, Bronx Borough President Adolpho Carrion, Brooklyn Borough President Marty Markowitz, and Queens Borough President Helen Marshall. Commissioner Ray Kelly of the New York City Police Department has been a solid *Intrepid* supporter.

U.S. congressman Bill Young and his wife, Bev, have been tireless champions of *Intrepid*'s mission for many years and are great friends and patriots extraordinaire. Their work in support of military families is legendary.

James Ortenzio, Rob Balachadran, Connie Fishman, Trip Dorkey, Diana Taylor, and the entire leadership of the Hudson River Park Trust—*Intrepid*'s landlord—have likewise been outstanding supporters, and the *Intrepid* team is truly grateful for their help. We are also grateful to Sean Maloney and our governor, David Paterson, for believing in *Intrepid*.

Each mayor of New York City has been an unwavering champion of the museum, beginning in 1982 with Ed Koch, who provided critical help to Zachary Fisher in establishing the Intrepid Museum. Mayor Rudy Giuliani answered Fisher's personal appeal to eliminate the rent owed by the museum to the city, allowing the funds to be devoted to vital programming and educational goals. Speakers of the New York City Council have thrown their weight behind *Intrepid*'s causes, particularly Speakers Gifford Miller and Peter Vallone Sr. In recent years Mayor Michael Bloomberg and Speaker Christine Quinn have rallied behind *Intrepid* by providing funding in excess of $30 million for the *Intrepid* refurbishment project. Speaker Quinn and Mayor Bloomberg continue to be two of *Intrepid*'s most outstanding advocates. *Intrepid* could not be so well positioned without the deputy mayors, commissioners, and all within City Hall and the city administration who support her mission.

We want to thank the lobbyist firm of WEMED, led by Vicky Contino, Ken Shapiro, Peter Piscitelli, and Skip Piscitelli who have all served *Intrepid* with great character and integrity.

Because of the noble efforts of all these people, *Intrepid* has been able to continue her mission to honor our heroes, educate the public, and inspire our youth about the price of freedom.

In addition to those named here, the authors would like to thank some special people who have stood behind them and made the telling of this story possible.

FROM BILL WHITE:

I want to give thanks to some special friends who have supported me and the work of the Intrepid Museum Foundation. To my business partner and best friend of twenty-two years, executive vice president Dave Winters, a huge thank-you. My sincerest thanks to Linda Mellon and Violeta Prelvukaj, who, together with Kristen Kelly Fisher, Lisa Yaconiello, Gary Spampanato, Nicole Vaughan, Matt Krause, Keith Duval, Jed Candreva, Jason Wallace, Joe Pecoraro, Reid Price, Melissa Rosenbloom, Jim Formant, and Max Tapper, have put up with me for so many years.

To the entire Intrepid Museum family—our executive director, Susan Marenoff; our vice presidents, Pat Beene, Matt Woods, Fredda Plesser, John Zukowsky, and Rich Lisi; our AVPs and directors; all 250 of the dedicated and talented professionals who run the *Intrepid* team and have made the Intrepid Museum what it is today; and those who gave their time and effort—all of whom I truly wish I could name here—since the museum opened in 1982— thank you.

Eternal thanks also to *Intrepid* vice chairmen Denis Bovin, Steven Roth, and Bruce Mosler, and to *Intrepid* trustees and truly dear friends Joe Perella, Tony Sichenzio, Dick Farmer, Roe Stamps, Joe Plumeri, Bill Owens, Donald Trump, Jim Nederlander, Jim Carrier, Dave Turner, Jim Bishop, Dave DeLuca, Greg Cuneo, Andrea Jung, and the Avon Foundation. We could not do this without you: you are so bright, so generous, and so thoughtful—true leadership for which we are grateful.

Special thanks to Gen. Matt Caulfield and to my friend and fellow co-chairman of the Intrepid Museum Society, Kent Karosen, who both helped me to meet Zachary Fisher in 1991. More thanks to the Intrepid Museum Society for all its hard work.

I will always be grateful to His Eminence John Cardinal O'Connor, archbishop of New York, rear admiral, USN, and chief of Navy chaplains, who inspired me to start Operation Support, with cherished friends Tim O'Neill and Cliff Yonce, and to be more directly involved in charitable work.

My gratitude to Chaminade High School, Fordham University, and Billy Deegan for helping me to figure out so much about life.

Warm thanks to my friends Clive Davis, legendary music mogul, and John Sykes, cofounder of MTV, both great patriots to whom we are very grateful for assistance with *Intrepid*'s mission and its historic return.

To my dear friend Hillary Rodham Clinton, thank you for being such a true friend and compassionate supporter of our troops and their families. I admire and respect you; you are a great leader and we are so proud of you always.

Special thanks and grateful appreciation to my dearest friends Christine Quinn and Kim Catullo. You are an inspiration to us all.

A big thanks to His Excellency, the ultimate samurai warrior, Uncle Jimmy. Your introduction to the one and only Georgette Mosbacher is so treasured.

To Mike Stern, who at ninety-eight continues to amaze and impress me. Thank you for your partnership, your mentorship, and your teaching me about true friendship. And a special thanks to our Nobel laureate Dr. Paul Greengard, who is working to solve Alzheimer's, from which Elizabeth Fisher died. And to Dr. Moshe Shike—my dear friend and the greatest doctor on earth.

Special thanks to my dear friends Don and Deirdre Imus, esteemed philanthropists who care deeply about the important issues of our world, love to you, DnD. Thank you, Doug Grad, for encouraging me to write this book and for introducing me to Bob Gandt. The Imuses put me in touch with the one and only Esther Newberg, who, in turn, connected me with Charlie Conrad of Random House. Charlie saw the potential of this story, and I thank him for his vision, along with the entire team at The Doubleday Publishing Group, particularly Jenna Thompson for her insightful work on the manuscript and assistance in producing the book, interior designer Michael Collica, senior production editor Nora Reichard, jacket designer Michael Windsor, marketing associate Julie Sills, and associate director of publicity Joanna Pinsker.

My esteemed respect and admiration for His Excellency Shaikh Saud Nasir Al-Sabah and his son Shaikh Nawaf Saud Al-Sabah for their cherished friendship, their love of our American service members, and their thoughtfulness and generosity to them.

We are grateful to Bunny Murdock for enduring friendship and support.

I am grateful to Bob Gandt, for whom I have the utmost respect, for bringing the great stories of *Intrepid* to life in such a masterly way so that readers may appreciate the sacrifices of the brave men and women who served then and now.

Thanks to Richard and Peggy Santulli, who are dearest friends and who have taught us so much about quiet giving—the purest form of philanthropy, something his parents taught him.

Charles and Nathalie de Gunzburg, I am grateful to you for your love, dedication, leadership, support, and friendship.

Marty and Nancy Edelman, you are always there for our troops and are true friends. You are all *Intrepid*! To all the Fishers, my love and gratitude. I am eternally and deeply indebted to you for your extraordinary generosity and tireless support of our troops and their families. There is no other family in this country like you, who lead us all in our duty to care for and honor them.

Arnold, Ken, Steven, and Winston, thank you for all you do for so many—I am personally grateful for our friendship and your extraordinary support. A special thank-you to everyone at Fisher Brothers and at Plaza Construction for their tireless dedication to *Intrepid*.

Senator McCain, your heroism, patriotism, and service is a testament to your character and true love and dedication to America. Thank you for being such an integral part in supporting everything for which *Intrepid* stands.

To Bryan Eure, my life partner, I thank you for your unconditional support and love; you're an amazing man and I'm so very proud of you. ILUSM! To my parents, Patricia and Bill, I love and thank you so much, and I couldn't comprehend life without you. You are my inspiration and my greatest support. Donna, Joe, Adrienne, Todd—my family, you have all my love.

To Chelle Pokorney, Terri Seifert, Deon Ford, Stacey Sammis, and Kelli Harrell, we will never forget your loved ones. We honor and cherish their ultimate sacrifice to our nation and keep you, Taylor, Benjamin, Ashley, Austin, and all the families of our nation's fallen heroes in our thoughts and prayers, always.

Especially to my hero and mentor, Zachary Fisher, thank you for the priceless national legacy you created and left for us to continue. What an awesome responsibility! We will always be grateful for your timeless inspiration, extraordinary generosity, tireless dedication, undying patriotism, and love for America. Thank you for caring so much about our brave men and women in uniform. You are a great American patriot. I miss you very much.

Most important, I wish to personally thank the brave men and women who defended our freedom, and their families, aboard *Intrepid* and throughout the armed forces. We owe you our gratitude, respect, and love for all that you have done for America.

FROM ROBERT GANDT:

My sincere thanks to the many *Intrepid* veterans who generously contributed their time, stories, written accounts, photos, and suggestions. This story could not have been told without their help.

A few of these gentlemen deserve special mention. I am particularly indebted to Rear Adm. J. Lloyd "Doc" Abbot Jr., former *Intrepid* skipper, raconteur, and still-active pilot, whom I count as a friend and an ongoing source of Navy lore. Three heroes of the Pacific War, Alex Vraciu, Charlie Mallory, and Ben St. John, have my unending respect for their modest and dignified telling of some of the most dramatic exploits of our history.

Another friend and contributor to this story was Felix Novelli, plane captain, salty sailor, and storehouse of great stories. Big thanks, Felix. Thanks too to his shipmates and *Intrepid* "plank owners" Ed Coyne, Lou Valenti, and Ray Stone, whose love of their country, shipmates, and ship make them living emblems of the Greatest Generation.

Another icon of the Greatest Generation was Marine Tony Zollo, whose splendid work *USS Intrepid CV-11 CVA-11 CVS-11* (Turner Publishing, 1993) was an invaluable reference source, and who passed away while this book was being written.

My thanks and a salute to fighter pilot and former POW Cmdr. Bill "Country" Landreth for the kind and patient telling of his own heroic story.

For his spadework in the National Archives, particularly in retrieving *Intrepid*'s war diaries and the action reports of Carrier Air Groups 6, 18, and 10, I thank researcher John Bowen. Big thanks and compliments to naval aviator Cdr. R. R. "Boom" Powell and submarine officer Lt. Julian K. "Joe" Morrison III, eagle-eyed nitpickers and checkers of fact, who kindly reviewed the manuscript.

To my coauthor, Bill White, who invited me aboard *Intrepid* and entrusted me with the telling of her epic story, my thanks and sincere respect.

The work of researching the book could not have been accomplished without the ongoing assistance of Intrepid Museum executive vice president David Winters, chief curator John Zukowsky, and Matt Woods, vice president of facilities, engineering, and security. My sincere thanks, gentlemen.

Sincere thanks to Charlie Conrad, vice president and executive editor at The Doubleday Publishing Group, who shepherded this book with skill and precision along its journey to publication. Bravo Zulu, Charlie.

Another round of thanks to longtime friend and literary agent Alice Martell, of the Martell Agency, and to her assistant, Stephanie Finman, for their ongoing loyalty.

To Anne Busse Gandt, my wife, fiercest critic, and best friend, love and gratitude for patience above and beyond.

My most profound thanks, as always, go to the heroes who answered their country's call. May we continue to honor them and their valiant deeds.

★ THOSE WHO GAVE THEIR LIVES ★

World War II

Ship's Company

Raymond F. Adkins, S2C
Oswald S. Bauer, S1C
Royal H. Bender, S2C
James C. Bracken Sr., S2Cave
Leander Brewer Jr., STM1C
James E. Caskins, S1C
Charles H. Casteel, S1C
Alfonso Chavarrias, GM3C
Joseph W. Cody, ST3C
George B. Colwell, S2C
Clyde C. Compton, S1C
Odell H. Cooke, S1C
Hugh A. Cooper, S1C
Lawrence J. Covell Jr., S2C
Elton L. Darden, S1C
Henry F. Darnauer, S1C
Russell E. Davis, S1C
Edward Davison, STM1
Louis N. Defedele, S1
David Dermenegildo, S2C

Lt. Donald D. Dimarzo
Raymond H. Doulette, S1C
Willie E. Dousay Jr., S1C
James M. Duren, S1C
Harold C. Ellen, AOM3C
Everett J. Eure, EM3C
Vito T. Fiore, S1C
John F. Fischer, S1C
Grandville Fleming, STM1C
Emil V. Foletta, S1C
Lt. (jg) Howard P. Frank
Samuel W. Gant, STM1C
Ens. John B. Gattey
John W. Giddens, ST3C
Elmer P. Graves, ACM
Wallace D. Greig, S2C
Will C. Hamblin Jr., AM2C
John T. Hanke, S1C
Alexander F. Hentosh, S1C
Nathan B. Hecker, ACRT
Loumas E. Helms, S1C
Samuel L. Hitt, CARP

Elden S. Hjelmeng, ACOM

Raymond Hope, S1C

Delmar L. Huff, ARM1C

Donald C. Hurd, TM3C

Leslie E. Jones, RT3C

Rhett Jones, S1C

Vemon F. Kahler, EM3C

Dean R. Krouch, S2C

Robert B. Kuhns, TM3C

Harold R. Kurtz, S1C

Delmer B. Lasater, PHM3C

William H. Lear, EM1C

Jay M. McDonald, S1C

Claude E. Maddox, AOM1C

Joseph Mancini, F1C

Merl M. Martin, S1C

James Monroe, S1C

Robert P. Morgan, S1C

Alphonse V. Moscaritolo, S1C

William H. Mottaz, HA1C

Sem C. Nelson, AMM1C

Richard L. Nieto, RDM3C

Robert H. Norris, BM2C

Mike L. Oritz, AOM2C

John Paksi, GM3C

Cecil D. Peterson, S1C

Raymond A. Ray, S2C

Laurence J. Robinson, RDM3C

Raymond J. Rucinski, COX

Robert L. Schug, MM2C

Burhl A. Schultz, S1C

Walter M. Schulz, S1C

Horace J. Sides, S1C

John Z. Sliger, F2C

Fred L. Smith, STM1C

William D. Smith, PHM2C

Earl E. Sorenson, S1C

Robert M. Stallins, F1C

Eskew R. Steffens, S1C

Kenneth C. Steffens, S1C

Lee E. Stull, AOM3C

Archie L. Svec, CWT

Edward F. Tarvainis, AMM2C

James Taylor, STM1C

Robert L. Taylor, FC2C

Harold L. Tucker, S2C

Norvel L. Van Every, S2C

Reginal E. Wallace, ACMM

John B. Ward, PHM3C

Albert J. Watson, AMM1C

Gilbert L. Weiss, S1C

Harry E. Wells, S2C

George C. Whatley, Jr., S1C

Albert M. White, S2C

Harold V. White, S1C

Ralph A. Whittington, S1C

Lyle W. Willey, S1C

Earl E. Williams, S2C

James A. Winslow, PHM2C

Lt. Henry H. Whitmer

Charles W. Yoder, RDM3C

Harold L. Zieg, RDM3C

Air Groups

Air Group 8

Kenneth W. Johann, AP1C

Ens. William A. Preston

Air Group 6

Lt. (jg) Dale A. Barrows

Lt. James E. Bridges

Robert E. Bruton, AM1C

Gilbert J. Farmer, ACRM

Lt. Robert E. Gardner Jr.

James A. Green, ARM2C
Ens. Thomas A. Hall
David E. Jensen, ARM1C
Harold F. Leach, ARM1C
John F. McCormack, ARM1C
Lt. (jg) Robert W. Neel Jr.
Ens. John R. Ogg
Cdr. John L. Phillips Jr.
Lt. John P. Phillips
Lt. Paul E. Tepas
Lt. (jg) Thomas M. Vaughn

Air Group 18

J. R. Adams, ARM3C
G. L. Anderson, ARM1C
Harry M. Bearden Jr., ART1C
Michael J. Benak, ARM2C
William H. Besoain Jr., AOM3C
Ens. John J. Boyle
George E. Christman Jr., AMM2C
Tom V. Collins, ARM2C
Donald R. Cooper, ARM2C
Frank P. Crevoisier, ARM2C
James D. Cropper, ARM1C
Harlan R. Dickson, LCMR
Rodrick L. Duchesne, ARM2C
Lt. (jg) Ralph C. Dupont
Lt. Edward H. Eisengrein
Clarence F. English, ARM2C
Lt. Cdr. Mark Eslick Jr.
William C. Ewart, ARM3C
Lt. Cdr. John W. Fish
Edward Fussell, ARM3C
Bryon B. Galbreath, ARM2C
Ens. Delbert C. Goodspeed
Sterling E. Graham, ARM1C
Lt. George A. Griffith Jr.

Lt. John W. Gruenewald
Frank L. Haynes, ARM1C
Ens. James P. Hedrick
Edward Hlywa, ARM1C
Raymond V. Hopkins,
    ARM3C
Billy G. Hunter, ARM3C
Lt. (jg) David L. Johnson
Lt. (jg) Isaac W. Keels Jr.
Francis R. Krantz, AOM3C
Ens. Daniel Laner
Alfred B. Lankford, ARM2C
Lt. (jg) Leger
Lt. (jg) F. A. McAllister
Frederick E. McCreary,
    ARM1C
Lt. Wilson C. McNeil
Lt. Walter J. Madden
Ens. Harold S. Meacham
Ens. Arthur P. Mollenhauer
Lt. (jg) John Morelle
Lt. Elmer C. Namowski
Lt. Fred Navas
Lt. James B. Neighbours
Elmer E. Nutgrass, ARM2C
Ens. Walter Passi
Robert H. Paulson, ARM2C
Ens. Piercell
Lt. (jg) Andrew H. Rohleder, III
Ens. Clarence Rolka
Albert P. Rybarczyk, ARM2C
Lt. (jg) William H. Sartwelle
Lt. (jg) John J. Savage
Harold H. Schnack, AMM3C
Ora H. Shaminghouse Jr.,
    AOM2C
Lt. (jg) Raymond J. Skelly

Lt. (jg) Ernest A. Smith
Theodore A. Smith, ARM2C
William J. Telliard, AOM2C
Lt. William B. Thompson
Louis D. Vaughan, ARM3C
Ens. A. E. Watkins
Ens. Harry R. Webster Jr.
Robert G. Westmoreland,
 ARM3C
Lumpkin Wood, ACM
William P. Young, ARM2C
Lt. (jg) William C. Ziemer

Vietnam and Cold War
HC-2 Det. 11
Richard R. Buszko, ADRAN
Frank D. Marvaso, ATN3
LT (jg) Richard K. Melcher

Ship's Company
CS3 David L. Broudeur
FN Joseph R. Cain
AN Frank L. Cantlon
HM3 Richard H. Gauthier
DC1 William F. Hawes
AB3 Ross Allen Picket
E Div Fred J. Pietras
ABE3 Bobby L. Spencer
Richard F. Urban

Air Wing Squadrons
VA-15
Cdr. LeGrande O. Cole Jr.

Cdr. Philip C. Craig
Lt. Cdr. Richard A. Moran
VA-34
Raul E. Carrion, SA
VA-76
Lt. Cdr. James J. Peddy Jr.
VA-106
Lt. Cdr. David F. Callahan Jr.
Cdr. Kenneth K. Knabb Jr.
VF-33
Lt. (jg) Dale Robbins
VF-162
Ens. Fred A. Gayer
Lt. (jg) James R. Stratton
VSF-3
Lt. Frederick M. Kasch
VA-65
Orville D. Butler, AD2
VA-66
Lt. Cdr. Edward J. Broms Jr.
VA-176
Lt. Charles A. Knochel
VAW-121
Lt. Robert W. Harris
VS-24
James E. Carmack, AE1
Lt. (jg) Jerry A. Kincaid
Lt. George M. Wise

Appendix

★ THE INTREPID MUSEUM EXHIBITS ★

Since the museum opened in 1982, a variety of ships and vessels have been displayed along with *Intrepid*. The museum complex includes *Intrepid*—a National Historic Landmark—as well as the missile submarine *Growler* (acquired 1988) and G-BOAD, a British Airways Concorde (opened 2004). *Growler* is a unique surviving example of the American nuclear cruise missile submarines of the late 1950s, predecessors of the Polaris missile submarines of the early to mid-1960s. The Concorde is one of only three supersonic airliners on display in the United States. This one holds the transatlantic speed record for a Concorde, set on February 7, 1996, in two hours fifty-two minutes and fifty-nine seconds.

One of the most popular display aircraft is the A-12 Blackbird, the super-secret Mach 3 spy plane from the early 1960s that could outrun Soviet-made missiles when it flew reconnaissance missions during the Cold War. The museum's example is the first production unit placed into service. With the Blackbird and the Concorde, the museum has two of the three fastest production aircraft in the world.

The permanent collection of foreign jet fighter aircraft includes a Russian-designed MiG-21, an Israeli Kfir, and an Italian Aermacchi MB-339, gifts of the Polish, Israeli, and Italian governments, respectively. Other aircraft such as the French Etendard and the

British Scimitar are on extended loan to the museum. The collection of foreign jets makes a good comparison with the American aircraft on display and provides visitors with an opportunity to see aircraft rarely shown in American museums. The museum has more than twenty aircraft that document the history of the Cold War, from the early jets of the post–World War II era through supersonic fighters of the 1980s.

The museum has hosted exhibits and related commemorations during the 1980s and 1990s, including fiftieth anniversaries of major historic events including the invasion of Poland and the beginning of World War II (1939), the attack on Pearl Harbor (1941), the D-Day invasion (1944), the Battle of Iwo Jima (1945), and VE-Day and VJ-Day (1945).

The first decade of the new millennium saw a change in the scale and professionalism of the exhibitions on the *Intrepid*. One of the most impressive is the kamikaze multimedia experience created, in part, by Chedd Angier Production Company. Entitled "Kamikaze: Day of Darkness, Day of Light," this dramatic 2004 audiovisual presentation re-creates the disastrous kamikaze attack on the *Intrepid* of November 25, 1944, when sixty-nine officers and crew gave their lives for their country. The stories of two crew members—one who lived and one who died—set the tone for the museum's tagline, "humanity behind the hardware." Individuals who served and made a difference were the theme of the museum's 2004 documentary, created with American Rogue Films, *The Story of Intrepid*.

The creation of those sophisticated visitor experiences parallels the construction of important contemporary spaces within the *Intrepid* which set the museum apart from other naval ship museums. The Allison and Howard Lutnick Theater opened in 2000, and the Michael Tyler Fisher Center for Education in 2003. Both serve museum visitors and the metro New York community with high-level educational programming reaching an audience of more than 700,000 annually.

The theme of "humanity behind the hardware" underlies the 2006 exhibition "Heroic Journeys: Ordinary People, Extraordinary Stories." The museum staff worked together with young designers

Molly Lenore and Joey Stein of Moey, Inc., to create a dynamic experience, examining heroic decisions by average Americans who went above and beyond in the service of their country. The exhibition was made possible through the generosity of the Military Order of the Purple Heart Service Foundation, Inc., and Reba White Williams in memory of her brother, Lt. (jg) Alexander Jacob "Punk" White Jr., USN, a Navy pilot wounded in action in Korea in 1952.

After the museum's closing in late 2006 for the pier reconstruction, the exhibits department staff inventoried the large collection that had been assembled over the past twenty-five years. Restorations were made to areas of the ship such as the anchor chain room, the junior officers' quarters, and previously unopened areas of the mess deck. Working with award-winning architects and designers Eva Maddox and Ralph Johnson of the Chicago office of Perkins & Will, the staff created an exhibition design that respected the historic interior of *Intrepid*'s hangar deck.

Funding for the new exhibition was spearheaded by Charles de Gunzburg, his fellow Intrepid Museum Foundation trustees, and other friends. New acquisitions include two Russian-designed fighters, the MiG-15 and MiG-17, and two helicopters, a Piasecki HUP and a Sikorsky HO4S. Both helicopters are of a type that flew from *Intrepid* in the 1950s. These new machines joined the family of *Intrepid* aircraft that were restored for the museum's 2008 reopening.

★ THE INTREPID SALUTE AWARD ★

Over the years, the Intrepid Museum Foundation has presented the Intrepid Salute Award to outstanding citizens in recognition of their business achievements and their support of important philanthropic activities.

The recipients of the Intrepid Salute Award:

Mr. Denis A. Bovin, Vice Chairman, Investment Banking, Bear, Stearns & Co., Inc.—Salute to Freedom 1995

Mr. Daniel Burnham, Chairman and CEO, Raytheon Company—Fleet Week 2000

Mr. August Busch IV, President, Anheuser-Busch Companies—Salute to Freedom 2003

Mr. Nicholas D. Chabraja, Chairman and CEO, General Dynamics Corporation—Salute to Freedom 1998

Martin L. Edelman, Esq., Counsel, Paul, Hastings, Janofsky & Walker LLP—Fleet Week 2002

Mr. William T. Esrey, Chairman and CEO, Sprint Corporation—Salute to Freedom 1992

Mr. John S. Hendricks, Founder, Chairman and CEO, Discovery Communications, Inc.—Fleet Week 1995

Mr. Thomas G. Labrecque, President and COO, The Chase Manhattan Corporation—Salute to Freedom 1997

Mr. Howard W. Lutnick, Chairman and CEO, Cantor Fitzgerald LP and eSpeed, Inc.—Salute to Freedom 1994

Mr. Bruce Mosler, President, U.S. Operations, Cushman & Wakefield—Salute to Freedom 2001

Mr. Terrence Murray, President and CEO, Fleet Financial Group—Fleet Week 1996

Adm. William A. Owens, USN (Ret.), President and CEO, Nortel—Salute to Freedom 2004

Mr. Joseph Perella, Vice Chairman of Morgan Stanley—Fleet Week 2005

Mr. Dennis J. Picard, Chairman and CEO, Raytheon Company—Fleet Week 1997

Mr. Joseph J. Plumeri, Chairman and CEO, Willis Group Holdings—Salute to Freedom 2007

Mr. Steven Roth, Chairman and CEO, Vornado Realty Trust—Fleet Week 2001

Mr. William C. Steere Jr., Chairman and CEO, Pfizer Inc.—Salute to Freedom 1996

Mr. Michael Stern, President and CEO, Fisher Center for Alzheimer's Research Foundation—Fleet Week 1998

Mr. Steven C. Witkoff, President, The Witkoff Group—Salute to Freedom 2004

★ THE INTREPID FREEDOM AWARD ★

The Intrepid Freedom Award is presented by the Intrepid Museum Foundation to national or international leaders who have distinguished themselves in promoting and defending the values of freedom and democracy, the core beliefs of our nation.

Those who have received the Intrepid Freedom Award:

The Honorable William Clinton, 42nd President of the United States—Fleet Week 1996

The Honorable George Bush, 41st President of the United States—Fleet Week 1994

The Honorable Ronald Reagan, 40th President of the United States—Salute to Freedom 1993

His Excellency Silvio Berlusconi, Prime Minister of the Republic of Italy—Salute to Freedom 2006

His Excellency Yitzhak Rabin, Prime Minister of the State of Israel—Salute to Freedom 1995

The Right Honorable Baroness Margaret Thatcher, Prime Minister of the United Kingdom—Salute to Freedom 1994

His Excellency Boris Yelstin, President of the Russian Federation—Fleet Week 1993

His Eminence John Cardinal O'Connor, Archbishop of New York—Fleet Week 1999

The Honorable Eliot Spitzer, 54th Governor of New York—Salute to Freedom 2007

The Honorable Michael Bloomberg, 108th Mayor of the City of New York—Fleet Week 2005

The Honorable Rudolph W. Giuliani, 107th Mayor of the City of New York—Salute to Freedom 2001

The Honorable Newt Gingrich, Speaker of the House of Representatives—Fleet Week 1995

The Honorable C. W. Young, Chairman, House Appropriations Committee—August 2004

The Honorable Hillary Rodham Clinton, United States Senate—Salute to Freedom 2004

The Honorable John McCain, United States Senate—Salute to Freedom 1999

The Honorable Madeleine Albright, Secretary of State—Fleet Week 1997

The Honorable Donald Rumsfeld, Secretary of Defense—Salute to Freedom 2003

The Honorable William Cohen, Secretary of Defense—Salute to Freedom 1997

The Honorable Richard Cheney, Secretary of Defense—Salute to Freedom 1992

The Honorable Robert Rubin, Secretary of the Treasury—Fleet Week 1998

The Honorable Tom Ridge, Secretary of Homeland Security—Fleet Week 2004

General Richard B. Myers, USAF, Chairman of the Joint Chiefs of Staff—Salute to Freedom 2004

General Henry Hugh Shelton, USA, Chairman of the Joint Chiefs of Staff—Salute to Freedom 1998

General Colin Powell, USA, Chairman of the Joint Chiefs of Staff—Salute to Freedom 1996

General Tommy R. Franks, USA, Commander in Chief, U.S. Central Command—Salute to Freedom 2002

The Honorable Raymond Kelly, Commissioner, New York City Police Department—Fleet Week 2006

Mr. Arnold Fisher, Chairman Emeritus, Intrepid Museum Foundation—Salute to Freedom 2006

The Honorable William Clinton
presented during Fleet Week 1996

The Honorable Ronald Reagan
presented during Salute to Freedom 1993

The Right Honorable Baroness
Margaret Thatcher presented during
Salute to Freedom 1994

His Eminence John Cardinal O' Connor
presented during Fleet Week 1999

The Honorable George Bush
presented during Fleet Week 1994

The Honorable Hillary Rodham Clinton
presented during Salute to Freedom 2004

General Henry Hugh Shelton presented
during Salute to Freedom 1998

His Excellency Yitzhak Rabin presented
during Salute to Freedom 1995

★ THE INTREPID FAMILY OF FOUNDATIONS ★
Supporting the Men and Women of the United States Armed Forces and Their Families

INTREPID SEA AIR & SPACE MUSEUM *Adventures in Heroism* The INTREPID SEA, AIR & SPACE MUSEUM is centered on the aircraft carrier *Intrepid*, one of the most successful ships in U.S. history, which is now a National Historic Landmark, and one of the unique attractions in New York City. The museum attracts more than 750,000 visitors each year with its range of interactive exhibits and events providing a snapshot of heroism, education, and excitement. More than 50,000 schoolchildren participate in *Intrepid*'s unique educational programs every year. The museum also hosts the annual Fleet Week celebration in honor of our military personnel, and more than 150,000 troops have visited for Fleet Week in the past twenty years.

www.intrepidmuseum.org

 The INTREPID FALLEN HEROES FUND is a leader in supporting the men and women of the Armed Forces and their families. Begun in 2000, the fund has raised over $100 million in support of thousands of families of military personnel lost in service to our nation, and for thousands more severely wounded military personnel and veterans. The fund is currently constructing the National Intrepid Center of Excellence, a premier research, diagnosis, and treatment center for military personnel and veterans suffering from traumatic brain disorder. This $75 million project will be complete and operating by the end of 2009. These efforts are funded entirely with donations from the public, and hundreds of thousands of individuals have contributed to the fund. One hundred percent of contributions raised by the fund go toward these programs; all administrative expenses are underwritten by the fund's trustees.

www.fallenheroesfund.org

The FISHER HOUSE FOUNDATION is a unique private-public partnership that supports America's military in their time of need. Because members of the military and their families are stationed worldwide and must often travel great distances for specialized medical care, the Fisher House Foundation donates "comfort homes," built on the grounds of major military and VA medical centers. There are currently approximately forty Fisher Houses, with more in planning and under construction. Annually, the Fisher House program serves more than 10,000 families, and has made available nearly 2.5 million days of lodging to family members since the program began in 1990. The foundation's Hero Miles program has provided thousands of airline flights to military families.

www.fisherhouse.org

The INTREPID RELIEF FUND is dedicated to supporting the men and women of the United States Armed Forces and their families. The fund is focused on several areas of need in the military community: hardship support, education, and military health care. The fund's primary program is supporting Operation Mend, which provides advanced plastic surgery care to troops severely disfigured in combat.

www.irfund.org

★ SOURCES ★

By far the single greatest reward in researching this book was the privilege of hearing the firsthand accounts of *Intrepid*'s World War II veterans. We listened in awe as these living icons of history recalled their trials by fire at Truk, Leyte Gulf, and Okinawa. Through their stories we have been able to glimpse the drama, terror, and exhilaration of the greatest sea battles ever fought.

The story of *Intrepid* was derived from multiple sources, including interviews and correspondence from crew members, formerly classified air group action reports, ship's war diaries, numerous historical works on the campaigns in which *Intrepid* was involved, memoirs by crew members and airmen, newspaper and periodical articles about *Intrepid*, the many cruise books produced in the style of school yearbooks as mementos of each major deployment, and the plethora of excellent historical and military sites on the Internet.

Of *Intrepid*'s "plank owners"—original crew members—only a few remain. Three of these, Ed Coyne, Ray Stone, and Lou Valenti, are actively involved in the preservation of *Intrepid*'s history. With remarkable clarity of recall, these gentlemen helped reconstruct the events of *Intrepid*'s commissioning and her wartime exploits in the Pacific. Their recall of the day-to-day, mundane details of their ship and shipmates was an invaluable source of information.

The description of the Kwajalein and Truk actions was derived from formerly classified air group action reports and *Intrepid*'s war diaries as well as personal recollections of numerous crew members. One of these, Alex Vraciu, was *Intrepid*'s first ace and the Navy's fourth-highest-scoring fighter pilot. From his point of view came the vignettes of *Intrepid*'s first combat actions over Roi and Namur, and the dramatic strike on Truk when Vraciu's tally swelled to nine downed Japanese airplanes.

The night of *Intrepid*'s first blooding—the torpedo strike off Truk—was vividly described by Ray Stone and his fellow plank owners. The circumstances of *Intrepid*'s destroyed rudder and the perilous voyage back to Hunters Point were distilled from several excellent online histories and from the published memoirs of crew members Ray Stone and Tony Zollo.

The actions of Air Group 18 aboard *Intrepid* were based, in part, on the air group history, which was made available to me by Torpedo 18 pilot Ben St. John. Fighting 18 pilot and double ace Charlie Mallory contributed his own firsthand account of the deadly air battles over Formosa and the Philippines. Action reports and recollections of squadronmates were consulted in depicting the character and career of Fighting 18 pilot Cecil Harris, the second-highest-scoring Navy ace of World War II.

Air group action reports and ship's war diaries were used to verify dates and specifics of the actions in the Palau Islands, the Philippines, and Formosa. The convoluted circumstances of the Battle of Leyte Gulf were drawn from a number of published histories, referenced in the selected bibliography in this section. Of particular value were the personal accounts of Air Group 18 airmen, including the excellent memoir *Hell Divers* (Motorbooks International, 1991), by Bombing 18 pilot and Navy Cross recipient John F. "Jack" Forsyth, whose recollections are quoted with the permission of Zenith Press.

The impressions and details of the kamikaze strike on Gun Tub 10 were derived from numerous eyewitness accounts, including that of Navy Cross recipient Alonzo Swann Jr. The story of the ditching of the six Avengers in the Philippine Sea was contributed by one of the pilots in the episode, Ben St. John. The devastating kamikaze attacks of November 25, 1944, were described in chilling detail by various crew members and air group aviators and are well documented in published and online war histories.

The exploits of Air Group 10 and the air battles at Okinawa were poignantly rendered by VBF-10 pilot Roy "Eric" Erickson in his memoir, *Tail End Charlies*. Another VBF-10 pilot, Bill "Country" Landreth, contributed details about flying the F4U Corsair from *Intrepid* and the story of his downing and capture by the Japanese. Air group action reports and *Intrepid*'s war diaries were consulted for details about specific engagements off Okinawa and Japan.

Former plane captain Felix Novelli was a source of anecdotal material about flight deck operations in the Okinawa campaign and during the show-of-force deployment at war's end. As an active former crew member, Novelli also contributed to the latter-day account of *Intrepid*'s 2006 grounding and rescue.

Information about *Intrepid*'s postwar years was drawn mostly from the ship's histories as well as the various cruise books. Former 1950s crew members Marino DiLeo, Bob Dougherty, and Skyraider pilot John "Pygmy" Paganelli contributed valuable anecdotal material. The details of *Intrepid*'s modernization came from the ship's histories and the SCB-27 program descriptions at the Naval Historical Center, the Patriot Files site, and other excellent Web sites dedicated to preserving military and naval history.

Rear Adm. J. Lloyd "Doc" Abbot Jr., who commanded *Intrepid* in 1961–62, provided a rich slice of *Intrepid*'s Cold War history. The former skipper filled in details about deployment to the Mediterranean, harrowing operational incidents, and the dramatic recovery of astronaut Scott Carpenter.

Intrepid's cruise books were used to document the ship's ports of call and the day-to-day aspects of carrier operations in the 1960s. The most informative of these was the twentieth-anniversary book, available online at www.navybuddies.com/cruisebooks/cv11-63/index.html, containing a voluminous photographic history of *Intrepid* from her commissioning through 1963.

Another valuable source was the USS Intrepid Association, which maintains a Web site at www.wa3key.com/intrepid.html for

Intrepid former crew members and is a storehouse of both historical and contemporary information. The energetic association president, Mike Hallahan, provided a priceless service by connecting
the authors with dozens of former *Intrepid* crew members.

The accounts of the two astronaut recoveries—Aurora 7 in 1962
and Gemini 3 in 1965—were gleaned in part from cruise books
and numerous histories of the early U.S. space program, including
Tom Wolfe's *The Right Stuff,* Scott Carpenter's memoir *For Spacious Skies,* and *How NASA Learned to Fly in Space* by David M.
Harland.

Many of the facts and impressions of *Intrepid*'s first Vietnam deployment were provided by crew members and Carrier Air Wing
10 airmen. Lt. Cmdr. Scott Allen, *Intrepid*'s air intelligence officer,
was especially helpful with explanations of how the ship was configured and deployed as a "special" attack carrier. Former VA-15
pilot and *Aviation Week* editor in chief Dave North related details
about combat operations from Dixie and Yankee Stations. Aircraft losses and the fates of aviators involved were substantiated by
personal accounts and in various histories of the Vietnam air war,
listed in the selected bibliography. The details of the MiG shoot-
down by an A-1 Skyraider from *Intrepid* came from recorded interviews of the pilots, available at the Skyraider Association site, www
.skyraider.org. Again, *Intrepid*'s official cruise books were useful in
documenting each of her three Vietnam tours.

VSF-3 Skyhawk pilot and writer Cmdr. R. R. "Boom" Powell
was a source of valuable anecdotal material about *Intrepid*'s second
Vietnam deployment and her last passage through the Suez. Other
pilots, including VA-34 pilot Bernie Fipp, shared colorful anec-
dotes, and the official cruise book was consulted for details about
ports of call and periods on line.

Intrepid's air wing on her third combat deployment included
VA-36 (coauthor Gandt's squadron in the early 1960s), from which
came much of the information about combat operations in North
and South Vietnam. The details of VF-111 pilot Tony Nargi's MiG
kill were distilled from the several histories of the air war listed
in the bibliography. The 1968 cruise book not only documented

Intrepid's third Vietnam deployment but contained an excellent twenty-fifth-anniversary overview of the ship's career.

The 1969 grounding incident in Narragansett Bay was reconstructed from the accounts of eyewitnesses, including former crew members Bob Frederickson, Joe Richardson, and Charlie Wladyka. *Intrepid*'s return to anti-submarine duty and details of the 1971 deployment to northern Europe, the intercepts of Russian bombers, and the purloined sonobuoy affair were distilled from information provided by Cdr. Boom Powell, Capt. John Paganelli, and Capt. M. R. "By" Byington.

Intrepid's last cruise and her return to Quonset Point were described by ship's navigator Byington and former executive officer and skipper Rear Adm. Lee Levenson, and were documented in *Intrepid*'s final cruise book. Captain Byington made available *Intrepid*'s official inactivation report, newspaper clippings, and programs from the ship's last change of command, her thirtieth anniversary, and her decommissioning ceremony.

The events of *Intrepid*'s mothballed years at Philadelphia and her rescue by Zachary Fisher and the Intrepid Museum Foundation were drawn from archived newspaper accounts, an April 1990 *Reader's Digest* article by John Culhane, "The Man Who Bought an Aircraft Carrier," and from the Fisher biography on the Intrepid Museum's Web site. *Intrepid*'s career as a sea, air, and space museum has been well documented in New York newspapers and periodicals and reconstructed in detail by coauthor Bill White and the staff of the museum. The drama of *Intrepid*'s grounding and ungrounding received voluminous press coverage and was the theme of a *Megamovers* segment on the History Channel.

The following is a partial list of the contributors, published works, Internet sites, and other sources that were consulted in the writing of *Intrepid: The Epic Story of America's Most Legendary Warship*. The list of selected books covers the technical and historical range of *Intrepid*'s story and is offered as a guide to researchers interested in further information.

Books

Astor, Gerald. *Wings of Gold.* Presidio Press, 2005.

Carpenter, Scott, and Kris Stoever. *For Spacious Skies: The Uncommon Journey of a Mercury Astronaut.* NAL Trade, 2004.

Erickson, Roy D. *Tail End Charlies! Navy Combat Fighter Pilots at War's End.* Turner Publishing, 1995.

Forsyth, John F. *Hell Divers.* Motorbooks International, 1991.

Harland, David M. *How NASA Learned to Fly in Space.* Collectors Guide Publishing, 2004.

Heiferman, Ronald. *U.S. Navy in World War II.* Chartwell Book Sales, 1978.

Hornfischer, James D. *The Last Stand of the Tin Can Sailors.* Bantam, 2004.

Jablonksi, Edward. *Airwar.* Doubleday, 1971.

Levinson, Jeffrey L. *Alpha Strike.* Random House Value, 1991.

Mersky, Peter B., and Norman Polmar. *The Naval Air War in Vietnam.* Nautical and Aviation Publishing Company of America, 1986.

———. *F-8 Crusader Units of the Vietnam War.* Osprey Publishing, 1998.

———. *US Navy and Marine Corps A-4 Skyhawk Units of the Vietnam War.* Osprey Publishing, 2007.

Morison, Samuel Eliot. *Leyte, June 1944–January 1945.* Castle, 2001.

———. *The Two-Ocean War: A Short History of the United States Navy in the Second World War.* Little, Brown, 1963.

Nichols, John B., and Barrett Tillman. *On Yankee Station.* Naval Institute Press, 1987.

Parrish, Thomas. *The Simon and Schuster Encyclopedia of World War II.* Simon & Schuster, 1978.

Reynolds, Clark G. *The Carrier War.* Time-Life Books, 1983.

Roberts, John. *The Aircraft Carrier Intrepid.* Naval Institute Press, 1982.

Steinberg, Rafael. *Return to the Philippines.* Time-Life Books, 1980.

———. *Island Fighting.* Time-Life Books, 1978.

Stone, Raymond T. *My Ship.* G.P. Books, 2003.

Thomas, Evan. *Sea of Thunder.* Simon & Schuster, 2006.

Tillman, Barrett. *Corsair: The F4U in World War II and Korea.* Naval Institute Press, 1979.

———. *Hellcat Aces of World War 2.* Osprey Publishing, 1996.

Toliver, Raymond, and Trevor Constable. *Fighter Aces of the U.S.A.* Schiffer Press, 1997.

Wolfe, Tom. *The Right Stuff.* Farrar, Straus and Giroux, 1979.

Zollo, Anthony F., Sr. *USS Intrepid CV-11 CVA-11 CVS-11.* Turner Publishing, 1993.

Contributors

J. Lloyd "Doc" Abbot Jr.	Jeff Morgan
Scott Allen	David M. North
M. R. "By" Byington	Felix Novelli
Ed Coyne	John Paganelli
James Crum	Robert R. "Boom" Powell
Marino DiLeo	Robert Rani
Bob Dougherty	Joe Richardson
Bernard Fipp	Ben St. John
Robert Frederickson	Ray Stone
Richard T. Holden	John Sumner
James Holbrook	Lou Valenti
William Iams	Alex Vraciu
William "Country"	Lance Winer
Landreth	Dave Winters
Sam Lev	Charles Wladyka
Lee Levenson	John Zukowsky
Charles Mallory	

Web Sites

www.acepilots.com. World War II aviation history and key figures.

www.navybuddies.com/cv/cv11.htm. Excellent reference site for USS *Intrepid* data.

www.history.navy.mil. Web site of the Naval Historical Center.

www.patriotfiles.com. Source of extensive World War II, Korean War, and Cold War data.

www.skyhawk.org. Home page of the A-4 Skyhawk Association.

www.wgordon.web.wesleyan.edu/kamikaze/museums/intrepid/index .htm. Discussion of kamikaze attacks and the current display in the Intrepid Museum.

www.wa3key.com/cvsdata.html. USS *Intrepid* service data.

www.intrepidmuseum.org. Home site of Intrepid Sea, Air, & Space Museum.

www.skyraider.org. Skyraider Association site, with much detail about Vietnam War actions.

Other Sources

The National Archives. Repository of most of the war diaries and aircraft action reports consulted in the writing of this book. Address: 700 Pennsylvania Avenue, NW, Washington, DC 20408–0001. For information about conducting research, visit www.archives.gov.

New York Times. Archived articles about *Intrepid* and her evolution as a sea, air, and space museum. The complete back file can be searched at www.nytimes.com, more than 13 million articles in all. Articles from 1851 to 1922 and from 1987 on are free.

U.S. Naval Institute. Extensive collection of oral histories covering World War II, Korea, Vietnam, and later. For information about researching the collection, go to www.usni.org/navalinstitutepress/OralHistory.asp.

★ INDEX ★

★ PHOTOGRAPHY CREDITS ★

Endpapers:	All photos courtesy of the Intrepid Sea, Air & Space Museum
Frontispiece:	Courtesy of the Naval Historical Center

Text
page

6:	U.S. Navy/Courtesy National Archives
160:	U.S. Navy/Courtesy National Archives
324, top left:	Courtesy of Intrepid Sea, Air & Space Museum
324, top right:	Steve Friedman
324, bottom left:	Herald Hechler Photography
324, bottom right:	Herald Hechler Photography
325, top left:	Herald Hechler Photography
325, top right:	Herald Hechler Photography
325, bottom left:	Herald Hechler Photography
325, bottom right:	Herald Hechler Photography

First insert
page

1, top:	Naval Historical Center
1, bottom:	National Archives

2, top:	Naval Historical Center
2, bottom:	Intrepid Sea, Air & Space Museum
3, top:	U.S. Navy/Courtesy National Archives
3, bottom:	Naval Historical Center, courtesy of Adm. Nimitz
4:	Intrepid Sea, Air & Space Museum
5, top:	U.S. Navy/Courtesy National Archives
5, bottom:	U.S. Navy/Courtesy National Archives
6, top left:	Robert M. Cieri
6, top middle:	Robert M. Cieri
6, top right:	Robert M. Cieri
6, bottom:	Naval Historical Center
7:	Intrepid Sea, Air & Space Museum
8, top:	Intrepid Sea, Air & Space Museum
8, bottom:	Intrepid Sea, Air & Space Museum

Second insert
page

1, top:	Intrepid Sea, Air & Space Museum
1, bottom:	Intrepid Sea, Air & Space Museum
2, top:	Intrepid Sea, Air & Space Museum
2, bottom:	Intrepid Sea, Air & Space Museum
3, top:	Intrepid Sea, Air & Space Museum
3, bottom:	Intrepid Sea, Air & Space Museum
4, top:	Intrepid Fallen Heroes Fund
4, bottom:	Intrepid Fallen Heroes Fund
5, top:	*L'Osservatore Romano*, The Vatican Newspaper
5, bottom:	Intrepid Sea, Air & Space Museum
6, top:	Intrepid Sea, Air & Space Museum
6, bottom:	Intrepid Sea, Air & Space Museum
7, top:	Intrepid Sea, Air & Space Museum
7, bottom:	Intrepid Sea, Air & Space Museum
8:	Herald Hechler Photography

★ ABOUT THE AUTHORS ★

BILL WHITE is president of the Intrepid Sea, Air & Space Museum and the Intrepid Fallen Heroes Fund.

ROBERT GANDT is a former U.S. Navy fighter/attack pilot and international airline captain. His numerous previous books include the definitive work on naval aviation, *Bogeys and Bandits*, which was adapted for the television series *Pensacola: Wings of Gold*.